JOHN MACLEAN

JOHN MACLEAN

Nan Milton

Pluto Press

First published December 1973 by Pluto Press Ltd
© Copyright Pluto Press 1973

ISBN 0 902818 38 4 paperback
ISBN 0 902818 39 2 hardback

Designed by Andrew Dark

Printed in Great Britain by Bristol Typesetting Company Limited,
Barton Manor, St Philips, Bristol

JOHN MACLEAN

Contents

Contents

Contents

Acknowledgements

Most of the research for this book was carried out so many years ago, in 1937-38, that it is both difficult and painful to record here those who helped me, simply because the majority are now dead. First and foremost was James D MacDougall, jocularly named 'Maclean's First Lieutenant', without whose dictated recollections the early part of the book could not have been written with any accuracy. Without the constant encouragement of my sister Jean, my mother Agnes Maclean and my first husband Tom Mercer, I would not have persisted. The latter's rocklike conviction that John Maclean had been the victim of a character assassination designed to obscure the magnitude of his contribution to the international socialist movement and that it was my duty to right that wrong, was an inspiration. The help given by James Clunie was crucial. He put at my disposal all the letters written to him by John Maclean during the years he was supposed to be 'unbalanced'. Many years later he published them in his memoirs *The Voice of Labour*. Other letters written by Maclean were given to me by W P Coates, Peter Marshall, Will Montgomery and Will Lawther. I received help also from James Maxton, who passed on to me all the material he had gathered in 1924 when he contemplated writing a biography. I received additional information from Peter Marshall, Joe Payne of the Scottish Labour College, and E C Fairchild. The pamphlets written by Tom Anderson and Guy Aldred in 1930 and 1932 respectively and William Gallacher's book *Revolt on the Clyde*, gave me guidance as well as information; although the latter did nothing to right the wrong.

In recent years the documents and information contributed by Harry McShane have proved invaluable; his help has been equalled only by that of Walter Kendall. Very special thanks are due to Thomas Phelan, who made available to me the text of his thesis on the history of working-class education in Scotland, which contained a chapter on John Maclean and the Scottish Labour College; in addition he gave me copies of all the relevant research material. Also due special thanks is James Downes, who preserved intact for fifty years the important leaflet, 'All Hail! The Scottish

Workers' Republic!' Other members of the John Maclean Society who provided information were Samuel Stewart, Charles Doran, John Mitchell, Mary Cordiner, Peter Jamieson, Dr Archie Lamont, Seamus Reader, and Jenny McNeill (who gave me the Minute Book of the Townhead Branch of the Scottish Workers' Republican Party).* Tom Bell's book, *John Maclean, a Fighter for Freedom*, published in 1944 by the Scottish Committee of the Communist Party, also provided some additional items of information. I am also indebted to the Librarian at William Gallacher's House for permission to copy one of Maclean's essays, 'The First Great "Pacific" Conference of Powers' and to the staff of the Manuscripts Department of the National Library of Scotland for courteous service.

Ten years ago John L Broom wrote a biography of Maclean from a different standpoint—that of an anti-Marxist socialist and ardent Scottish Nationalist—which I hope will be published soon. All additional material collected by him he very kindly put at my disposal, including the testimony of the Assistant Chaplain at Barlinnie Prison during Maclean's last imprisonment.

* Jeannie Payne.

Introduction

On 7 October 1917, immediately prior to the Bolshevik Revolution, Lenin wrote:

> There can be no doubt that the end of the month of September marked the beginning of a new period in the history of the Russian Revolution; and, very probably, of the world revolution.
>
> The world working-class revolution was first begun with engagements by isolated combatants representing with unequalled courage all the honest elements of official 'Socialism'—a socialism rotten to the core, which is in reality nothing but social chauvinism, Liebknecht in Germany, Adler in Austria, Maclean in England, such are the best known of these isolated heroes who assumed the heavy task of precursors of the revolution.

He went on to point out that the tiny trickle of revolutionary opposition to the war initiated by these men had swelled to a great flood. Had Lenin and the Bolsheviks not thought then that behind them stood the revolutionary workers of Western Europe, would they have had the courage to go forward? That is why, after the Revolution, the men Lenin mentioned were selected along with the Russians, Lenin, Trotsky, and Spiridonova, as honorary presidents of the First All-Russian Congress of Soviets. And that is what John Maclean himself meant when he proudly boasted at his trial in 1918 that the Red Clyde had helped to win the Russian Revolution.

Red Clyde

How the Clyde broke with a hundred years' tradition of backwardness, became the centre of working-class struggle in Britain, and helped to win the Russian Revolution, is also the story of John Maclean.

The first and most important element of the Red Clyde was its economic structure: its high concentration of heavy industry massing together the most advanced sections of the proletariat—the engineers, the dockers, the shipyard workers, and the miners.

The second element was its racial composition. A large percentage of the working class was Highland or Irish of the first or second generation, driven to the Clyde by the Clearances and the Famines of the nineteenth century. This was significant because, as Trotsky pointed out in 1925:

> the most radical elements of the contemporary British Labour Movement are mostly of Scotch or Irish race. The union in Ireland of social with national oppression, in face of the sharp conflict of an agrarian with a capitalist country, gives the conditions for sharper changes in consciousness. Scotland set out upon the road of capitalism later than England; the sharper break in the life of the masses of the people causes a sharper break in political reaction.

This shrewd comment was marred only by a failure to realize that in Scotland national oppression, of a more subtle nature than in Ireland, was also added to social oppression.

These two elements alone, however, were not sufficient. Social oppression produced a high degree of trade union consciousness; national oppression resulted in a lack of the fervent 'patriotism' found in England. Socialist consciousness required more than that, and it was John Maclean who, more than any other single individual, gave the Clyde that.

Maclean's Role

When he joined the socialist movement at the beginning of this century, the Scottish working class was notorious for its backwardness, in spite of the fact that Scotland was one of the most advanced capitalist countries in the world. The class struggle had produced well-organized trade union and co-operative movements, but beyond this the proletariat, stunted by its indifference to theory, had scarcely developed. It was almost completely absorbed in narrow, defensive, practical activity.

Maclean, steeped in Marxist knowledge, knew that when working-class activity was not guided by working-class theory then, whether the persons engaged in it were aware of it or not, the activity would be carried on under the influence of orthodox capitalist theory. He realized that there could be no revolutionary action without revolutionary theory. And he knew that this kind of theory could not, like trade union consciousness, develop spontaneously. It would have to be taught.

So for many years, at street corners, in lecture rooms, in village halls, at work-gates, and at pit-heads, wherever workers gathered, he hammered the basic principles of Marxism into the heads of his listeners. As a good teacher, however, he knew that the majority of ordinary people learn best through active participation, and he encouraged them to take part, at every level, in the 'day to day struggle'. He himself, in true Marxist tradition, became the embodiment of the unity of thought and action.

The Legend

John Maclean's untimely and totally unexpected death at the early age of forty-four on 30 November 1923, was a traumatic shock for large sections of the Clydeside people. His funeral was the most spectacular ever to be held in Glasgow. Tom Anderson, who organized it, described it in a pamphlet written seven years later:

> At least 5,000 comrades took part in the march from Eglinton Toll to the Cemetery, a distance of four miles; and double that number followed the funeral, which was led by the Clyde Workers' Band.
> The march was known as 'The Silent March', each comrade marching with his head uncovered and observing due silence . . . A film was made of the funeral . . . and was shown in most of the cinemas; and each year on the first Sunday of December we march to Eastwood to Comrade John's grave and hold our annual service. Nearly 500 have marched every year since 1923 the distance of four miles, and in the evening we hold a Remembrance Service at which the film of the funeral is shown, and we sing 'The Silent March'.

These ceremonies were held every year until 1947, when Tom Anderson died, but the legend did not die away. In 1948, the twenty-fifth anniversary of his death, a huge mass meeting organized by the Scottish-USSR Society was held in St Andrew's Hall. A unique feature of this event was the presence on the platform of some of Scotland's foremost poets and literary figures, including Hugh MacDiarmid and Sydney Goodsir Smith, who gave readings of poems which they themselves had composed in honour of John Maclean. Thus as a result of the Scottish literary renaissance, which he himself had helped to inspire, the legend took on a new, immortal form.

Although the annual ceremonies ceased until 1968, when Tom Murray founded the John Maclean Society, the legend persisted also at grass roots level. As James D MacDougall, Maclean's closest friend and colleague, told me on one occasion:

> On a whole generation of men he left such an impression that they

will carry the memory to their grave. More than that. He is already to tens of thousands of men such an idol that they have conveyed to their children, who never saw him or heard him, a clear idea of this great working-class fighter, so that to this new generation his name and figure is almost as familiar as to the men whom he enthused and inspired.

One of that new generation, James D Young, while studying during the fifties at Ruskin College, Oxford, was so exasperated by the almost complete ignorance of Maclean's work manifested in England that he wrote an indignant letter to *Forward*, of which the following is an extract:

A great army of orthodox historians have done their level best to cover John Maclean in obscurity. Most of the historians of the Labour Movement have not done any better, for they have almost completely ignored his immeasurable contribution to British Socialism. He was even ignored by G D H Cole in his monumental book *A Short History of the British Working Class Movement*.

In Scotland the man's name is a legend; indeed, his incredible stature, his wonderful simplicity and unselfish devotion to a great cause have become part of our Scottish folk-lore. All the debunking in the world and all the attempts to surround his life and deeds in darkness cannot conceal his essential greatness.

Biography

Many of his contemporaries had no doubts about his greatness. Soon after his death, James Maxton began to write a biography but, immersed as he was in the turbulent politics of those days, found the task beyond him. Ten years later, Hugh MacDiarmid also made a beginning, but ill-health overtook him, and he contented himself with writing some remarkable essays and two memorable poems, in one of which he asserted:

> Scotland has had few men whose names
> Matter—or should matter—to intelligent people.
> But of these Maclean, next to Burns, was the greatest.

The ideal biographer would have been James MacDougall, who took part in most of the events recorded in this book, and who was as able a writer as he was an orator. To help and encourage him I undertook to gather information and do the necessary research, and managed on several occasions to persuade him to recount some of their earlier experiences. I wrote a skeleton book, hoping that he would cover the bare, factual bones with the flesh of his vast knowledge and personal experience. However, he never recovered the health shattered by early persecution and the book remained uncompleted.

Many years later, I pleaded on first Walter Kendall and then Harry McShane to undertake this task. Walter, however, had a more important book to write, *The Revolutionary Movement in Britain 1900-21*, and Harry, who could have written a magnificent book because of his personal association with Maclean and his sixty years' experience in the working-class movement, insisted with typical modesty that he was an engineer not a writer.

Probably a daughter is the last person to write the biography of a controversial figure like Maclean, but I do not see him in that light. I do not care whether he was a genius like Marx and Lenin—the 'Scottish Lenin'—or a 'fool of the most colossal dimensions' as Philip Snowden called him. I see him as Guy Aldred saw him:

> The workers' message dominated and consumed him until that message became his personality. Apart from his class, he was nothing, because of his class, its sorrows, its struggles, had become his life and being.

**Dedicated to the
Scottish working class**

1/Childhood and youth

The key to the drama of John Maclean's life is found in his early environment. Born on 24 August 1879, he was the sixth child of working-class parents and grew up in Pollokshaws, then a busy industrial town in Renfrewshire, near Glasgow.

His parents, Daniel Maclean and Anne MacPhee, had both been child victims of the Highland Clearances. They had been driven with their parents from their homes and crofts, his father from Mull, and his mother from Corpach, a small village at the foot of Ben Nevis.

Many years afterwards his maternal grandmother used to take 'wee Johnnie' on her knee and tell him how the wicked landlords had taken the farms and crofts of the poor people of the north, so that they had nowhere to sleep, nothing to eat, and no means of earning an honest living. She told him how many had been forced to take ship to America, and how often parents never again saw their children, and husbands were parted for ever from their wives. She told him how his grandfather, Donald MacPhee, had been forced to make his way down to the Clyde industrial belt to find work, and was eventually taken on as a quarryman at Paisley. Then she and her little daughter Anne, who could not speak one word of English, had to make the long journey south on their own, walking great parts of the way, to join him in Paisley. We can be sure that these stories sank deeply into the boy's mind, and when, years later, he read *Capital*, he was able to appreciate to the full Marx's harrowing description of the notorious Sutherland Clearances.

My grandmother Anne died one year after I was born, so I have no memory of her, but her other grandchildren retained a vivid impression of a typical Highland woman, stout and large-boned, with a rosy face, high cheekbones and twinkling blue eyes. She had more than her share of courage, determination and independent honesty—qualities which she passed on to her son.

Little is known about Daniel Maclean, as he died when John was only eight years old. It is said that he had a very active mind and was fond of discussion and argument. He and Anne were married in 1867 at Nitshill, near Pollokshaws. He had become a potter, and for a while worked in a pottery at Bo'ness, Linlithgowshire. Eventually he obtained work at Lockhart's Pottery, Pollok-shaws, and there John was born in 1879, the sixth of seven children. Only four survived, but that was a typical survival rate for those days, and four children were quite plenty to bring up on the small wage of a potter who was very often on short time.

Many of these dispossessed Highlanders adapted themselves remarkably well to their new environment. They had been accustomed to poverty and hardship, and most of them were Calvinists. Calvinism exalted those self-regarding virtues which tended to make and save money—hard work, thrift, and sobriety. Any kind of light-mindedness or frivolity was anathema to the Calvinist, who regarded feelings of joy and pleasure as evil in themselves. This was carried to such an extent that in some Highland villages even to smile on a Sunday was sinful! The Original Secession Church, the sect to which the Macleans belonged, would not allow even an organ inside the church.

The Macleans were good Calvinists, but they never managed to 'get on'. They remained well-respected members of the working class, with the usual hard struggle to make ends meet. As time went on, Daniel Maclean was afflicted with what used to be called 'the potters' trouble', but which we would now call silicosis, and was often unable to work at all at his trade. Anne Maclean had to go out nursing to augment the small income he received as a labourer, and at the early age of forty-three he died, in 1888.

If life was grim for the working-class wife with a family to rear, it was ten times worse for the widow—no pensions in those days. The hard struggle of his mother to provide for herself and her children was one of the strongest influences on Maclean's development. Mrs Maclean had been a weaver before marriage, so she now obtained employment at Auldfield Mill, Pollokshaws, while her old mother came to look after the children. But women's wages in the textile industry were then based on the bare needs of a girl living with her parents or of a married woman working in addition to her husband. They were insufficient to keep the family.

Her next venture was to take over a small newsagent's and general store. She was too soft-hearted to make a good business-woman, but the shop gave them a living until her eldest daughter, Margaret, was old enough to work. By moving into a small room-and-kitchen house and keeping a lodger, she was able to give up the arduous life of a small shopkeeper.

John's older brother Daniel had become a pupil teacher before his father's death, and his mother refused to remove him to more immediately remunerative employment when she became a widow. He did his two years at the Teachers' Training College, and ultimately took his MA, but he had no sooner begun his teaching career in earnest than he was found to have developed tuberculosis. The only hope for sufferers in those days was removal to an easier climate, and many went to South Africa; so that is what Daniel did, teaching there until his early death.

This was a big blow to Mrs Maclean, but she was determined that young John should have his chance of education, cost what it may. He had to do his bit, of course. He worked as a message boy before and after school hours, earned money as a caddie at the Thornliebank Golf Course on Saturday afternoons, and gained first-hand experience of factory life by working in Thornliebank Print Works during school holidays. His Sundays were, of course, spent in going to Church and Sunday School, so there was little time for play in his childhood.

He received his elementary education at Pollok Academy, and, in spite of his hard work outside school, is reported to have been a very bright pupil. Instead of setting him to work as soon as he was twelve, his mother kept him on, and he received his secondary education at Queen's Park School. In 1896, when he was seventeen, he went to Polmadie School as a pupil teacher, and remained there until the summer of 1898. From 1898 to 1900 he studied at the Free Church Training College, from which he emerged as a certificated teacher.

Meanwhile, his real, as apart from his academic, education was proceeding apace. Since his early teens he had been attending the Sunday morning meetings for young men, as well as the usual Church services, but young John began to think for himself.

His growing experience of life soon showed him that the poverty suffered by the Maclean family was by no means exceptional. He found that the pillars of the Church, those most looked-up-to by the congregation because they gave most money, were the very factory-owners, landlords and business men who were responsible for the miserable conditions of the ordinary worker. Their 'Christian charity' consisted in giving back with their left hands a tiny portion of the wealth they had taken with their right hands. Hard and self-righteous, they maintained that God had given all their places in the world, rich and poor. So it had always been, and so it would always be. Therefore when some of his more thoughtful contemporaries began to leave the Church, young John soon followed.

By this time he was preparing to attend the Teachers' Training College, and was nineteen years old. A letter from his older brother Daniel, from South Africa, dated October 1898, shows how he was maturing:

'I was extremely pleased and, I may say, somewhat surprised on receipt of the two letters from you lately' wrote Dan, in fatherly fashion. 'My reason for feeling so was that your former epistles had been full of plenty of good-natured fun and nonsense, but very little information or sense. However, you seem to have got over the natural calfish sprightliness of youth, and from the tone of your letters seem to have become imbued with some sense of manhood and the responsibilities, troubles and pleasures accompanying that condition. I am glad, also, to note the strong enthusiasm and ambition which pervade your remarks about yourself. The enthusiasm, I daresay, will become considerably toned down as your experience grows riper, but the possession of enthusiasm, especially in regard to things worth striving for, is much more to be desired than the want of it.'

John was determined to avoid Dan's fate, and to the end of his life retained a fervent belief in the benefits of open-air exercise. He walked to College every morning, during the two years of his teacher training. During the summer he worked as a farm labourer, and as a postman during the other holidays. That was how he obtained his exercise—not for him the expensive games and athletics of his middle-class fellow students. Whether his own, conscious efforts had anything to do with it or not, there is no doubt that he was outstandingly successful in maintaining good health. In later years his extraordinary energy and strength were to astonish all who knew him.

2/The Progressive Union

1900 marked quite definitely the beginning of John Maclean's adult life. He celebrated his twenty-first birthday, he successfully concluded his teacher training, and obtained his first post as assistant master at Strathbungo School. More important than these facts, however, was his connection with the Progressive Union. That was the real beginning of his manhood.

It was early in the year that the respectable, God-fearing inhabitants of Pollokshaws were startled by the formation of the

Progressive Union. Founded on the initiative of Will Craig, who appears to have been the brother of John's best friend Jim, the objects of this novel Society were, as described in the local *Pollokshaws News*, 'the social intercourse and mutual improvement —materially, mentally and morally—of the members; the discussion of philosophic, scientific and literary subjects, and all problems of present-day interest, especially those which concern the social and religious life of the people'.

To the great horror of the 'unco guid' their meetings took place on a Sunday afternoon. As the members made their way through the somnolent streets, they formed a target for the bitter disapproval of large sections of the population. Such was the interest created, however, that their activities were reported in great detail in the local press.

Socialism, anarchism, Henry George's single tax theory, Malthusianism, co-operation, were among the social problems discussed. The natural sciences, with particular emphasis on astronomy, together with the whole field of imaginative literature, were covered. The chief interest, however, centred on religion. The majority of the members, although they might not have called themselves atheists, hated the churches and their superstitious doctrines. They believed that the first step towards a better life was the breaking of religion's yoke. Then the eyes of the poor, ignorant, priest-ridden proletariat would be opened to the wonders of the universe and to the potentialities lying dormant in each individual.

John Maclean developed rapidly in this stimulating environment. He learned to speak in public by taking part in the discussions and was soon himself giving lectures. Among those recorded are 'Poverty, Drink and Crime' (16 January 1901), 'Shelley' (November 1901), and 'Plato and the Republic' (3 February 1902). All his youthful enthusiasm was poured into the organization and in 1901 he was appointed secretary.

By this time he had adopted a completely secularist outlook and he remained an uncompromising atheist during the whole of his life. Soon after he began teaching he was in conflict with headmaster George Watson over the teaching of the Bible. He objected strongly to pumping what he considered false and insidious doctrines into the plastic minds of his pupils. He was eventually transferred to Rutland Crescent School—but Govan School Board, his employers, composed mainly of priests and ministers, did not forget him.

For a short time John, like the majority of his Progressive

Union associates, was inclined to over-estimate the importance of anti-religious propaganda. He soon realized, however, that whole sections of the community could cast off religion and yet remain the most hidebound social reactionaries. Secularist teaching, while important, could not cure the social evils he loathed. He turned more and more towards the ideas of socialism.

This was almost inevitable. Most of the leading lights of the Union were socialists. Chief among them was John MacDougall, a stonemason, and uncle of James MacDougall who became Maclean's chief assistant in his socialist pioneering work throughout Scotland. John MacDougall was a real 'character'. At the age of forty he refused to remain a wage-slave any longer, but settled himself in an armchair surrounded by books and papers, and refused to budge, except to go to bed, and visit the PU meetings once a week. He lived with his brother Daniel, a cripple, who was a cobbler, and, like John, a bachelor. Daniel was interested in psychology, rather than sociology, and eventually wrote a series of novels which were published after his death. Another of the members was Willie McGill, an anarchist, who later became famous in the Glasgow revolutionary movement. The most important among the younger men was Bill Stewart, who became one of Maclean's closest friends, and was for a short time later on, the editor of *The Socialist*, organ of the Socialist Labour Party.

According to the report made by the *Pollokshaws News* about young John Maclean's lecture on 'Poverty, Drink and Crime', January 1901, he was already a convinced socialist at that time. 'The writer of the paper attributed poverty to the unequal economic conditions. Socialism would cure this. He argued that in a state where the Government was a Socialist one there could not be the same opportunities for drink, and the diminution of drunkenness would result in the diminution of crime.'

Twelve years later, during a lecture, he declared he had been a convert of Robert Blatchford's book *Merrie England* in the first place. 'All honour to Robert Blatchford,' say I. 'He has given us the finest elementary introduction to Socialism that I know of. *Merrie England* is the primary school of Socialism, but *Das Kapital* is the university.' (*Forward*, 1 March 1913.)

It can't have been long after reading *Merrie England* that he was introduced to *Das Kapital* by John MacDougall. At this time, John Maclean was taking early morning and evening classes at Glasgow University for his MA, one of them being on political economy, so he had every chance to examine both sides of the question. It is not surprising that he did particularly well in his final examination on this subject at the university, taking second place to a young man who became well-known in academic circles.

By September 1902, Maclean had become a convinced Marxist, according to a very long letter of his in the *Pollokshaws News*:

> To make wealth rapidly, capitalists have wrought men, women and children long hours at high speed and for wages that just keep them alive. Here the class struggle begins with the desire to steal the maximum from the workers. The workers feel the necessity for united effort, so that they may resist the attacks of the enemy, the capitalists. Trade Unions are formed, and the strike is used to get as much of the wealth produced as possible. But wives and children starve, and the Unions must yield. Though united, the workers still fight an unequal battle. Hunger brings them to their knees, and so most strikes have resulted in loss to the men. Whatever gain is got is soon lost at times of depression, when masters need only threaten the lock-out to reduce wages.
>
> Instances of strikes: The Belgian workers recognized that politics is closely related to economics, and so they struck work to force the capitalists to give them the political right of universal suffrage. Lord Penrhyn, trying to exercise feudal tyranny over his Welsh quarrymen, forced them to strike. The struggle has lasted two years, and is not settled yet. The Progressive Union felt it obligatory to help the workers in both cases . . .
>
> That the class struggle is bitter, we need only reckon the annual death roll of the workers, the maimed, the poisoned, the physically wrecked by overwork, the mentally wrecked by worry, and those forced to suicide by desperation. It is a more bloody and more disastrous warfare than that to which the soldier is used. Living in slums, breathing poisonous and carbon-laden air, wearing shoddy clothes, eating adulterated and life-extinguishing food, the workers have greater cause for a forcible revolution than had the French capitalists in 1789.

Here followed a statement of faith in constitutional, parliamentary methods of struggle, engendered by the formation of the Labour Representation Committee in 1900, and worth repeating because the hopes expressed were echoing throughout the labour movement at that time:

> But the workers need not that method. Their hope lies in carrying the class struggle into the political field, and there they will meet and defeat the capitalists, when all the workers see the need for solidarity and for loyalty to their class. The efforts of the masters to end the use of the strike through the Taff Vale decision has caused the miners to save their funds for labour representation. Next election we shall see a complete change in politics. The

inevitable outcome will be the formation of two new parties with opposite interests, the parasites including capitalists, landlords, etc., on the one side and the workers gathered round the Trade Unions and Co-operative Movements, on the other, the Haves versus the Have-nots. Socialists have pointed out this line of action and the masters have compelled its adoption.

When in Parliament, the new Labour Party will find its true mission to be not the shortening of hours, increasing of wages, and bettering of conditions, but the overthrow of the capitalist class and the landlord class, so that land and capital be used to produce for consumption and not for profit. Remember, the capitalist does not benefit the worker by giving him work, the worker benefits the capitalist by making him rich.

These hopes were, of course, not fulfilled, but by the time the LRC had developed into the Labour Party, in 1906, John Maclean had identified himself with a very different kind of organization.

While there has been some controversy about the actual date John Maclean joined the Social Democratic Federation, there seems little doubt that he did so some time in 1903. James D MacDougall assured me that he did not join until after the break-away of the Socialist Labour Party which took place at the annual conference of the party that Easter. What is quite certain is that, although young John had been a convinced socialist for some years, he was quite determined to achieve as much economic security as he could manage—this meant security for his mother and sisters as well—by obtaining his MA before devoting his energy to what became his life-work.

He had been taking classes for his degree from 1897, when he was still a pupil teacher, and by 1902, had passed them all except Higher Latin, which had become his *bête noire*. A teaching colleague recorded that he used to sit this exam twice a year and used to talk jocularly about taking out a season ticket. He did not formally become an MA until October 1904, but by 1903 obviously felt himself entitled to devote the largest part of his energy to the socialist cause. However, he continued to take evening classes in chemistry, physics, and mathematics at Glasgow Technical College until 1907, purely for his own information.

Before we begin the record of John Maclean's work for the socialist movement, some readers may be interested to know more about the kind of young man he was at this crucial period of his life. By good luck, information of this kind has been preserved. At the beginning of 1903 Daniel MacDougall, who was very interested in psychology and especially in the novel doctrines of Freud, began what he called a 'character album'. Each subject had to answer twenty-five questions, revealing his likes and dislikes. One page was devoted to young John's answers and after Maclean's death, on 8 December 1923, an article appeared in the *Pollokshaws News* giving Daniel's own summary of the answers:

> His favourite quality in man is 'sincerity of purpose', and in woman 'cheerfulness'. His most loved activity would be that of 'a worthy citizen of a Co-operative Commonwealth'. His idea of happiness is 'long life with a woman I admired'. The calling that appeared to him the best is 'dispeller of ignorance'. If not himself, he would like to be 'one as good as himself'. He could live anywhere 'with true friends'. He would like to be living 'when Socialism is established'. His idea of unhappiness is 'a life without friends'. His chief character inclination is 'nobility of ideal'. His favourite painter is 'Sam Bough'. His favourite authors are 'Marx, Blatchford, Shelley'. He has no favourite musical composer. His favourite colour and flower are 'pink and white and forget-me-not'. (If his followers wish to adopt a flower in memory of him, here is a hint.) His favourite heroes in history are 'John Ball, Socrates, and Jesus'. His favourite heroines in history are 'Lady Macbeth, Rosalind, Miranda'. The historical characters against whom he feels antipathy are 'Queen Victoria and Edward VII'. The greatest mistake he made was 'entering life'. His greatest antipathy is to 'selfish rivalry'. He fears most 'poverty, false friendship, being misunderstood'. His favourite food and drink are 'porridge, water'. His temperament he describes as 'serious'. His motto is: 'To thine own self be true, and it must follow, as the night the day, thou can'st not then be false to any man'.

I do not suppose that the people who contributed to Daniel's album took it at all seriously, but there are enough indications that some of the answers at least were quite accurate, and a picture is formed of an earnest and idealistic young man, very much of his time and place, in spite of his advanced ideas. Although he had cast off the religious teaching of his early upbringing, he was at the same time very much its product. His puritanical personal behaviour—he did not smoke or drink, was conventional as regards sex, and found it difficult to tell even the 'little white lies' of social tact—lasted throughout his life. His own personal interpretation of Marxism was obviously, whether he realized it himself or not, affected by the general ethos of the Presbyterian Church. Its ultra-democratic form of Church government, and its passionate belief in universal education—both stemming directly from John Knox and the social revolutionaries of the seventeenth century—found a reflection in his emphasis on 'power from below upwards' and on the supreme importance of independent working-class education.

3/The Socialist Movement

After John Maclean's conversion to Marxism, it was prac
cally certain that he would eventually join the Social Democra
Federation. At that time it was the only Marxist organization of a
account in Britain, and was, indeed, the pioneer of the mode
socialist movement. It had been founded, as the Democra
Federation, by H M Hyndman in 1881. Two years later the ne
body, having by this time agreed to adopt and propagate t
principles of Marxian Socialism, changed its name to the Soci
Democratic Federation.

Marxism, contrary to the frequent charges levelled against
of being a foreign import and alien to the British working cla
was very much part of the British scene. Marx himself lived
London for the greater part of his life (1849-83), and the maj
part of his scientific investigation into the nature of capitalism w
carried out during this period. His magnum opus, *Capital*, was
Critical Analysis of Capitalist Production' as found in Britain, a
was based on the work of the classical political economists, Ada
Smith and Ricardo. Their basic conclusion that labour was tl
source of value had now been rejected by the new orthodox scho
of political economists like Marshall and Jevons, who had form
lated the new 'marginal utility' theory of value, which of cours
had been studied by Maclean at Glasgow University.

A brief account of these developments in economic theory w
given by Maclean in the address prepared by him for the inaugur
meeting of the Scottish Labour College in 1916. I have includ
the following extract now, because I think it is important at tl
stage to understand why John Maclean considered 'independe
working-class education' as important as 'independent working-cla
representation':

The next source of opposition to a Labour College will be t
Curriculum. In the city where Adam Smith discoursed on 'T
Wealth of Nations' a full century-and-a-half ago, it should hardly
necessary to insist that the principal study ought to be Economi
I fancy we are largely agreed on that. The difficulty arises as to t
kind of Economics. At a Labour College Economics must l
taught fundamentally from the Labour standpoint. Otherwise v

ought to send our students to the capitalist universities. Our students must make the writings of Marx and Marxian scholars the basis of their studies; otherwise the College becomes an expensive tragedy. That does not imply the exclusion of the study of Marshall, the pontiff of present-day capitalist Economics, or the other great writers who have influenced or are today moulding economic thought.

Many people are horrified to hear it said that the working-class standpoint in economics is bound to be different from that of the capitalists. . . . True! The professors of political economy in the Universities claim to be impartial men of science. But nobody believes them: their attitude is recognized as a necessary, professional pose. Their teaching has become a mere system of apologetics, by means of which they reveal the moral reasons that justify the plundering of the working class.

In this respect it is as different as night from day, when compared with the work of the economists of the Classic School from Smith to Ricardo. These truly great men earnestly sought for the hidden forces operating the mechanism of society; they tried to discover the tendencies that introduced a semblance of regularity into the chaotic anarchy of manufacture and commerce. They classified economic facts, and, in doing so, discovered and defined some of the principal categories of political economy. . . .

They could afford to be quite frank, for in those days there was no need for hypocrisy, because the working class, as we know it, was hardly in existence, and where it had appeared was devoid of consciousness. And so the economists in their researches into the nature of value had no class prejudices to obscure their vision, any more than has the chemist of today when he carries out an experiment. They proclaimed Labour to be the source of value.

But very soon the working class had developed and even had secured literary champions—such as Thomson, Hodgskin, etc—either from its own ranks or from other classes, and they asked the question: if Labour produces all value, why does the labourer not receive the full value of his product? Thus they made a moral application of Ricardian Economics, and severely criticized the competitive system.

Then came Marx, who set aside moral considerations as out of place in such a study, and, in a strictly scientific manner, dealt with the economic facts: the same man who, starting from the Ricardian theory of value, which he criticized and put upon a scientific basis, burst through the economic concepts of the time and discovered a new category, which he called surplus value, by means of which he explained the origin and formation of profit, interest, and rent.

It was then that the demoralization of economic science set in. When the working class was to some extent awakened and had even produced its theoretical writers, safety demanded that political economy should cease handling the real facts of Capitalism, and should deal only in the vaguest generalities and sophisms. Now we can read in the writings of such shining lights as Lord Cromer of 'that unfortunate statement of Ricardo's that labour is the source of value'.

Almost twenty years prior to the foundation of the SDF, Karl Marx had taken the initiative in drawing together the different threads of British and European working-class thought by the formation of the International Working Men's Association (the First International). Max Beer in his *History of British Socialism* summarizes its policy as follows:

The emancipation of the working classes must be achieved by the working classes themselves. The struggle for that emancipation means not a struggle for class privileges and monopolies, but for equal rights and duties, and the abolition of class rule. The economic subjection of the man of labour to the monopolizer of the means of production or the sources of life is the foundation of servitude in all its forms, of all social misery, mental degradation, and political dependence. The economic emancipation of the working classes is, therefore, the great end to which every political movement ought to be subordinated as a means. The emancipation of labour is neither a local nor a national, but a social, problem, embracing all countries in which modern society exists, and depending for its solution on the concurrence, practical and theoretical, of the most advanced countries.

I have included this statement, because it appears to me to be the foundation on which Maclean's political thinking was based. He was not an original thinker. His talent lay in his application of Marxian principles to the circumstances of time and place, and in his outstanding ability to communicate them in the simplest terms to the uneducated Scottish working class.

Radical ideas had died out during the decade prior to the formation of the SDF. The leaders of the rapidly-expanding trade union and co-operative movements were thoroughly wedded to the Liberal Party and to the capitalist system, as were the great mass of workers. The SDF brought a revival of socialist thought, and one of the first reactions was the formation of another socialist organization, the Fabian Society, in 1883. It was founded with the express purpose of eradicating Marxism from the British labour movement. While it was never successful in this aim, it was completely successful in dominating the outlook of both the existing labour movement and of the Labour Party that was formed. Thus Edward Pease could write in 1916 in his book *The History of the Fabian Society* that its first achievement 'was to break the spell of Marxism in England'.

Here it should be noted that Scotland (whether intentionally or not!) was left out of this sweeping assertion—and rightly so, for this book is the story of how Marxism became more deeply rooted in Scotland than in any other part of the British Empire.

It is hardly necessary to go deeply into Fabian philosophy, as we are all so familiar with its products, such as Harold Wilson and most of the leaders of the Labour Party, both past and present. We are also only too familiar with the concrete results of its policies—the welfare state or 'welfare capitalism'. It is necessary to emphasize, however, that the fundamental root of Fabianism was the rejection of any kind of socialist theory ('pragmatism'), and in particular the repudiation of Marxism, the labour-time theory of value, and the theory of the class struggle. No systematic criticism of Marxism was ever made, but it was simply stated that its theories no longer applied in a society which had granted universal suffrage (except for women!) and other democratic rights to the workers. As regards the economic base of society, the Fabians simply stated that they accepted the findings of 'the accredited British professors', and supported the marginal utility theory of value as expounded by them.

The policy of the Fabians was directed at first towards 'permeating' the Liberal Party, of which most were members. Because of this belief in the Liberal Party as an effective instrument of social reform, the Fabians at that time were called the 'possibilists', from the definition of politics as 'the art of the possible', in contrast to the 'impossibilists' of the SDF, and others like Keir Hardie and Ramsay MacDonald who were by then coming to the fore. The latter, however, while also repudiating Marxism, were convinced that the working class must have separate representation, and must therefore be weaned away from the Liberal Party. They thought it was much more important to fight for this kind of independence than to emphasize or propagate socialist aims. Thus the result of their efforts was the formation, at Bradford in 1893, of of Independent Labour Party (independent of the Liberal Party), which was to become the ideal working-class vehicle for Fabian ideas.

Seven years later the ILP was successful in forming the Labour Representation Committee, a federal body to which were affiliated some trade unions, the SDF, the ILP, and the Fabian Society. In 1900, 375,931 people affiliated to the LRC. They included 13,000 members of the ILP, 9000 members of the SDF, and 861 members of the Fabian Society. So, in spite of its ten years' start, the SDF was already falling far behind the ILP in attracting members and this trend was to continue.

Two years later, in 1902, because of an influx of new left-wing members, the SDF annual conference voted to disaffiliate from the LRC, because of its refusal to accept socialist principles, and thus left the field open to the ILP and the Fabian Society. John Maclean considered this a very grave error of judgement, and did his best throughout the years to get the party to reverse this decision.

4/The SDF in Scotland

By the end of the nineteenth century, the SDF had achieved some measure of success in England. Some of its leaders, such as Tom Mann, Ben Tillet, and John Burns, had gained fame through their leadership of the campaign for the 'new unionism', the organization of unskilled workers in general unions. In Scotland, however, after twenty years of stormy existence, little impact had been made.

Some branches were formed as early as 1883. One in Glasgow was founded by Bruce Glasier, later to become famous as one of the leaders of the British ILP. Within a year, however, Glasier and a number of others left to join William Morris's Socialist League.

After that blow, there was a steady growth until the formation of the Scottish Labour Party in 1888, subsequent to the famous mid-Lanark by-election when Keir Hardie stood against the Liberal as an independent Labour candidate, but failed to win. The Scottish Labour Party might be called the prototype for the ILP, its members being primarily concerned with 'independent working class representation' rather than with the propagation of socialist ideas. There was one difference however. In Keir Hardie's election address he stated:

> I am strongly in favour of Home Rule for Scotland, being convinced that until we have a Parliament of our own we cannot obtain the many and great reforms on which I believe the people of Scotland have set their hearts.

Home Rule for both Scotland and Ireland was one of the

aims of the first Labour Party in Britain, and all the officials elected were well-known as both nationalists and socialists—the famous R B Cunningham-Graham, Dr G B Clarke, John Ferguson, leader of the Glasgow Irish, and, of course, Keir Hardie himself.

The Scottish Labour Party naturally stole a great deal of the SDF's thunder, especially because of its support for Home Rule, a very popular cause, particularly among the miners. However, it did not remain long on the scene. With the formation of the ILP at Bradford in 1893, the Scottish party was dissolved and re-constituted as the Scottish Council of the ILP. The new association of Scottish nationalism with the labour movement did not end, however. Scottish Home Rule was an integral part of Labour Party policy until after the formation of the 1945 Labour government. One of the last things Keir Hardie did before his death in 1915 was to prepare a draft Home Rule Bill for Scotland.

Little is known about the early SDF pioneers in Glasgow, but John Maclean's first biographer, Tom Anderson, wrote:

> Long before Comrade Keir Hardie we had Comrades Willie Nairn and Bob Hutchison, two veteran members of the SDF—to name two only—who held meetings in the Jail Square on the Sundays, from ten o'clock in the morning till ten o'clock at night. The meetings were carried on by the relay system, and were well known.
>
> Comrade John had often listened to these comrades, and it was from them he received his first lessons on Scientific Socialism.

Among other early members were the Irish martyr James Connolly, then a carter employed by Edinburgh Corporation; John F Armour, a Glasgow stonemason; George Yates, an engineer; J Carstairs Mathieson, a Falkirk schoolteacher; John Leslie, an Edinburgh insurance agent, and Tom Bell, an ironmoulder, who later became president of the British Communist Party.

In Scotland the attack on official SDF policy came most strongly from the left. At this time revolutionary syndicalism had put down no roots in Britain. It had originated in France and was basically a plan for turning trade unions from organs of defence into organs of attack on capitalism. The trade unions were to take over industry and run it themselves in the interests of the workers, completely by-passing political action, which was regarded as worse than useless.

The syndicalist ideas which were now beginning to flow into Scotland did not come from France, however, but from America, and were allied with Marxism. American syndicalism, in response to a highly-developed capitalism dominated by huge, highly-centralized trusts, favoured large-scale industrial unions (as opposed to trade unions), highly centralized and well-disciplined. These ideas were embodied in the Socialist Labour Party, whose outstanding leader was Daniel de Leon.

When the majority of the Scottish branches of the SDF seceded at the Easter conference in 1903, they lost no time in constituting themselves as the British Socialist Labour Party (although there were hardly any English members!), receiving intellectual guidance and inspiration from the American party. John Maclean was never a syndicalist, and was always very impatient with those socialists who wanted to limit socialist activity to the industrial sphere. However, he never at any time, as far as I am aware, criticized either the organization or its members in a systematic fashion, as he did the ILP. That was because its members were avowed Marxists, and the differences between them were those of tactics rather than principle.

5/Pioneering work

When Maclean arrived at the end of 1903, the Scottish SDF was at a very low ebb, after the secession of the majority of the branches at Easter. He joined in Glasgow, where there was only one small branch left. Hutchison and Nairn were dead by this time.

Maclean immediately plunged into activity of every kind. With members so scarce, there could be no division of labour. The first priority, however, was to build up the party again, and Maclean set about helping the Scottish Organizer, Tom Kennedy (later to become Labour MP for Kirkcaldy in 1921, and Chief Labour Whip in the 1929 Labour government), to form new branches and resurrect old ones. Together with James Burnett he formed the Glasgow Press Committee, the duties of which were to write letters to the press, draft leaflets, manifestos, and election literature. He helped to organize demonstrations by the unemployed. He played an active part in trade union and co-operative circles, always as a revolutionary socialist. From spring to autumn he conducted intensive open-air propaganda all over the country, pioneering in many districts. During the winter months he took classes in Marxian economics and industrial history.

His tremendous vitality and allied qualities—self-confidence,

...n Maclean (far right middle row) when a teacher at Lorne Street School, ...sgow, 1915. He was sacked later. Far left: Anne MacPhee, John Maclean's ...ther. Left: Agnes Wood, his wife. Overleaf: before the 1916 trial.

GLASGOW EX-TEACHER.

AMERA PRIOR TO TRIAL.

SSIAN PEOPLES'
EMBASSY AND
SULATE GENERAL
VICTORIA STREET, S.W.1

Telephone : VICTORIA 3960

5/1/18

Dear Comrade Maclean, I am writing to
the Russian Consul in Glasgow (I am
not sure that there exists such a person)
informing him of your appointment
& ordering him to hand over to you
the consulate. He may refuse to do so,
in which case you will open a new consulate, & make it public through the
press. Your position may be difficult
somehow, but you will have my full
support. It is most important
to keep me — informed (and through
me the Russian Soviets) of the Labour
movement in N. B.

I am writing in all haste, as
I wish not to miss the occasion.
It is not very safe to write
per post. With best wishes
Yours sincerely
Maxim Litvinoff

e Round Toll, Pollokshaws. Peter Petroff stayed with John Maclean when he
ed in the house on the right. Far left: letter from Litvinov on John Maclean's
pointment as Russian Consul in Glasgow. Left: William Gallacher. Overleaf:
al speech 1918.

Release from jail, 4 December 1918. In front row: Mrs William Gallacher, Jam⟨

laxton, Agnes Maclean, John Maclean, William Gallacher, and Dora Montefiore.

The banished Clyde workers: J. M. Messer, James Haggerty, A. Macman

. Shields and David Kirkwood.

The Tramp Trust Unlimited: left to right: Peter Marshall, Sandy Ross, Joh

The TRAMP TRUST Unlimited

...Maclean, James D. MacDougall and Harry MacShane.

John Maclean speaking at Glasgow Green, May Day 1923.

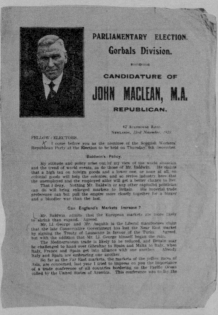

PARLIAMENTARY ELECTION.

Gorbals Division.

CANDIDATURE OF

JOHN MACLEAN, M.A.

REPUBLICAN.

42 Auchmead Road,
Newlands, 23rd November, 1923.

FELLOW - ELECTORS,—

X I come before you as the nominee of the Scottish Workers'
Republican Party at the Election to be held on Thursday, 6th December.

Baldwin's Policy.

My attitude and policy arise out of my view of the world situation
and the trend of world events, as do those of Mr. Baldwin. He claims
that a high tax on foreign goods and a lower one, or none at all, on
colonial goods will help the colonies, and so revive industry here, that
the unemployed and the employed alike will get a better chance to live.

That I deny. Nothing Mr. Baldwin or any other capitalist politician
can do will bring enlarged markets to Britain. His imperial trade
preference can but pull the empire more closely together for a bigger
and a bloodier war than the last.

Can England's Markets Increase?

Mr. Baldwin admits that the European markets are more likely
to shrink than expand. Agreed.

Mr. Ll George and Mr. Asquith in the Liberal manifestos claim
that the late Conservative Government has lost the Near East market
by signing the Treaty of Lausanne in favour of the Turks. Agreed,
but with the addition that Mr. Ll George himself began the ruin.

The Mediterranean trade is likely to be reduced, and Britain may
be challenged to hand over Gibraltar to Spain and Malta to Italy, when
Italy, France and Spain get into alliance with one another. Already
Italy and Spain are embracing one another.

So far as the Far East markets, the markets of the yellow races of
Asia, are concerned, last year I tried to impress on you the importance
of a trade conference of all countries bordering on the Pacific Ocean
called by the United States of America. This conference was to lay the

Up Ireland!   Up Scotland!   Up India!

Right: John Maclean with a friend at a
holiday camp on the Solway Firth, not
long before his death in 1923. Top: last
election manifesto. Above: the Vanguard.

Previous page: John Maclean's funeral. The rear pallbearer shown is Jame
and double that number followed the funeral, which was led by the Clyde Workers

...xton, leaving 42 Auldhouse Road. Above: five thousand took part in the march
...nd.

The ballad of John MacLean

Words and music by Matt McGinn
© Heathside Music 1967

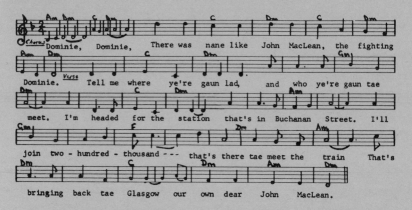

Chorus: Dominie, Dominie, There was nane like John MacLean, the fighting Dominie. Verse: Tell me where ye're gaun lad, and who ye're gaun tae meet. I'm headed for the station that's in Buchanan Street. I'll join two-hundred-thousand --- that's there tae meet the train That's bringing back tae Glasgow our own dear John MacLean.

Tell me whaur he's been, lad, and why has he been there.
They've had him in the prison for preaching in the Square,
For Johnny held a finger at all the ills he saw,
He was right side o' the people, but he was wrong side o' the law.

Johnny was a teacher in one o' Glasgow's schools
The golden law was silence but Johnny broke the rules,
For a world of social justice young Johnny couldnae wait,
He took his chalk and easel to the men at the shipyard gate.

The leaders o' the nation made money hand o'er fist
By grinding down the people by the fiddle and the twist,
Aided and abetted by the preacher and the Press —
John called for revolution and he called for nothing less.

The bosses and the judges united as one man
For Johnny was a danger to their '14-'18 plan,
They wanted men for slaughter in the fields of Armentiers,
John called upon the people to smash the profiteers.

They brought him to the courtroom in Edinburgh toun,
But still he didnae cower, he firmly held his ground,
And stoutly he defended his every word and deed,
Five years it was his sentence in the jail at Peterheid.

Seven months he lingered in prison misery,
Till the people rose in fury, in Glasgow and Dundee,
Lloyd George and all his cronies were shaken to the core,
The prison gates were opened, and John was free once more.

courage and determination—made him admirably suited for a pioneer. He had already gained some experience of public-speaking at the Progressive Union, and soon after joining he was thrown in at the deep end. On 4 April 1904, *Justice*, the SDF organ, reported:

> The first outdoor meeting was held on Sunday last in St Enoch Square, when, owing to the unavoidable absence of Comrade Johnstone, Comrade J Maclean delivered a stirring address on the elementary principles of socialism to an audience of about 200.

During that summer he helped in the formation of a new branch at Greenock, a large industrial town down the Clyde famous for its sugar refineries and shipyards. He met for the first time there, Hugh Hinshelwood, who was to become a lifelong friend and good comrade. It was in connection with the new branch that Maclean's courage and determination first became manifest. One of its first actions was to apply to the authorities for permission to hold meetings at Cathcart Square, an ideal stance for drawing large crowds. The police refused permission, and suggested an alternative stance quite away from the main thoroughfare, where there was little chance of holding a good meeting. The branch meekly submitted, but when Maclean came to speak later in the summer he insisted on defying the police, spoke at Cathcart Square, and held a triumphantly successful meeting. On this occasion, audacity won, for the police said not one word.

Maclean became very well-known in Greenock. His first pamphlet, *The Greenock Jungle*, inspired by Upton Sinclair's famous novel *The Jungle*, was written about the criminal traffic carried on in diseased carcases by a number of Greenock butchers. It sold remarkably well and resulted in an enquiry by the Local Government Board. Eventually a meat inspector was appointed for the town's slaughter-house. Nowadays, of course, this is a statutory duty carried out by the public health authorities, but at the time it was a real victory. Maclean also conducted an agitation about the bad housing conditions in Greenock, which resulted eventually in the formation of a Greenock Housing Council.

In 1906 he began taking weekly economic and industrial history classes in Greenock every winter, which were so successful that, prior to the formation of the Scottish Labour College in 1916, the number of regular students was 121.

It was a great disappointment to Maclean that the SDF continued to remain disaffiliated from the Labour Representation Committee (which I shall now call the Labour Party). All his activities were founded on the fundamental belief that socialists

B

were not a sect apart from the working class, and this decision seemed to him to drive a wedge between the SDF and the developing labour movement. He himself tried to make up for it by playing an active part in the co-operative movement. Because of his profession, he was unable to take part in the trade union movement, except from the outside, so he made strenuous efforts to turn the co-operative movement in a socialist direction. He had, of course, no illusions about it. Excluded as it was from the most important branches of production, it could not be seriously considered as an instrument of general social transformation; but it could be a valuable ally.

He became a member of the Pollokshaws Co-operative Society, and was devoted in his attendance at the quarterly meetings, where he took a great interest in all the business that arose. He ended by gaining the approval of the old Liberals who were the dominating force. His ideas of political action for the working class on a gigantic and frightening scale had to be overlooked because of his practical value, and in 1905 he was elected as a delegate to the British Co-operative Congress which met that year at Paisley. Determined that SDF action should be of an organized nature, he put a notice in *Justice* inviting all members who were to attend to get in touch with him 'with the view to some arrangement being made for united action among socialists on matters of socialist importance'. Jimmy MacDougall told me how he fared:

> At this great gathering John Maclean, then a very young, inexperienced man, fought out a wordy duel with Fred Maddison MP, a veteran of Lib-Labism, on the matter of class-collaboration versus class conflict. It was a famous tourney, and many an honest old co-operator chuckles yet as he remembers how Maclean 'gied it' to the great man from the South.

When ordinary people are no longer dazzled by bourgeois standards and values, the parliamentarians and trade union leaders they have honoured as the great pioneers of socialism, will be revealed as nothing but insignificant bureaucrats or 'labour fakirs' as the SLP members called them at that time. They will realize that the socialist movement was built up outside at the street corner, by the real heroes and pioneers, the despised 'tub-thumpers'. It is no doubt difficult for the younger generation, accustomed to a house-bound, television-watching proletariat, to realize just how important this kind of propaganda was in the early days of the socialist movement. A flamboyant kind of oratory had to be used to draw the crowds, and all the outdoor speakers soon developed a quick wit to deal with constant heckling from the crowd. Maclean rapidly became an expert, as MacDougall told me:

> The fixed pole around which all John Maclean's aspirations and plans for the advancement of socialism in Scotland revolved was the street-corner meeting. He was like a charged body at this time, a young, vigorous man, who had undergone an almost religious conversion to a noble doctrine, and the whole remainder of his life was the incessant pouring out of this charged energy in a sustained series of street-corner meetings.
>
> He spoke in every quarter of Glasgow, in every industrial town in Scotland from Hawick in the south to Aberdeen in the north—aye, and further than Aberdeen, for he addressed the fishermen in the summer herring season at Lerwick. He devoted his two months' summer holidays as a teacher for many years to tours of propaganda systematically conducted and organized over the industrial areas.
>
> He became a masterly speaker. It has long been the habit of our critics and opponents, to refer to such men as Maclean as street-corner spouters. . . . Had they listened to John Maclean's addresses instead of abusing him as they so often did, they would have been astonished to find that, at these rough, scrappy meetings, in the middle of the roar of the traffic, and with crowds of casual people constantly changing and being renewed, he was in the habit of delivering masterly speeches having logical form and structure.

He received his introduction to parliamentary electioneering during the General Election of January 1906. After pressure from Maclean, the SDF contested North Aberdeen with Tom Kennedy as candidate. Maclean, of course, gave all the help that he could, and Kennedy polled a respectable vote of almost 2,000. It was clear from the election results, however, that the Scottish people were still loyal to the Liberal Party, to a much greater extent than the English. The Scottish Workers' Representation Committee ran, unsuccessfully, five candidates, all nominees of the miners, but its English counterpart, now called the Labour Party was successful in getting two of its Scottish nominees elected—George Barnes in Glasgow and Alex Wilkie in Dundee, and twenty-seven were successfully returned in England.

After another summer tour of Scotland, this time assisted by two other members (Morrison of London, and McNabb of Beith), he concentrated during the autumn of 1906 on local politics. After a series of outdoor meetings at the Shawbrig in Pollokshaws, he managed to secure the support of about thirty recruits and the new Pollokshaws Branch was formed, with James MacDougall, the son of the Provost, as secretary. MacDougall was just sixteen years old, but he was the only clerk among them, the others being stone-masons, engineers and so on. He subsequently became Maclean's first lieutenant, as he liked to call himself, and was associated with him in every aspect of his work, as we shall see.

That winter Maclean was launched on that part of his socialist career which was to become his unique contribution to the Scottish movement. He began taking classes on Sunday afternoons at the branch rooms at 17 Cromwell Street. This was part of an educational programme which was quite ambitious for such a small party. During the week a class on English and English literature was taken by Miss C H Jockel MA, and one on elementary economics by A Russell. On Sunday afternoons there was one hour of constitutional history taken by William MacDougall MA and Maclean's hour of advanced economics. John F Armour also took a class on public speaking during the week. That winter Maclean also took over a Saturday evening class in economics under the auspices of the Greenock Branch.

James MacDougall told me how John F Armour and the others tried to keep the educational tradition of the SDF going after the SLP split, when most of the able men deserted the ranks:

These men, and others like them, self-educated, had with painful striving acquired for themselves a certain knowledge of Marxism, but their range was so limited, they felt so insecure in their grasp of the leading principles that, with the best zeal in the world, they were not particularly successful as teachers of others in the various classes which were conducted. In this respect, the advent of Maclean was an absolute godsend.

He formulated a method of teaching Marxian economics. He drew out for his own teaching purposes a series of lecture notes in which he had compressed the whole original scope of Marx's thought. These lecture notes, with the passing of the years and continual teaching of the subject, were polished, amplified with illustrations drawn from the active pulsating life of capitalist business, and in the natural course of events were cyclostyled. The notes then became a perfectly suitable instrument to be used by the school of teachers whom John Maclean himself had educated.

6/More pioneering work

The year 1907 proved to be a momentous one for Maclean, for during that year he was introduced for the first time in a personal way to the developing socialist movements in Ireland and

Russia—movements which were to have a profound effect on his political career.

One of the first of the sporadic strikes that heralded the great industrial unrest of 1911 and 1912 was that of the Belfast transport workers in the summer of 1907. The main leader was James Larkin, the organizer of the dockers, and also a staunch socialist. He had met Maclean the previous year when he was in Glasgow organizing the Clyde dockers, and now he invited him, through the Belfast Socialist Society, to speak on behalf of the strikers in Belfast. Maclean remained there from 3-6 August, and, through Jim Larkin, was allowed to sit in during the union negotiations. This was his first thrilling experience of a big strike.

Not long after Maclean returned to Glasgow, the whole labour movement was shocked to hear that strikers had been killed and injured by soldiers in the streets of Belfast. As the man who had first-hand experience and who had been warning his meetings ever since that all the conditions for a civil conflict were present in Belfast, he was called upon by the SDF to defend the Belfast workers against the slanders of the capitalist press. He wrote a long article, 'Reflections on Belfast', in which he blamed the Liberal government and especially the secretary for Ireland, Birrell, for the deaths. Philip Snowden, one of the leading members of the ILP took up the cudgels on behalf of the government. Maclean defended himself against Snowden in the *Co-operative News*:

> 'I am willing', he wrote, 'that this "Labour Leader" should call me "a fool of the most colossal dimensions"' . . . I am one of those who hold Birrell with his party partially responsible for the dastardly deed perpetrated against the working-class of Belfast. I lectured the strikers nine days before the murder, and I lectured the citizens a week before. More than that, when giving my experiences to a vast audience in Carlisle the day before the event, I pointed out that the situation was such that a petty incident might culminate in such a civil conflict as actually took place on that fateful Monday night. Who are to blame? In my estimation, the capitalist class. The strikers had arrayed against them three wealthy English railway companies, the Shipping Federation, the local employers, the British press, the local Council, the capitalist Liberal Government. . . . The Monday prior to the street fight, negotiations were set on foot to bring about arbitration. The men were willing, if allowed meantime to return to work under the same conditions as those prevalent when they came out. But the masters wished union men to work alongside non-union men. The men refused arbitration under such unfair conditions. The masters broke off further negotiations. Now I maintain it was Birrell's duty to get the Board of Trade to step in and compel the masters to accept

arbitration under the conditions agreed upon by the men. The Government had a week to think and act, and it should have acted. I knew sufficient of history to foresee some tragic event. Birrell knows more about history than I do, and therefore I am entitled to hold him and his party partially responsible for the murder— for murder it was, no matter by whom committed.'

This strike was the beginning of the modern Irish labour movement.

Some time during 1907 a young Russian political prisoner escaped from Siberia and reached Leith, where he made himself known to members of the SDF. He was directed to John Maclean, who by that time had become well-known for his generosity and hospitality. The young man's name was Peter Petroff, and he was to play a big part in Maclean's political life. A member of the Russian Social Democratic Labour Party, he had led three workers' battalions in the 1905 Revolution, been severely wounded, imprisoned, and sent to Siberia.

Maclean welcomed the destitute young man to the room-and-kitchen tenement flat at Low Cartcraigs, Pollokshaws, which he shared with his mother. He kept him there for almost two months, and taught him to speak English. A warm friendship developed, which lasted until Petroff was deported to Russia in 1918. Maclean gained much from this association, including an inside knowledge of Russian affairs. At that time Germany was the leader of world socialism, and Karl Kautsky was regarded as the 'Pope of Marxism'. Plekhanov, the leader of the Menshevik section of the Russian party, was quite well known in Britain; some of his writing had been translated and published by the SDF. Very few had ever heard of Lenin or Trotsky. The differences between the Menshevik and Bolshevik sections of the party were not regarded as important, and little understood.

After leaving Pollokshaws, Petroff went to London to join the large circle of Russian political refugees, and became a very active member of the SDF, which changed its name to the Social Democratic Party (SDP) in 1908. He was much in demand as a speaker on the 1905 Revolution, in which all Marxists were intensely interested, and later on became a member of the executive committee of the London Division. He also wrote articles in *Justice* on the situation in Russia which were a model of Marxist analysis, and became John Maclean's ally in his fight against the chauvinist Hyndman clique.

Maclean spent six weeks of his summer holiday in 1907, for the third year in succession, on a propaganda tour, covering every area in which a branch existed, and doing pioneering work in many others, like Lerwick in the Shetlands. There he gave evening lectures for a week under the auspices of the Lerwick Working Men's Association. His subjects, as advertised in the local newspaper, were: 'The Inevitability of Socialism', 'The Basic Principles of Socialism', 'Socialists and Education', 'Socialism and the Trusts', 'The Class Struggle', and 'Socialism and Morality'.

The following tribute was paid to him by one of his audience on that occasion, as told to Peter Jamieson of Lerwick in 1948:

> Maclean was an outstanding personality. I have pleasant memories of he and I strolling out the North Road, he with *Capital* firmly held under his arm, listening eagerly while I tried to demonstrate some of the enormities of landlordism and the iniquities of 'Fishing Tenures' in Shetland. He was most attentive and the tenderness of his heart was outstandingly apparent when there was mention of oppression and hardship.

After his return to Glasgow, the following appreciation appeared in *Justice* (Scottish Notes, 14 July 1907):

> It is often said that to mention names is invidious, especially in a democratic body like the SDF, and particularly here where all our members from the indefatigable organiser, McPhee, to the members who sell literature or take collections, outvie each other in their efforts to push the movement ahead. Nevertheless there are a few comrades who highly deserve special mention for their herculean efforts and self-sacrificing devotion in spreading the truths of social democracy.
>
> First and foremost among these is John Maclean, than whom no better man has ever been produced by the SDF, and that is saying a great deal indeed. It is quite safe to say that Maclean has addressed meetings in various parts of the country at the average rate of one per day since the beginning of May. He has sometimes held as many as five meetings in one day! And two or three a day is quite a usual thing for him to hold. Nor is he less active in the winter, as in addition to addressing indoor meetings, he usually conducts as many as four economic classes—all of them meeting once a week—while at the same time he will teach an evening continuation class under the School Board. How he manages to get through such an extraordinary amount of work, no one can tell. In fact, I doubt if he could do so himself. But how he can stand the strain of such a pace is a still greater wonder. Just think of the sum total of the work he gets through year after year. Daily he follows his profession as a school teacher, with so much success as to earn the highest merits from the Chief Inspector of Schools. Every evening he is engaged in SDF work of one kind or another, or

is teaching a continuation class. The whole of his vacation is devoted to propaganda—in fact, as Peipes of Inverurie remarked to me the other week—'Maclean does the work of three good men'. Well may we exclaim, 'Eh, but our Mac is a bonnie fechter!' Maclean however, really ought to ca' a little more canny. The most iron-like constitution could not stand such a strain indefinitely.

The concrete results of his summer tours were new branches, and new members for the established ones. Thus before leaving Shetland that year a new branch had been formed in Lerwick, and one report from Carlisle as early as 1905 mentioned that twenty new members had joined the branch there as a result of Maclean's meetings. It appeared to have been his custom to address six or seven meetings at each place he visited, and probably his subjects were similar to those at Lerwick. It is a great pity that these different lectures were never recorded, because they would have been an accurate statement of his fundamental beliefs at that period. As it is, his ideas have to be deduced from the occasional articles and so on, which he wrote during these early years.

His theoretical writing is very limited, and the reason for that is that he was concerned with converting and educating the working class of Scotland, not any other section of the population. The Scottish working class was poorly educated. After leaving school, very few read anything but newspapers, although all respectable households contained at least two books—the Bible and the poems of Robbie Burns. Maclean's educational work had to be done orally, and he never at any time wrote more than a short pamphlet.

Unemployment was very bad in 1907 and at that time there was neither government nor municipal assistance for the tens of thousands of unfortunate men in Glasgow and other industrial towns who could not find work. Those who belonged to some of the older trade unions or were members of Friendly Societies received unemployment benefit, but for the vast majority it meant starvation or indoor relief, the dreaded workhouse. Maclean had already been initiated into the socialist fight on behalf of the unemployed in 1905 and had helped to organize meetings and demonstrations.

The battle was renewed in 1907. Keir Hardie unsuccessfully introduced a Bill in the Commons for the 'Right to Work', and the attack was passed back to the localities. An amusing incident took place during one demonstration headed by Maclean and John F Armour. When it passed near the Stock Exchange it occurred to Maclean that it would be a good move for the unemployed to invade the sacred precincts. Word was quickly passed along the ranks with instructions to be orderly at all costs. As the head of the procession came to the entrance, it suddenly wheeled to the right, marched up the steps, passed inside the building right round the floor, and out into the streets again. Glasgow's financiers were horrified, and after that day the doors of the Stock Exchange were kept shut whenever there was any trouble around.

Just as the riots of the unemployed during the eighties had frightened the upper-class into providing some palliatives, so actions like this stirred the Tory Glasgow Corporation into some activity.

7/In Pollokshaws

It was only natural that Maclean should devote a large part of his efforts to his own home town, Pollokshaws, which had not yet been assimilated into Glasgow. Immediately the new branch had been formed in October, 1906, at least one open-air meeting was held every week, either at the Shawbrig or at the Townshouse. In MacDougall's words (taken from a letter written by him to James Maxton dated 24 February 1924, when Maxton was proposing to write Maclean's biography):

> Of the feverish activity kept up in Pollokshaws for years, mainly through the enthusiasm and largely on the money of John Maclean, through door-to-door distribution of the *Pollokshaws Review*, the *Vanguard*, and special leaflets on other matters as they arose, through a perpetual agitation at street corner meetings, through fighting every election, and utilizing every opportunity for further-ing the cause, you already know.
>
> It was characteristic of John, that every time we were organizing a public meeting, with a speaker from outside, he would be for taking the large Burgh Hall. The rest of the branch, afraid of failure and a deficit, would reply to John's enthusiasm and optim-ism, with that kind of Scots commonsense that can only count in pennies, but very often he had his way, and when there was a deficit, which was 'gie often', John had the pleasure of footing the bill. Sometimes, however, John's tactic of making a thing big by preparations on a large scale, was justified, and then his air of triumph was a pleasure to see.*

---

* The *Pollokshaws Review* was the organ of the Pollokshaws SDP, founded about 1909. The *Vanguard* was the organ of the Scottish District Council of the BSP and appeared a few years later.

According to MacDougall, Maclean had the greatest difficulty in finding candidates for the various elections. He generally had to teach them how to speak a few sentences without stumbling badly, and until he had trained young James MacDougall, George Pollok (a Co-operative shop assistant), and Robert Blair (an engineer), to assist him, he naturally had to bear the brunt of the propaganda work himself.

The first election events were forlorn hopes, yet they were very much worthwhile, in terms of winning recruits to the SDP. Thus Maclean wrote triumphantly in *Justice* at the end of 1908,

> We did very well at the election in the First Ward considering that our comrade's election address was issued six days before the election, and we had therefore time to hold only four meetings and no canvass. . . . We have doubled our membership, and soon will touch 100. Not bad for a small town.

During the early months of 1908 socialist schoolteachers like Maclean were intensely interested in the Education Bill being prepared by the new Liberal government, supposed to be for the radical reform of the educational system. He agitated all over the country for a 'real Education Bill for Scotland'. Clydebank Branch reported that at a meeting on 12 March a resolution was adopted, 'proposed by our comrade John Maclean and seconded by comrade Tom Anderson—"that this meeting calls upon the Government to introduce an Education Bill for Scotland embodying in it clauses providing for secular education, free books, medical attention for all children, sanatoria for summer recreation, free maintenance for all, with the extension of the school age to 16 years and maintenance bursaries to enable working-men's sons to attend secondary schools, technical colleges, and universities." ' A resolution along the same lines was carried at the May Day demonstration, and Maclean wrote an article in *Justice* called 'Education in Scotland'.

Needless to say, the new Education Act did not contain these items, but it did contain some of the clauses which were to prove very useful to socialists. For instance, it conferred many new powers on the School Boards, such as the power to feed and clothe necessitous children and provide them with free books; and also the power to provide continuation classes of any kind which might be requested by groups of people numbering twenty or more. Of course, the majority of School Boards in Scotland were dominated by reactionaries, who had no intention of using these new powers. This gave the SDP an added incentive to ensure that socialists were elected more and more to the Boards.

In the meantime some of the young members of the Pollok-shaws SDP, prompted by Maclean, requested Eastwood School Board for a continuation class in economics. When, after some demur, this was granted, they asked that the tutor be Maclean. The board eventually yielded to rising socialist pressure in the district, and John Maclean was appointed tutor, and paid the full standard rate per hour for teaching Marxist doctrines. This was probably the only case in Britain in which Government funds were used to teach what were in effect 'subversive' doctrines, *Capital* being the main textbook.

Forward had now been in existence for a few years as an independent socialist weekly, with Tom Johnston, later to become the first Secretary of State for Scotland, as editor. Helping him was R E Muirhead, who later became the Grand Old Man of Scottish Nationalism, whom I remember striding down Sauchie-hall Street, complete with long white beard, when he was over ninety, heading one of the first anti-Polaris demonstrations in the sixties. *Forward* gave a glowing account of the Pollokshaws class, which began in the winter of 1908:

> Even more will be gained in one session at this class than in a lifetime at Ruskin College, and so it is incumbent on all who aspire to eminence in Trade Union, Co-operative or Socialist circles to seize hold of this glorious opportunity. Maclean possesses a certificate of special distinction from Professor Smart in his University Arts Class. To thorough knowledge he adds power of lucid and interesting exposition acquired as a consequence of almost a decade's practice as a teacher. To this may be added a generally recognized reputation of being one of the ablest expounders of the *mysteries* of Marx in Scotland. His course includes not only the elucidation of basic economic principles, but also a criticism of the various schools and theories of economics, domestic and foreign, a brief history of economics and a skeleton course of industrial history from primitive society up to the present day. Attention to the development of Trade Unions and Co-operation will form special features.

This class, which continued until Maclean's imprisonment in 1916, had from time to time the assistance of James Maxton, who had been a socialist convert of Maclean in his student days and was now a teacher. Maxton had been born in Pollokshaws not far from Maclean's own birthplace, and they had been boyhood friends. Tradition has it that the older boy Maclean taught the young Maxton to smoke, which, if true, seems rather ironical, as Maclean in adult life was a non-smoker and Maxton an excessively heavy one.

What is certainly true is that he came under Maclean's political influence and 'Maxton himself has told us that it was Maclean who influenced him most and who was responsible for his conversion to socialism.' (John McNair, *James Maxton, the beloved rebel.*) Maxton, however, joined the ILP, as did most of the young students and teachers whom Maclean first converted. Later we will see that many of them accepted some of the teachings of Marx for instance, the labour theory of value in economics and the theory of the class struggle in politics, but they drew the line at dialectical materialism. The Christian religion, in both Catholic and Protestant versions, was deeply rooted and widespread all over the country, and the explicit materialist philosophy of the SDP antagonized many. Among other young teachers converted by Maclean were Bob Nicholl (afterwards an ILP MP), Joe Maxwell and Hugh Guthrie. A Scottish Socialist Teacher's Society was founded by Maclean and Maxton shortly after this period, and, according to McNair, the Society's 'record in educational emancipation was one of the great formative influences in the spread of Labour and Socialist ideals in the whole of Scotland, and whose object was to interest educationists in Socialism and socialists in Education'.

A much more famous event took place in the educational world in 1908. This was the strike of students at the working-man's college at Oxford, Ruskin College. The students wanted to learn Marxian economics as well as the orthodox political economy which was exclusively taught. The Plebs League was formed to promote this aim, and in 1909 breakaway students formed the Central Labour College in London, which had the following guiding principles:

1 The College to be based upon the recognition of the antagonism of interests between Capital and Labour. 2 The aim to be the imparting of education of a definitely utilitarian character, *viz*, the training necessary to equip workers to propagate and defend the interests of their class against the dominant ruling class ideas and theories prevalent in capitalist society. 3 The College to be owned and controlled by the representatives of organized labour, *viz*, the trade unions, socialist and co-operative bodies.

From that time onwards, Maclean's educational work was aimed towards the formation of a Labour College in Scotland after the style of the CLC.

It was just about this time also that the Workers' Educational Association, founded in 1903, tried to make a start in Glasgow. Maclean attended a West of Scotland Conference held in St Andrew's Hall, and was elected to the Executive Committee.

Attempts were made to establish classes under the School Boards in and around Glasgow. The Boards were willing, but no classes could be formed, so no more was heard of the WEA for many years. Maclean was quite willing to help in this venture, but the WEA never had his whole-hearted support. It was concerned with extending orthodox education to the adult members of the working-class, whereas Maclean was concerned about the extension of the 'Independent Working-class Education' of the Labour College movement.

Maclean persuaded the branch to contest the Eastwood School Board Election in 1909, for nobody knew better than he how Scottish education had suffered from the narrow tyranny exercised over it by the parsons for many years. He found in Robert Blair a very suitable candidate, for this young man, after a little coaching by Maclean in public speaking, had revealed a natural eloquence which was impressive. After strenuous and self-sacrificing efforts by the whole branch, Blair was elected. It was a remarkable event, because he ran not as a Labour candidate but as a Socialist, and did not shirk the difficulties of winning the workers by a frank statement of socialist principles.

Blair proved an energetic and conscientious member of the Board, and at the next election, MacDougall also stood.

MacDougall, in his own words 'presented the Marxian doctrine in the most rigid terms possible, explicitly affirming himself to be an atheist and that his intention was to abolish Bible teaching in the schools. To the horror of the local vested interests, this, instead of causing his certain defeat, seemed to be the very thing that rallied the electors to his support.' Both candidates were triumphantly elected, and MacDougall told me that this was probably the happiest day in John Maclean's life.

During the winter of 1908-09, Maclean, with the assistance of young MacDougall, was now taking classes every week in Central Glasgow, Pollokshaws, Greenock, Burnbank (Lanarkshire), Govan, Paisley, and Falkirk, the last-named receiving assistance from the Central Ironmoulders' Union. There had been a division of labour, and it was customary now for Maclean to take economics and MacDougall, industrial history. Dialectical materialism was not dealt with as a separate subject, but explained in simple terms by Macdougall when dealing with the development of industrial society. Maclean also gave a short explanation before beginning his course on economics.

8/Socialist unity

In the midst of his almost incessant practical activity, Maclean found time at the beginning of 1909 to write a letter on theoretical lines to *Forward* challenging a regular contributor, who wrote under the pseudonym 'Rob Roy', about his support for the Austrian economist Bohm-Bawerk, one of the 'marginal utility' school. He defended Marx along his usual lines, and ended:

> If rent and interest are not due to class robbery then we must seek elsewhere the sources of the wrongs done the workers. The Socialist theory is then false, and we must give it up and seek the true one. If BB's theory is true, then the ownership of capital by the few is not the ultimate source of interest and profit—in fact interest is quite natural and just. If that be so we have no reason to believe that the workers will be any better off in the future society than they are today.

Strangely enough, in his reply to Maclean, 'Rob Roy' quoted Marx to defend the conduct of the Labour MPs who were very much under fire from socialists at the time. The Liberals had such a large majority in parliament that they did not require help from the small Labour group, who found themselves without power of any kind, except to take a principled socialist stand. Most of them, however, were afraid to do this, as they were dependent on the Liberal vote in their constituencies. The only exception was young Victor Grayson, who had won his seat on a straight socialist programme.

Maclean replied to 'Rob Roy' indignantly:

> It shows a frightful chaos when professed Socialists defend BB against Marx. This parallel can only be found when professed Socialists appeal to Marx to justify the conduct of the Labour MPs who, whilst claiming political independence, silently listen to a wearisome discussion of the Licensing Bill during a period of almost unparalleled unemployment and starvation for the workers, and who strut about on Liberal Temperance platforms, exhorting the starving to end their drunken habits.
>
> These phenomena result from the fear some men have of fully studying the Marxian theory of value in economics and the Marxian theory of the class struggle in politics, and accepting them as the basis of thought and action.

Marx could never brook sycophancy, and mercilessly flayed economic and political charlatans. The Labour MPs have fawned upon Asquith and his crew whilst at the same time using the vilest language against Grayson, Blatchford, Hyndman and others. They have created and aggravated schisms by trying to prevent the SDP putting up parliamentary candidates, and to that end have even gone against payment of members; or, where SDP candidates have been put up, have done all they could to prevent the workers supporting them. Whatever is proposed by the SDP is mis-represented, caricatured or opposed; but whatever comes from the Liberals receives adulation. It is a scandal to quote Marx as one who would support such a line of conduct . . .

The probability is that 'Rob Roy' in his attempt to justify the Labour Party by quoting Marx wishes to nullify the criticisms of those who are said to swear by Marx. Unfortunately for him, Marxians do not fall back upon what Marx said here or there, but apply his principles to each set of circumstances as it arises. 'Thus spake Marx' is not the Marxian but the anti-Marxian method . . .

The method of Marx, in testing the Labour Party and its leaders is to examine whether they are constantly fighting in the interest of the wage-earning class. We Marxists are in favour of the Labour Party because it is working-class; but we oppose the conduct of the MPs because it is reactionary and tends to lead the masses to Liberal petty patch-work rather than to the class struggle ending in the revolution of property-ownership which must inaugurate Socialism.

This attack did not mean that he no longer supported SDP affiliation to the Labour Party. In some correspondence which took place in *Justice* the previous year, he had stated that the Pollok-shaws Branch was unanimously in favour of joining the Labour Party. But he was very sceptical of the campaign which had been begun by Grayson calling for socialist unity and the merging of the ILP and SDP into one really effective Socialist Party. The previous year he had written a letter to *Justice* on this subject, denying that the continued separation of the two parties was due to spleen and jealousy on the part of a few leaders in either party, but saying that the fundamental difference in outlook and methods made it appear like that:

But the same divergence exists amongst the rank and file where branches of both exist side by side. The ILP are loving brothers when they wish SDP members to aid in open-air summer propa-ganda. They work separately when the indoor season begins, and when the selection of constituencies and candidates arrives, they carefully avoid taking the SDP into consideration until the candi-date has been put in the field, and then again they become anxious for socialist unity to return their man. . . . Those who dream of the accomplishment of a single socialist party by a kindly feeling being fostered between the leaders, etc, are Utopians ignorant of history, ignorant of men, and ignorant of the material forces that compel unity for any purpose.

As we shall see, his scepticism was to be fully justified.

It was a busy year in Pollokshaws, and the surrounding district. The *Pollokshaws Review* of May announced:

The *Forward* Van has given a good send-off to our summer propaganda. See to it that you get your friends to turn out with you to our regular open-air meetings during the summer. Every Tuesday a meeting will be held at the Town's House; every Wednesday at Langside Halls; every alternate Thursday at Thornliebank. Other meetings will be held at Mearns, Nitshill, Cathcart, and Queen's Park Gate.

The same issue of the paper also announced that the work of the SDP in holding huge demonstrations the previous year and keeping up constant pressure on the town council had produced practical results. The town council had been forced to give work to more than a quarter of the unemployed, 'beating any other town in Scotland in proportion to its size. Agitation pays.' However, the paper made quite clear that this kind of shoring up of capitalism was not what the SDP was after. The only cure 'is socialism, when land and capital shall be used to create wealth for human satisfaction and not to make millionaires of a few stupid, though cunning, tyrants. Wage-slaves, arise like men, and with your fellows fight shoulder to shoulder for a reconstructed society!'

Glasgow was notorious for its terrible housing conditions, reputedly the worst in Europe, and the smaller towns in the west of Scotland were not much better—the same ramshackle, insanitary tenements huddling round each factory. The housing question therefore played a large part in the SDP agitation. A Housing Council had been organized by the Pollokshaws branch some time before and consisted of delegates from the trade unions, the Co-operative Society, the Liberal Association, the United Irish League, the Third Ward Committee, and the SDP. Its purpose was to expose the dreadful slum conditions so prevalent in the town, and to force landlords either to do necessary repairs or to have the buildings closed. All the time a constant agitation for the building of council houses was kept up. Jimmy MacDougall was elected secretary of the Housing Council.

It happened that one of the slum landlords most bitterly attacked by the Housing Council was one of the main clients of the local branch of the Clydesdale Bank, where MacDougall was just finishing his apprenticeship as a bank clerk. The landlord brought pressure to bear on the bank manager, and soon Jimmy was facing the alternative of giving up his socialist activities or being dismissed. Jimmy, being the dedicated socialist that he was, chose dismissal, but that was not the end of the matter. A bitter agitation was kept up by Maclean and Pollokshaws SDP for retaliation against the bank. 'We in Pollokshaws intend to pursue the slum-owners all the more keenly . . . and we would appeal to all socialists in Scotland to spread the news of this action of the bank, and use such influence as is possible to get Co-operative Societies, Trade Unions, Friendly Societies etc, to withdraw their deposits.'

One of the most striking solidarity actions was in Falkirk, where young Jimmy had become the idol of many of the rough, uneducated ironmoulders who attended the weekly class in industrial history which he now took. It happened that the funds of the Falkirk branch of the Central Ironmoulders' Union were deposited in the Clydesdale Bank. Many of the most influential members belonged to Jimmy's class, and one day the members marched in a body through the streets of Falkirk to withdraw their money from the bank.

One of the most significant events that year was the formation of the Catholic Socialist Society by John Wheatley, who had joined the ILP in 1908. This was of great importance, because of the large proportion of Irish workers in the west of Scotland. Wheatley was one of the ILP-ers who was influenced by Marxist teaching, except by the materialist conception of history. That year both MacDougall and Maclean spoke to the Society.

The amount of work Maclean had been doing since he joined the SDF seems, in retrospect, almost inhuman, but the fact was he enjoyed it, as he did his work as a teacher. He had been teaching at Kinning Park School since 1902, and, according to one of his colleagues, Harry Ross, in a letter to James Maxton, he

> was one of the most popular members of the staff. There were about half-a-dozen of us who did not go home for dinner and John was one of our most enthusiastic whist and nap players. Latterly we dropped cards for chess, and John soon became quite a fair player. After 1908 I did not see him so often unless on Christmas Day which he usually spent at the football match followed by pantomime, with myself and some of my bosom friends. He was always true to his small lemonade or ginger ale, and I'm sure he must often have suffered from the number of gaseous refreshments which he consumed for company's sake.

So he managed to get some recreation during his school dinner hour, but I have often wondered where he got the time to do his courting, which had been going on since 1905. During his summer propaganda tour that year he had spent some time in Hawick, where a group of advanced thinkers, some of them socialists, were anxious to become organized. Maclean naturally tried to interest them in joining the SDF, and received hospitality during his stay at the house of James Stothart, who had a shoe shop in the town. Stothart was a widower, and his niece Agnes Wood kept house for him. He did not succeed in persuading the Hawick group to join the SDF. His Marxism was too advanced for them, and they finally formed a Social Reform Society. One positive result did accrue, however, because a close friendship began between him and Agnes. In 1906 this was cemented when she came to Stobhill Hospital in Glasgow to train as a nurse. They became engaged, in conventional style, Christmas 1908, and arrangements were made for their marriage in 1909.

The future Mrs Maclean had no illusions about the part she had to play as the wife of a single-minded socialist. She knew she would have to play second fiddle to the socialist movement, and she was prepared to do so. She had been very religious as a young girl, and was steeped in ideals of unselfishness and self-sacrifice, and was as fervent a socialist as Maclean himself. She was, however, a very shy and retiring person, and made up her mind that she could help most effectively not by taking part in public life but by making his home life as smooth and as comfortable as possible.

That year, in 1909, in the columns of the *Pollokshaws Review* he made a call to hold May Day in future on the first day of May— a call he was to make many times again:

> In 1889 the International Socialist Congress determined to call upon the workers to strike work on the first day of May. This is done on the Continent, where hundreds of thousands in Berlin and Paris and other huge centres lay down their tools and come out to demonstrate the growing force of the revolutionary Socialist spirit that now inspires the workers of Europe. We in Scotland have, so far, selected the first Sunday in May. *This year the fine weather enabled over 40,000 to muster on Glasgow Green. Such a huge turn-out indicates the growth of militant Socialism in and around Glasgow.* (My emphasis.) Ere long we expect the workers to follow their Continental Comrades and celebrate the first of May as the workers' self-elected holiday.

By this time the SDP had about forty branches in Scotland, and the ILP about fifty. As in England, the ILP was gaining ground much more rapidly than the SDP, partly because it had a purely Scottish paper *Forward* (which, although calling itself independent, was more or less an ILP organ), and partly because the SDP had cut itself off from the mainstream of the labour movement by disaffiliating from the Labour Party. Because of this, also, it was inevitable that the growing Labour Party should become imbued, not with Marxist ideas, but with the Fabian ideas of the ILP.

9/Industrial unrest

By this time Marxist ideas were being received much more sympathetically by the more advanced sections of the working class all over the country. In 1910, with prices rising, unrest was rapidly growing, and strikes broke out among cotton workers, miners, railwaymen and shipbuilding workers. However, Maclean was concerned at first only with action on a much smaller scale. This was described to me by Jimmy MacDougall, who, of course, also took part:

One of the villages in the East Renfrewshire area where he carried on systematic propaganda was the mining village of Nitshill. Like many other mining villages and towns throughout the country, the men and boys found employment in the mines while the girls travelled to the nearest textile factories. These happened to be thread mills situated at Neilston some miles away. This was a very large factory employing thousands of girls, and of course they were on piecework. One or two of the Nitshill girls, daughters of socialist miners, worked in the Copwinding Department, and they put forward demands for better prices.

When the demands of this department were refused, the whole mob of girls streamed out of the mill, shouting defiance of the management. Many of them were quite young; none of them had any experience whatever of organization, but their fathers at Nitshill knew that to carry on strikes there had to be meetings, and so they went for Maclean and his friends to come up to organize the girls.

Maclean came and infused his own vigour and courage into these girls. He instructed them how they must act in order to win, not only this immediate wage demand, but to be able in the future to protect themselves against the tyranny of the foremen or any unjust demand that might be made upon them. They must get into a Trade Union. Maclean himself took the initiative in writing to the

Federation of Women Workers, and very soon a whole array of women organizers and speakers, including the famous Mary MacArthur, were on the scene. Miss Kate Maclean, afterwards Mrs Kate Beaton, took a prominent part in organizing the girls.

The Manager lived many miles away in Pollokshields, a 'posh' Glasgow suburb. The most prominent incident of the strike was when it was decided to have a march from Neilston right through all the intervening towns and villages to Pollokshields in order to interview the manager. It can be understood that to lead such a disorderly, undisciplined horde of young girls, to whom the thing was more of a joke than anything else (they were carrying effigies of the manager which were intended to be burned) was by no means an easy job, but Maclean was equal to anything of that kind. He was full of fun and chaff, and so took the hearts of the girls that they would have done anything for him, with the result that no serious trouble occurred.

The march, with a great banging of tin cans and shouting and singing pursued its noisy way from Neilston to Pollokshields, where the respectable inhabitants were thoroughly disturbed. The meeting was held in a field adjacent to the manager's house, and then the weary strikers dispersed to find their way home as best they might. The wage demands were won. The whole of the girls in the factory were organized, and a great mass of virgin minds received a favourable impression of their first real contact with Socialism.

It should be noted that even in this traditional women's industry, women received only about one half of a man's earnings for doing the same work. In this way, management naturally preferred to employ women, who were often actually more efficient than the men. Since the middle of the nineteenth century, the employment of women in light industry had therefore been increasing much more rapidly than that of men. Even in the heavy industries, the introduction of more and more elaborate machinery was making heavy physical work unnecessary, and the inevitable tendency of capitalism to employ cheap female labour instead of male, was making itself manifest.

It should also be noted that it soon became evident that the purely female unions were not a success, for much the same reasons as they are not today, and Maclean and MacDougall advocated later on the union of men and women in the same organization. The whole question of women in industry became, of course, of very great importance during the war. MacDougall and Maclean, because of their involvement in the co-operative movement, through which women were organized in the guilds to a greater extent than in any other part of the labour movement, were to play a leading part in the campaign for votes and equal pay for women.

The SDP, of course, was also very much involved at this time in the struggle for feminine emancipation. The first paragraph of the party's recorded *Objects* was as follows:

> The Socialization of the Great Means of Production and Distribution under a Co-operative Commonwealth, the complete Emancipation of Labour from the domination of Capitalism and Landlordism, with the establishment of *Social and Economic Equality between the Sexes*. (My emphasis.)

Other strikes similar to the Neilston one began to take place all over the west of Scotland, as women and unskilled workers having no tradition of organization were being forced to resist the lowering of their standard of living. The most significant was the strike of a few women polishers at Singer's Sewing Machine Factory at Clydebank, a few miles down the Clyde from Glasgow, which employed 12,000 people and belonged to an American trust.

The propaganda of years spent nursing the class solidarity of the workers showed itself in a spectacular manner. Immediately the whole three thousand women in the factory came out in sympathy, to be followed by all the men not in trade unions.

It was during this strike that the new tendency manifesting itself in the British labour movement towards syndicalism and direct action first found concrete expression in Scotland. Since its foundation in 1903, the SLP had been preaching the paramount importance of industrial action. A few of the unskilled workers at Singer's belonged to the Industrial Workers of Great Britain, and the strike was certainly their big chance.

John Maclean was always to be found in the midst of any strike, holding meetings, distributing propaganda leaflets, and so on, but he was especially interested in what he called 'this rather romantic effort', and wrote about it at length in *Justice*.* Beginning by deprecating the 'black-legging' of the orthodox trade unionists who did not come out in support of the girls, he went on:

> The whole circumstances are uniquely appropriate for the immediate application of industrial organization of the up-to-date type—a monopoly centred in one workshop; minute division of labour; unskilled labour; absence of trade unions; a sudden and spontaneous strike of unprecedented dimensions. . . . Should success be attained by the workers, then nothing will stand in the way of an immediate organization embracing the workers in every part of the factory. . . . It is my earnest desire that all this should happen . . . as it certainly will act as an incentive to comrades in

---

* 1 April 1911.

old unions to proceed with the utmost rapidity in the agitation for the fusion of all unions engaged in the same and closely allied industries. Trustification of industries, through fusion, must obviously bring in its train trustification of already existing unions and the closing of their ranks internationally.

Although most of the trade unionists (certainly all the socialist ones) eventually came out in solidarity, the strike was in the end defeated when the management resorted to a common American stratagem—the referendum. Forms were issued to the strikers, stating that if 6,000 signed them as willing to restart work, operations would begin as usual. This was, as Maclean said, 'no other than a veiled threat':

> It says in effect, send back this paper signed to show that you are willing to return. If you do, we assure you that the strike committee will not know. If you do not, you had better look out for another place elsewhere, the which you may get—if it pleases us to let you. Choose!

The management succeeded. Six thousand men signed and went back, and the strike failed. Discussing the failure and the methods which must be used in future to combat this new menace of the referendum, Maclean insisted that incipient industrial unionism must not be condemned as useless. At the same time he outlined the social-democratic objection to syndicalism:

> All social democrats are industrial unionists. We differ from others in that we insist real industrial organization must arise out of the fusion and federation of already existing Trade Unions . . . And, furthermore, we rightly insist that economic organization is subject to political organization. . . . The workers, here having the completest basis of unity, are better able at once to form a party representative of the interests of the workers as a whole, and affording an outlet for the energies of many capitalists and intellectuals who cannot very well come within the scope of a purely economic instrument . . .
>
> Again as politicians we rightly hold that the socialization of industry cannot be accomplished by the direct seizure of the factories and the land by the unions. This latter method denies (tacitly, of course) the naturalness of the state and politics, that which we as scientists cannot uphold. The state is the natural outgrowth of a growing economic structure of expanding society, and upon it, in rapidly increasing numbers, devolves duties formerly undertaken in a voluntary manner. It is only consistent with impartial scientific survey to carry forward this growth of the duties of the state until the social revolution has been accomplished. And this course is the only true one for the party that claims to be Marxist and believes in the class war. (15 April 1911.)

Although a failure, this strike had one important result. The leaders, most of them SLP-ers, were sacked, and ultimately found work in various shops in the Clyde area. Thus, instead of their influence being diminished, as had been hoped, it was spread over a much wider area, and when the industrial upheavals of war-time took place, these revolutionary socialists occupied strategic positions throughout the whole Clyde district.

It should be realized at this point that not only the SLP, but also the SDP, objected to the ILP panacea, nationalization, which all Marxists considered would lead to a kind of state capitalism, rather than to state socialism. The SDP advocated 'socialization' rather than 'nationalization', the difference being, as Maclean put it very briefly, that nationalization implied the payment of interest and socialization did not. As is obvious today, actually 'centralization' would be a more accurate description for the kind of nationalization brought in by the 1945 Labour government. All the Marxists fore-saw that the nationalization and the municipalization which were advocated so fervently by the ILP would not end the system of wage-slavery, and would put power into the hands of petty officials and big-time bureaucrats. They believed that the socialists must work towards what became widely known as 'workers' control' of both industry and government.

10/The British Socialist Party

Industrial unrest plus the bitterly disappointing performance of the new Labour Party in parliament swung the whole labour movement towards the left. In the summer of 1910 *Forward* was again claiming that the British Labour Party was the heir of the Marxian tradition, because it was the party of the wage earners. An outraged Maclean replied:

The Labour Party is a miserable caricature of Marxism. . . . The ILP have strenuously opposed the raising of the principles and programme of socialism inside the Labour Party. The result is that the reactionary Liberal element in the Labour Party has carried the day and has swept it into Liberalism of a dangerous kind. (20 August 1910.)

Later he returned to the attack in the columns of *Justice*. A Liberal railwayman, W V Osborne, had sued his union alleging that its compulsory political levy was illegal, and his claim had been upheld in the courts. Naturally other claims followed, and in 1909 and 1910 the Labour Party had been suffering severe financial losses. Maclean wrote, pulling no punches:

> It is with the deepest interest we Social Democrats must watch the campaign over the Osborne decision. For the first time since the formation of the Labour group in the House of Commons, the Labourists now have begun to realize the genuine importance of a national campaign. From now on till the autumn session begins, they are going to stump the country to create a public opinion that will cause the Liberals (their dear friends who love their presence in the House!) to reverse the 'awful' decision that will deprive them of their wages.
>
> Why did they not do that on behalf of the unemployed millions two years ago? . . . Why did they not fight for the Tyneside engineers or the Belfast dockers? Their only excuse was that such was not statesmanlike, or not practical. Yet all the time they could stand on Liberal platforms and write in Liberal 'rags' for Free Trade, temperance, and a change of the human heart through a Christianity they use but do not believe.
>
> What did not become them to perform on behalf of the class that put them into Parliament and kept them there, seems plainly to suit them now that their personal interests are affected. The political hypocrisy of the whole thing certainly will not blind the rank and file who so frequently have been betrayed this last four years by the group of swelled-headed mediocrities whose sole object seems to be to grovel at the feet of one of the most tyrannical Governments of modern times.

It was this continuing Labour dependence on the Liberal Party which prompted the Executive Committee of the SDP that year to advise members during the General Election to adopt a Parnellian tactic: to urge the workers to vote against the sitting Liberal member, where branches could not manage to put up their own candidates. The Scottish SDP could manage only one candidate, again Tom Kennedy in Aberdeen, so Maclean loyally followed this line, and shocked the public by issuing an SDP election manifesto maintaining that the Liberals were worse enemies of the working class than the Tories.

Maclean and the SDP were subjected to a great deal of abuse, not only from Liberals but also from Labour Party and ILP members, who made the usual insinuations about Tory gold. Maclean defended himself:

> We are all agreed that the workers are robbed by a class whose various interests are safeguarded by the Liberal and Tory Parties. The Tories openly declare that they are out to protect the society in which we all live. . . . The Liberals, just as strenuous in the preservation of exploitation, pretend in a vigorous manner that they are out for the 'people' . . . Our every experience proves that they do not step aside, that they fight us more immorally—with more contemptible lies—than even the Tories. . . . The average man can quite easily follow our tactical moves; our hope lies in his grasping our principles . . . As believers in political action, we socialists have as a duty the kindling of enthusiasm for the study of economics, history and politics in particular, and once we get our class versed in them, tactics in politics will become just as easy as tactics in bowling, chess or football.

It seems to me that the fallacy in this reasoning is to assume that ordinary people will be able to follow these rather confusing tactics more easily than basic principles.

Nevertheless, Maclean's approach did indeed have some effect. More than fifty years later, I had an argument with an old Labour Party stalwart, an ex-miner, and maintained that at that period (1963) the Labour Party was in some respects more reactionary than even the Liberal Party. He turned to me indignantly: 'But it was *your* father that taught us that there was no difference between the Liberals and the Tories!'

There is no doubt that the rank and file of the ILP were becoming much more interested in Marxist theories, and especially in syndicalism. That year Keir Hardie issued a statement defending Marxism, even the materialist conception of history, and ended up with the familiar claim that the ILP was the Marxist party:

> The Trade Union Movement is the real movement of the working class and the ILP is the advanced wing . . . that was what Marx intended the Socialist section of the working class to be . . . He did not ask the working class to unite as class conscious socialists, but only as working men. He knew the class consciousness would come in good time.

This development in the ILP encouraged the campaign for uniting the two parties, and Maclean, although still with doubts about the practicality of the project, followed party policy and supported the campaign. In 1911 Unity Committees were set up all over the country, and at a Unity Conference at the beginning of October, called by the SDP, delegates from branches of the ILP, the Fabian Society and the Clarion Scouts, met SDP delegates, and the new British Socialist Party (BSP) was launched. In actual fact, time was to show that it was more or less the old SDP with some new adherents: *Justice* remained as the party organ, Hyndman remained as chairman and everything went on as before, including the reactionary militarist policy so fervently supported by the Hyndman clique, the 'old guard' of the SDF.

I shall deal with this disgraceful episode in socialist history in the next chapter, but here I will point out that on this really important point of principle Maclean made known very emphatically his opposition to party policy, and on 17 September 1910, a notice appeared in *Justice*:

> Pollokshaws Branch has passed the following resolution—'That this branch recognizes the international solidarity of the working class and therefore deprecates Comrade Hyndman's agitation for a big Navy as tending rather to break down than to build up the essential unity of the workers of the world.'

At about this time a debate was raging about the causes underlying the constant rise in prices. George Bernard Shaw, a leading light of the Fabian Society, had been claiming that higher wages would end destitution. The usual capitalist argument that higher wages would only lead to higher prices and that a campaign for higher wages was therefore futile had been used against Shaw.

Maclean pointed out in *Justice*:

> During the last 14 or 15 years, prices have almost steadily risen, whereas wages, though fluctuating, have rather on the whole tended downwards. And had we the absence of Trade Unions, wages would markedly fall without at all affecting the upward movement of prices. The reverse of this we see in the increasing wages of German comrades organized into unions, unaccompanied by price increases greater than obtaining in other fully evolved capitalist countries.
>
> Wages simply being the specific name for the price of labour-power, it must be theoretically apparent that a price cannot regulate prices in general. The above illustrations bear witness. (12 November 1910.)

At the same time he did not agree with Shaw that higher wages alone would cure unemployment, which he maintained was an integral part of the capitalist system.

In the same letter he affirmed his support for two of the items in the SDP's Transitional Programme—a 'minimum wage for all workers, with equal pay for both sexes for the performance of equal work', and 'a legislative eight hours' working day, or 48 hours per week, to be the maximum for all trades and industries':

> I am one of those who believe that we ought to have a law of minimum wages, but ever increasing with every increase in prices . . . and a law of maximum for hours, ever falling with increased productivity. Tom Mann does right to insist on this as work for the organized workers, after they have organized industrially for fusion of unions already existing, and the absorption of those as yet unorganized. But the supplementary effort of Parliamentary representatives I hold to be necessary and here it is that a real Labour Party could fight the class war effectively in the 'Temple of Time-servers'.

He went on to maintain that any attempt to limit prices inside the capitalist system was utopian:

> Prices are, under perfect free competition and uniform composition of capital, determined by the exchange of gold for other articles in proportion to the time necessary to produce them socially. Thus ten hours of gold will normally exchange for ten hours of any other product. This gold, converted into coin, constitutes the price of all products finished in the same time.
>
> If gold can be found abundantly in rich, easily accessible seams, or if by the application of improved mechanical and chemical agencies, it can be more easily produced, then its value declines, and prices generally rise. This is quite natural and is operating today; and laws to limit prices would be just as silly as laws to end trusts. An agitation for the limitation of prices would imply that we favour the point of view opposed to Marxism, that profits are the result of fleecing the consumer. Such a fight would blur over the class issue entirely, and would thus be as bad tactically as it would be economically.

He maintained that, on the other hand, a fight for a minimum wage and maximum hours 'would bring to the surface the fact that the producer creates profit, and would thus enable us to raise to eminence the fight of the workers against the capitalists'.

During the summer of 1911 Maclean began to write the regular 'Scottish Notes' in *Justice*, using the pseudonym *Gael*.

11/Anti-militarism

One serious issue of principle which divided the ranks of the SDP was that centering round the question of imperialist war. The policy of the Second International as expressed in the decisions of the various Congresses was (according to MacDougall) that 'each of the national Socialist Parties must find its primary task in exposing the military forces of its own nation. Moreover, on the question of the army, the socialists in the European parliaments, while fighting against the military estimates, put forward as their alternative for the defence of the country the substitution of a militia on the Swiss lines for conscript armies'. This was called the Citizen Army, and this policy was enthusiastically adopted by the SDF leaders as a reaction to the formation of the Territorial Army by Haldane in 1907, which was seen as 'an attempt to militarize the nation'.

The Citizen Army policy was progressive in countries like France and Germany, where military conscription was already in force, but it soon became obvious that in Britain it was irrelevant. As MacDougall put it:

> In Britain where the land army has never bulked large in the various wars that this country has carried on, the crux of the defence question has always lain in the possession of a large navy. H M Hyndman, equating in his mind the British Fleet to a continental national militia as a purely defensive weapon, imagined he was carrying out an international socialist policy when he supported the increase in the British Fleet which was being undertaken to meet the threat of German aggression. At the BSP conferences immediately prior to the war where this matter was discussed, the response to the jingoism represented by Hyndman was vigorously carried on by John Maclean and Peter Petroff.

As late as 1908 Maclean was still apparently under the influence of Hyndman and Harry Quelch, with whom he was, according to his friend Harry Ross, constantly corresponding. On 3 October, *Justice* reported that Maclean had moved the following resolution at a meeting of the Scottish District Council:

> That in view of the possibility of an attack on Britain by the German Empire, we demand that all citizens be trained in the use of arms and have each a rifle and ammunition ready for use at a

moment's notice. Furthermore, to provide energy and stamina requisite for the strain of warfare, we request the Government to bring forward at once a Bill making more adequate provision of work for the unemployed.

This resolution was carried.

The Citizen Army policy was attacked both by the SLP on the grounds that it was utopian to expect any capitalist government to arm the working class, and by the ILP on pacifist grounds. It is interesting to note that in Britain the only Citizen Army that ever materialized was James Connolly's Irish Citizen Army, but on an entirely different basis to that envisaged by the Social Democratic policy. The Irish Citizen Army was formed to defend the workers during the notorious 1913 transport strike in Dublin against the violence of the police and the employers. Socialists in Scotland ran guns illegally to Dublin just as they had done to Russia at the time of the 1905 Revolution.

Inside the SDP there was a constant battle against Hyndman's jingoism, being led mainly by the non-English members like Theodore Rothstein and Zelda Kahan.

Matters came to a head in the summer of 1910 when Hyndman sent a disgraceful letter to the Conservative *Morning Post* demanding an increase of £100 million in the navy estimates. He claimed to have inside knowledge that there would be no effective opposition to war in Germany—the leaders of German social democracy had told him that 'one and all they could not hope to check war . . . if the Emperor . . . decided upon it'. Sections of the party which had not taken part hitherto in the anti-jingo protests now came in, and letters poured into *Justice*.

The Pollokshaws Branch was among the first to protest. From then onwards Maclean lost any loyalty he may have had to Hyndman and his supporters and conducted an intensive anti-militarist campaign throughout Scotland. One of his most popular speeches was called 'Edward the Peacemaker', referring to Edward VII who died in the summer of 1910. According to J D MacDougall,

> While the press was eulogizing the monarch as the ambassador of peace, who had softened imperialist rivalries and nationalistic antagonisms in Europe by his peculiar diplomatic talent, Maclean found it necessary to point out that these regal activities were not to be taken at their face value. He implied that Edward's real mission was to find military allies for Britain and to secure, so far as might be possible, the encirclement of Germany.

Maclean denounced the title given to Edward VII, insisting

instead that it should be 'Edward the Warmaker'.

Later, in a pamphlet entitled *The Coming War with America*, written in 1919, he gave a brief account of the background to this whole business:

> We Marxists knew the war with Germany was coming, as both Germany and Britain were conducting a life and death struggle to dominate the world and its markets. From the Boer War onwards Germany began to build a fleet, whilst Britain enlarged hers and constructed naval bases on the North Sea; Germany perfected her army whilst Haldane gave us the Territorials; Germany built up the Triple Alliance, whilst Britain brought off the Entente with France and the Alliance with Russia; each riddled the other's territory with spies; J Chamberlain urged a tariff war against Germany, whilst Lloyd George imported German Insurance and other expedients to gain Labour support in case of war.

At the 1911 annual conference, Zelda Kahan moved a resolution from Central Hackney demanding opposition to all armaments. This was opposed by the Executive Committee, and was very narrowly defeated. Subsequently there was a plebiscite of the branches on the question of national defence, which resulted in a victory for the Hackney resolution. That was the situation prior to the formation of the British Socialist Party.

At the first conference of the BSP, which Maclean does not appear to have attended, his place was more than adequately filled by young William Gallacher, of Paisley. Gallacher had been a member of the SDF since 1905, and was a product of Maclean's Marxist training. He was the first to oppose a paper on 'Socialism and Patriotism' given by Harry Quelch in which he defended the old Citizen Army idea. Gallacher said:

> It was no use juggling with the word patriotism; they had to take it in its generally accepted meaning. They would have to dominate the entire country before they could force the masters to grant a Citizens Army which they knew would be used against them. A Citizen Army would be of very little use as a means of defence against aggression from without. The principal line of defence against aggression from without would be the Navy, and they could not have a Citizen Navy. They should condemn all idea of patriotism and all idea of militarism, unless it took the form of shooting down those who exploited them. They must stand as Internationalists, and not trouble about nationalism. (Official Conference Report.)

There was a ding-dong battle on this issue going on all the time up to the beginning of the war, but the great wave of strikes which reached its peak during the years 1911 to 1913 dominated the political scene, and shoved the anti-militarist struggle into the background.

12/Revolutionary ferment

Max Beer, in his *History of British Socialism*, described the years 1911 to 1913 as 'memorable in the annals of British Labour', and went on to outline the situation:

> The United Kingdom witnessed for the first time a class war in which all its component parts were involved; English, Welsh and Scottish miners, English railwaymen and Irish transport workers were joining hands across the borders and seas. Robert Smillie, Tom Mann, James Larkin, and James Connolly, all born fighters, marshalled and led the new forces in battle array. Nothing like it had ever happened before.

At the end of 1911, in his introduction to a famous speech given at the Renfrewshire Co-operative Conference, Maclean put it this way:

> The times we live in are so stirring and full of change that it is not impossible to believe we are in the rapids of revolution. Truly, the development in every branch of industrial, commercial, political, social, and intellectual activity is so apparently quick that even the dullest must admit that the old order of society is passing away, to give place to one that, with our aid, will eradicate for ever the inequalities, the injustices, and the oppression that characterize the present. We have but to think of the increasing thousands of inventions and discoveries that facilitate production; of the swift spread of the most perfect modes of transit and communication; of the amazing expansion of capitalism through the export of capital from developed to undeveloped countries; of the unprecedented grabbing of occupied lands for the extension of trade and empires; of the sudden arrival of mammoth trusts controlling colossal masses of capital and slaves; of the tremendous uprise of the masses in the Co-operative, the Trade Union, and the Socialist Movements, to find a growing expression in productive and distributive activity, economic revolt, and political agitation; of the modern political upheavals, starting six years ago in Russia, and passing in rapid

succession through Turkey, Persia, Portugal, and Mexico, to find a momentary culmination in China, in what may ripen into the most magnificent and dramatic transformation ever witnessed by man—I say, we have but to think of all this to catch but the faintest outline of a world change that is so truly indicative of the triumph of knowledge and its application over the chaos of the past, and of the ultimate ascendancy of the organized masses over the forces and the resources of the world.

A few months after the Singer strike, Maclean was again involved in an important strike. His usual summer propaganda tour led him in July 1911, to the Rhondda Valley, where the South Wales miners were forging that reputation for militancy which has made them a legend in working-class history. Many months previously, twelve thousand of them had downed tools in support of eight hundred fellow miners, who had been locked out by the employers, the Cambrian Combine, for refusing to accept their terms for working in abnormally bad places. The rank and file were demanding that the Miners' Federation of Great Britain (MFGB) should not only support them in this local issue, but should also extend the strike into one for a minimum wage for all miners. This was a cause after Maclean's own heart, and he wrote a letter to *Justice* appealing for nation-wide support for the Rhondda Valley men.

The MFGB were forced to take a ballot of the entire membership. The result was a decision to strike unless the owners granted a universal daily minimum. The owners refused, and a national strike of almost one million miners, the largest of the century, was called in February 1912.

The strike, which ended in April, was only partially successful. The men did not get what they wanted, for the Minimum Wage Act passed by the government did not prescribe a national minimum wage, but decided that minima should be decided locally for the various districts. The resulting discontent with the orthodox leadership of the MFGB, together with the general spread of dissatisfaction with parliamentary action and the rise of opinion in favour of direct action, crystallized into the South Wales Miners' Reform Committee.

The leading spirits were young students from Ruskin College who had taken part in establishing the Central Labour College: Noah Ablett, who afterwards became agent in Merthyr district; A J Cook, afterwards secretary of the MFGB, and Will Mainwaring, who eventually became a Labour MP. Maclean was on friendly terms with them all, and A J Cook, in particular, became a warm admirer. This rank-and-file movement in Wales had died down before war-time, but it left a valuable legacy in the shape of the pamphlet *The Miners' Next Step,* which contained a whole programme of proposed reform of the miners' organization and of aggressive syndicalist action against capitalism.

By 1911, Maclean had acquired a great deal of prestige and influence in the Scottish co-operative movement. When the massive use in the cost of living began to hit the pockets of the workers, the directors began to realize the necessity for a great increase in wages if progress was to be continued. They became very ready to welcome a theorist who could throw down the gauntlet to the authorities constantly flourished in their faces by capitalist opponents. Maclean was therefore asked to prepare a paper for the Renfrewshire Conference to be held at the end of November.

In a carefully prepared Marxist interpretation of the situation, Maclean analysed the rapidly-expanding multiple shop system as a serious menace to the co-operative movement:

> In the past the large-scale organization of the Co-operatives had enabled them to compete successfully with the small private shops, but these huge selling combines had grown up recently parallel to the growth of the great industrial trusts. By various methods such as sweating, adulteration, rationalization, they were under-selling the Co-operatives. They would have to be fought tooth and nail . . . I am out for the abolition of interest and dividend, with free capital and a national society as the best basic conditions in the struggle. I am out for high wages and short hours to all workers as long as capitalism lasts, and therefore, if we are going to do justice to our servants, we must have a fusion of the two trade unions and the growth of a solidified union for the whole distributive trade, linked up with the Transport Workers' Federation. By such means will we prevent the enemy beating us through sweated labour.
>
> Lastly, we will have to bring our methods up-to-date. A national society could do this better than individual ones, and hence I am confident that when we reach this stage of development we will not be defeated by the enemy carrying on trade at a less expense.

He described the attempts being made in Glasgow to weld the different Societies: 'The sooner this is done the better, and the sooner the Glasgow society evolves into a West of Scotland one the better still.' He fully comprehended the dangers to democracy in such proposals, but he was confident that the suggested amalgamation of co-operative organizations could ultimately be founded on a democratic base. He wound up by affirming his belief in the future:

C

Bear in mind I have no fear of the future. The working-class is going to win by the establishment of socialism even were co-operation to go under. But the working-class cannot afford to let this great popular movement sink before the opposition of the class that, having performed its work in history, must inevitably yield supremacy to ours, the last class to attain freedom.

In my eyes, just as trade unionism is playing its part, so also must Co-operation, in the great human impulse towards that time, when the world-wide Co-operative Commonwealth having been established, man for the first time shall rise dictator over the forces and resources of nature, and ensured through life of the material, mental and moral requisites of a grand and noble existence, shall also for the first time cease from robbery and cease from conflict.

It may be considered rather wishy-washy for a revolutionary socialist to be aiming at a 'Co-operative Commonwealth', but that was the phrase used in the constitution of the new BSP:

The object of the BSP is the establishment of the Co-operative Commonwealth—that is to say, the transformation of capitalist competitive society into socialist or communist society.

Methods The Education of the People in the principles of Socialism. The closest possible co-operation with trade union organizations, and the advocacy of industrial unity of all workers as essential to bring about the socialization of the means of production. The establishment of a militant Socialist Party in Parliament and on Local Bodies, completely independent of all parties which support the capitalist system.

Immediate Action The BSP will vigorously advocate and support all measures and activities that in the opinion of the Party will strengthen the workers in their fight against the capitalist interests.

Maclean's paper. 'Co-operation and the Rise in Prices', was read at numerous co-operative gatherings all over Scotland, and the gist of it reproduced in co-operative and socialist journals. It was eventually published as a pamphlet. So the theorist had come into his own. The political men in the labour movement who had derided his studies and his teachings as abstract and remote from everyday affairs were compelled to recognize that there can be no political activity, especially on a grand scale, without some theory.

As the hostility to Marxism began to break down in co-operative circles, Maclean's popularity grew rapidly. Jimmy Mac-Dougall told me that, very characteristically, he did not take advantage of it for himself, but pushed forward his young assistant. He neglected no opportunity of publicising the young lad, and, like himself, MacDougall received numerous engagements from

Co-operative Education Committees, and took every advantage to spread Marxist teachings. Thus in 1912 he was sent on his own initiative as a delegate from Pollokshaws Co-operative Educational Committee to the Renfrewshire Conference in order to move that School Boards be urged to start classes in Marxian economics and in industrial history if groups of twenty could be obtained. This was carried, and in addition, it was further resolved to carry on such classes if the Boards failed to do their duty.

Classes in economics, history and public-speaking were held under the auspices of some of the principal Co-operative Societies in the west of Scotland, such as Greenock and Clydebank, and during 1914 Maclean held a Speakers' Class for the Glasgow Guildswomen.

Meanwhile the BSP in Scotland had expanded to such an extent that at the Easter conference of the Scottish District Council, MacDougall was appointed organizer for Scotland. As he was still unemployed, this was a paid job.

That year 'Scottish Notes' was full of the record of strikes, most of them failures, because the trade union movement was not the power in the land that it is today. Although membership had almost doubled since the beginning of the century, it was, in the Britain of 1912, still only 3,416,000. John Maclean was not disheartened in any respect. While he welcomed wholeheartedly any improvement in the standard of living resulting from a successful strike, it was as a school for revolution that he saw, not only strikes, but every aspect of the 'day-to-day' struggle'. Hence his comment after the dockers' strike in Glasgow:

> My contention is that the forces brought out by our enemy—that must be brought out by our enemy—afford illustrations of the real class war that are more effective than all the theory we might fire at our benighted class from this till doomsday. Fighting leads to new facts, thus to our new theory and thence to revolution. On with the fight! (*Justice* 24 February 1912.)

13/Marxism takes root

By 1912 the industrial ferment had produced a soil which was becoming more and more favourable to Marxist ideas, and the seeds sown by the pioneers began to take firm root. This was particularly noticeable among the miners in Scotland. The Liberal government's Minimum Wage Act accomplished what twenty years of socialist propaganda had failed to do. It succeeded in driving a wedge between the Scottish miners and the Liberal Party. As MacDougall put it in an article, 'The Scottish Coalminer':

> The majority of the Scottish miners were against the calling off of the strike and received the leaders in a very hostile fashion when they appeared at mass meetings of the men to explain the beauties of the Minimum Wage Act . . . Several popular socialist propagandists began to criticize the action of the men's leaders, and, although not themselves miners, they were acclaimed at huge gatherings of miners in Fife and Lanarkshire as the true voice of rank and file opinions. In particular, their hearers were delighted with attacks, in the spirit of *The Miners' Next Step* . . . on the autocracy practised by the agents who, because of the anti-democratic character of the union constitution, were practically irremovable.
>
> The propaganda of John Maclean, J D MacDougall, and the speakers of the SLP and IWW . . . cultivated an intransigent psychology, suspicious of Labour parliamentarism and favourable to 'direct action' which already in 1912-1913 was predominant in certain important strategic centres in the minefields, such as Bowhill in Fife, Burnbank in Lanarkshire, and Musselburgh in the Lothians. (*Nineteenth Century*, December 1927.)

There had been an SDF branch in Burnbank for years, and Maclean and MacDougall had been taking classes since 1908. All the subsequent leaders of the Lanarkshire Miners' Union passed through their hands.

The mining area round Stonehouse in South Lanark was also by this time becoming a stronghold of Marxism. The schoolmaster there, Alexander Anderson, was one of the 'old guard' of the SDF, and had been a member of the national executive in 1902. According to MacDougall:

Anderson was as unresting a propagandist of socialism as Maclean himself. They were men after one another's hearts. From Stonehouse Anderson cycled to all the villages which he could reach, establishing contacts with local miners, holding meetings and succeeding in setting up branches of the party . . . He got a footing for socialism especially in a group of villages with Lesmehagow in their centre, the whole of the inhabitants of which worked a dozen miles or so from their dwelling-places 'up the line' in the Coalburn district. 2000 miners drawn from a wide radius worked in a matter of a dozen pits.

Until the 1912 strike, the Lanarkshire miners, especially the Irishmen among them, had a tradition of political Liberalism. Even their trusted leaders like Robert Smillie (ILP) and John Robertson (SDP/BSP) had been recently defeated when running against the Liberals. Now, however, the tide had turned and when Anderson's propaganda began to have a powerful effect, the vested interests of the district took steps to have him dismissed, although he was outstandingly successful as a teacher. By this time their action was too late. As MacDougall described it:

> No one who recalls the incident can fail to be affected by the memory of the Stonehouse handloom weavers and miners springing to arms at the news that 'auld Anderson wis to get the bag', and the women were even more excited than the men. By this time there was a whole brilliant galaxy of socialist teachers in Scotland, with John Maclean as their doyen. A great public meeting was held in the square at Stonehouse, addressed by a dozen graduates of Glasgow and Edinburgh Universities, protesting against the injustice.

And so Anderson kept his job.

Falkirk, the centre of the light iron industry in Scotland, and surrounded by the extensive Stirlingshire minefields, was also a stronghold of Marxism. There had been an SDF branch for many years, and it was one of the few Scottish branches represented that year at the first annual conference of the BSP. Nearly every worker in Falkirk belonged to the Central Ironmoulders' Union, and the branch members were all men highly respected and very active in its affairs. The classes taken since 1908 by Maclean and MacDougall had been very successful, and during the years before the war one of them was always the principle speaker at the Falkirk May Day celebrations. That year (1912) Maclean addressed a gathering of more than two thousand.

Later on in June there was a big lock-out of moulders, and, in return for the solidarity shown him when he was dismissed from

Clydesdale Bank, MacDougall spent a fortnight there helping the men, and the best speakers from Glasgow, including Maclean, also came down from time to time.

Maclean and MacDougall were as well-known in Fife as they were in Lanarkshire. They made the real beginnings of socialism in West Fife, in places like Cowdenbeath and Lochgelly, and consistent propaganda over the whole county. Just as Coalburn in Lanark was *their* village, so was Bowhill in Fife. It was a modern, up-to-date village, with a new colliery which employed 1,800 men. They made it a socialist community, and it was a great event when either of them came to speak. From round about 1910 Maclean took Marxist classes on at least one night a week, changing the venue from time to time—Bowhill, Dunfermline, Kirkcaldy or Cowdenbeath. There is no doubt at all that they prepared the ground that ensured the victory of Scotland's future Communist MP, Willie Gallacher.

Tom Bell records that during his traditional summer propaganda campaign Maclean 'averaged three meetings a week, and was the principal speaker at the end of August at Stonehouse, where a huge demonstration took place in memory of Wilson, the Strathaven martyr for political reform'. Here Bell was referring to the Radical Rising of 1820, for their part in which Wilson, Baird and Hardie were publicly hanged and then beheaded as traitors. This was the last armed uprising in Scotland, but it was much more than a working-class protest against the brutal and dreadful economic conditions that sent thousands to early graves. It was also a protest against the Union of Scotland and England in 1707, which had brought nothing but misery to the people of Scotland and had been effected in the first place by the bribery of the upper-class members of the Scottish Parliament.*

The most significant feature of the ill-fated 1820 Insurrection was that the half-starving working men who rose under the banners 'Scotland—Free or a Desert!' were betrayed into premature military action by agents provocateurs in the pay of the British government, who widely posted up proclamations of the setting-up of a Provisional Government which called the people to arms. The lesson of the rising has never been forgotten by revolutionaries in Scotland, and this must be borne in mind in relation to John Maclean's actions in the years ahead.

That autumn Maclean paid a tribute to the work of MacDougall in 'Scottish Notes' (12 October):

---

*   We're bought and sold for English gold—
        Such a parcel of rogues in a nation!   (BURNS)

Since the end of March when the miners' strike was still at its height, till the end of September, our comrade, with the utmost thoroughness, executed the work before him, a work that at times would break the heart of a Titan.

'Scottish Notes' went on to report the formation of a Scottish Federation of Tenants' Associations for the protection and advancement of the interests of tenants.

This was the result of an agitation which had been going on since the spring of 1912 over widespread rent increases. In January 1913, Maclean wrote a long article in *Justice* called 'The Law of Maximum', again opposing as utopian any attempt to impose a general law of maximum prices inside the capitalist system, except in the case of rents:

In relation to rent, limitation is quite practical. Rent forms a large part of expenditure, and every excuse is used to send it up while the house is deteriorating. Workmen take a keener interest in rent than in any other item of expenditure . . . because more immediately visible . . . and any increase usually meets with greater resentment. Proof of this is to be found in the meetings held all over Scotland against the universal raising of rents in the spring of the year, and a general growling has started that will not end, I trust, until houses are built by the local authorities and the state, and rent courts are established.

That was the beginning of the organization which led to the famous 1915 Rent Strike.

In the same article he made scathing remarks about half-baked socialists becoming unbalanced by a new phase of 'anarchist unionism under the stunning title of syndicalism', and went on to reiterate his support for the minimum wage policy of the BSP, although he knew that the state could not grant this, because of its capitalist structure:

But that is all the more reason why we should fight. If we get the masses behind us every capitalist resistance will bring us nearer to the revolution. It is not a minimum wage that worries me; it is getting the workers into line, and on the move. The aeroplane speed will soon follow, and then the masses become an irresistible force.

How to get the masses behind them was the problem! Bitter disappointment about the failure of the socialist parties to recruit members was the theme of an article 'Socialism and Pluck' which appeared in the third issue of *Vanguard* the 'Organ of the British

Socialist Party—Scottish Branches', which appeared for the first time in the spring of 1913, probably on the initiative of MacDougall and claimed a circulation of about 20,000. This article, by 'J G', underlines the situation prior to the war, and will arouse a fellow-feeling in activists who are frustrated by the apathy of their fellows:

> What's gone wrong with Scotland? Here have we Socialists been preaching Socialism for twenty to thirty years till we have everyone converted, or nearly, and yet we can't get the converts to join themselves on to Socialist branches. . . .
>
> The man in the street who toils for his living recognizes that his whole life is spent in a blind alley which steadily becomes more and more crowded. He will admit that neither Tory nor Liberal proposals will get him out of that blind alley, will save him from the eternal grind of monotonous and deadening labour. He admits, readily enough, that Socialism is the only plan put forward to get him out of that blind alley; he will even agree that Socialism is bound to come if the world is not to go to utter smash; yet he will not join the BSP or ILP and lend himself a hand to get out.

One of the reasons, of course, that prevented workers becoming active members of the BSP was the one which probably prevented 'J G' from signing his full name—fear of the sack, and the blacklist. It is perhaps difficult for young people of today, living in a world where the majority of workers are organized in powerful unions, victimization leads to solidarity actions and where unemployment means poverty but not starvation, to understand the real heroism of every rank and file member, and the great sacrifices each was called on to make for 'the cause'. It must have seemed, even to the most sanguine, that they were banging their heads against a stone wall. In the end, it took the cataclysm of the Great War to knock the wall down.

In a lecture on 'Marx and his Message', delivered to a crowded audience at the Pavilion Theatre, Glasgow, 23 February 1913, under the auspices of the Glasgow Clarion Scouts, Maclean is reported in *Forward* to have commented jocularly:

> Karl Marx is dead. He died in 1883. Since then he has been killed many times, quite recently by Ramsay MacDonald. He is killed every other week by 'Rob Roy' in *Forward* . . .

In more serious vein he wound up his speech by saying,

> I want you to go home and read the works of Karl Marx. If you read one or two good books they will do more good for your head and heart than a library of rubbish. What we want in this country today is an educated working class. The millenium, if it is to come,

must come from an educated working class. Today you can be swayed by speeches and pamphlets. But the person who has studied Marx and applied him to literature, to life in all its phases, can see things as they really are.

14/Before the deluge

By 1914 the great mass strike movement had died out, but at the end of 1913 one very unusual industrial dispute took place on Alex Anderson's home ground, the mining village of Coalburn.

A dispute arose between the Coalburn Co-operative Society and its employees. The directors, all of them socialist miners, dismissed for inefficiency two employees who were members of the National Union of Distributive and Allied Workers. The latter immediately brought all the employees out on strike, and demanded that the Lanarkshire Miners' Union (LMU) should expel the directors. Of course the members of the Co-operative Society were all members of the LMU, and half of them at least were socialists! The Quarterly Meeting of the Co-op endorsed, by a huge majority, the directors' action and gave them full power to fill all the strikers' jobs. It happened that some of the new employees engaged were unable to take up work immediately, and several of the miners, including the directors, absented themselves from the pits to distribute the food necessary to keep the village from starving. (The Co-op had a distributive monopoly, as in most Scottish mining villages.) The LMU expelled them as blacklegs.

The miners had taken Maclean to their hearts, so the expelled men immediately turned to him in their trouble and asked that he should take their part during the forthcoming official meeting of the LMU. MacDougall described the occasion to me:

A strange scene was witnessed on that bleak, cold upland that winter morning. It was an idle day. Smillie had come up from Hamilton to defend the action of the Executive of the LMU in acceding to the requests of the NUDAW that the miner Directors should be expelled from the LMU (which meant that there could be no employment for them in the mines). Smillie put up the orthodox case to the critical audience of 2,000 miners in their working garb, their piece tins in their pockets and their lamps in their caps. But when Maclean explained that this was not an ordinary strike, namely a conflict between capital and labour, but internecine strife between two sections of the working class itself, and therefore was not to be judged by ordinary rules, there was an immense shout of applause from the crowd.

Even the accumulated fame of such a veteran as Smillie could not stand against the influence that John Maclean had won with this body of Scottish workers. Had Maclean given his assent the Coalburn miners would there and then have separated from the LMU, formed a definitely socialist miners' union, and appointed MacDougall as their Secretary.

However, Maclean was against any kind of split in the union movement, which at that time was far too localized in any case. The rank and file movement which he and MacDougall later helped to initiate favoured amalgamation of the county unions into one national industrial union.

By this time the anti-war opposition to Hyndman and the old guard had not only grown in size but was changing in quality. Hyndman had resigned from the chairmanship of the party in 1913 because an anti-war resolution had been passed, but a compromise had been reached at the 1913 annual conference when a resolution was carried making the issue of militarism a matter of individual conscience. This was anything but satisfactory, but the general consensus of opinion was that it was preferable to a split in the ranks.

At the 1914 conference an attack was made on an entirely different front. The Twentieth Century Press had published *Justice* and all the socialist literature produced by the SDF since 1891. To raise the necessary money it was organized on a commercial basis. As Hyndman was himself wealthy, and many of his supporters were also in comfortable circumstances, the majority of the shares were in their hands, and so they dominated not only the policy of the Twentieth Century Press but also the policy of *Justice*, of which Hyndman's main ally, Harry Quelch, was the editor for over twenty years. Quelch died in 1913, but the position, as far as the party rebels were concerned, became even worse, because H W Lee, who proved to be more of a reactionary than Quelch, became editor.

Maclean and Petroff decided that something should be done. Maclean had been buying shares in the Twentieth Century Press whenever he had any spare money, which was very seldom, as he now had two baby daughters to support and had been giving his mother ten shillings a week ever since he was married. Most of his spare cash went, in any case, to the Scottish movement, but he

had used the money he earned as tutor of the Pollokshaws
Economics Class (still under the auspices of the Eastwood School
Board!) to buy shares. All, however, to no avail, as the Hynd-
manites made sure they always had a majority. At the 1914 annual
conference in May, Maclean moved a resolution requesting that
two members of the Executive Committee be empowered to act as
trustees of the Twentieth Century Press, and 'that the ownership
of *Justice* be taken in their names, the trustees and editor to be
elected annually by a ballot vote of the members'. This was
defeated by a large majority, but the whole question should be
remembered, because of the situation which arose in 1919 when
money came from the Bolshevik government to finance the working
class press in Britain. This was done, of course, in all good faith,
but Maclean used to say 'The man who pays the piper calls the
tune!' from the depths of his own bitter experience.

Maclean also tried, in vain, to get some party control over the
BSP election candidates. He moved 'that all candidates for the
party at the next General Election run on the same official election
address, and raise any subsidiary local points in extra literature'.
This was seconded by Petroff, but was also defeated by a large
majority.

That summer trouble was brewing among the engineers on
the Clyde. They were peacefully negotiating for an increase, but at
the end of July a small strike broke out at Weir's of Cathcart, at
which many BSP members worked, over an unjust dismissal of one
of the men. Maclean and MacDougall happened to be speaking
at the work-gates during the dinner hour, and heard all about it.
Maclean came to the conclusion that there was more in it than was
apparent, and described the situation in *Justice*:

> No British firm has been more Americanized than this pump-
> making monopolist, one that supplies the Navy as well as the
> Merchant Fleet. It is hustle, hustle, hustle, all the time and every
> time.
> By chance a circular meant exclusively for the foremen has
> fallen into my hands. . . . The socialist who reads this and denies
> the Marxian theory of value ought to hie him to a nunnery or
> hermit's cell until his trump blows. I reproduce it as I got it—
>
> *In view of the large increase in the size of the establishment the
> Directors desire to draw the attention of all foremen to the neces-
> sity of maintaining a high degree of discipline in their departments.
> . . . The following matters are specially insisted upon:*
> *All foremen to be in their departments before the second whistle
> is blown to see that the men start at the correct time.*

Until the whistle is blown no foreman to leave the department. He should see that no preparations for leaving are made by the men; in particular no hot water to be drawn by the men before the whistle blows.

The Directors must insist on greater efficiency, in view not only of the increase in the rates of wages, but also the increase of the ratio of labourers' charges in almost every department. The Directors feel that much greater care should be taken in the selection of labourers. Only strong and active men should be employed, and they suggest of each foreman that he should review most carefully his labourers' staff and bring up the efficiency by carefully weeding out all non-efficients, and at the same time concentrate his efforts on reduction in numbers without loss of efficiency.

Directors desire to draw the attention of foremen to the large increase in capital expenditure during the last three years. This expenditure has been largely incurred in providing improved facilities, and in the case of machine tools the foremen should insist on the co-operation of every man in the attaining of improved results.

This policy of rushing the men to get the work done more quickly, not only supports our contention that articles tend to sell according to the time taken to make them, but shows that in the process the men are nagged at until any excuse is seized to come out on strike. This clearly explains the strike.

In the meantime, although the great strike movement of 1911-13 had petered out, apparently defeated, in reality it had a tremendous impact. Although members were not flocking into the socialist parties, they were certainly flocking into both the co-operatives and trade unions. The pace was forced as regards the inevitable amalgamation of trade unions into industrial unions, to meet the challenge of the growing trustification of industry, and in April 1914, the Triple Alliance of miners, railwaymen and transport workers, was formed. The policy of 'direct action' in addition to constitutional methods of attack on capitalism was now widely accepted in the labour movement.

Thus at the beginning of 1914, at the annual conference of the Scottish Branches of the ILP, Keir Hardie said 'Socialism meant freedom and could only be secured by the abolition of class rule over land and capital'. During a lecture at the Glasgow Metropole, according to Maclean in 'Scottish Notes':

Keir got back to the same theme. They must not forget that socialism was a great principle, not a thing of patchwork reforms. It was a revolution they were out for. . . . We congratulate him on his conversion to the revolutionary position, our position.

There were small gains for the BSP that year, which delighted Maclean perhaps out of all proportion to their real importance, but he saw them as straws to show which way the wind was blowing. MacDougall was elected to Eastwood School Board in addition to Blair, and BSP members were also returned to School Boards in Aberdeen, Falkirk, Larbert and Newton Mearns. In Falkirk the result was free books and classes in industrial history and economics, while at Newton Mearns a new BSP branch was formed.

That summer Maclean welcomed Willie Gallacher home:

> What was my astonishment on Sunday to see W Gallacher of Paisley back from America. Lecture organizers pounced down upon him. And when they are at it, let them enquire for Paisley's new hopeful, Campbell,* whose only crime is that he is a second MacDougall. Nuff sed!

In actual fact, Maclean and Gallacher clashed a good deal after this, as Gallacher had become imbued with the syndicalist ideas so prevalent in America.

The scene in the working-class movement on Clydeside prior to the outbreak of war has been described so ably by MacDougall that no comment of mine is required:

> There was at this time no very active hatred of the employers as a class among the masses of the workers. . . . The majority of the artisans and labourers voted Liberal, as a matter of course, because their fathers had done so, without thinking very much about the matter. Any scepticism that might have been rising among them as to the sincerity of Liberalism . . . was effectively put to flight by the democratic tone of Lloyd George's speeches and the actual measures of social reform then placed on the statute book. But it would certainly be an exaggeration to say that the factitious interest in politics awakened among the workers at election times by the thaumaturgy of the press equalled in any degree their abiding passion for football and sport in general. They voted by habit, not from any strong conviction.
>
> Not that there was not a great deal of zeal expended to stir them from this apathy. The ILP had been originated in Glasgow and for almost a generation its lecturers and propagandists had been preaching at the street-corners the doctrine of independent working-class politics, insisting upon the essential unity of Liberalism and Toryism, and calling the workers to a new political crusade against poverty and suffering. The results of this strenuous and sustained

---

*   J R Campbell later to become one of the leaders of the CPGB.

activity were little enough; the ILP had enrolled a thousand members or so; a small group of labour 'stalwarts' had been elected to the Town Council, where they were successful in pressing forward schemes of municipalization; some of the Trade Unions had selected Socialists as organizers and secretaries; and that was about all.

The Labour Press was pitifully weak and was simply snowed under by the gigantic circulation of its capitalist contemporaries. The Socialist Movement of this time was really a sect, not a party. But if it had some of the narrowness and heresy-hunting spirit characteristic of a sect, it had, at the same time, all the warm enthusiasm and energetic conviction, the heroism and self-abnegation usually displayed by a small band of brothers in the faith.*

15/The great betrayal

In 1912 the International Socialist Conference at Basle put on record its uncompromising opposition to the coming war, the war which all knew must come as a result of sharpening imperialist conflicts between Britain and Germany over markets and colonies. The leaders of the Second International at every national and international meeting had pledged themselves to use the organized force of their followers against their different governments when war broke out.

In August 1914, these very same leaders fled before the rising storm of war madness, throwing principles, courage and honour to the winds, and dragging their followers after them. 'It seems only yesterday', wrote Lenin later in 1915, 'that Hyndman, having turned to the defence of imperialism prior to the war, was looked upon by all "decent" Socialists as an unbalanced crank, and that nobody spoke of him otherwise than in a tone of disdain. Now the most eminent Social Democrat leaders of all the countries have sunk to Hyndman's position, differing among themselves only in shades of opinion and temperament.'

The great German Social Democratic Party, the dominating force of the International, collapsed like a pricked bubble. On

---

*   'Clyde Labour: a study in political change'. Nineteenth Century, 5 February 1927.

1 August a Social Democratic member of the Reichstag visited the parliamentary group of the Unified Socialists in Paris. He assured it that, although his colleagues were divided as to whether they should abstain from voting for war credits or should vote against them, they certainly would not vote for them. He returned to Germany just in time to vote with his colleagues *for* the war credits and to cry 'Hoch!' in honour of the Kaiser. We must defend the gains of social democracy against Russian despotism, the workers were told; we must free the poor, crushed Russian people!

Kautsky, the great Marxist theoretician who had supported Rosa Luxemburg in her fight against the revisionism of Bernstein, used all his great knowledge and skill to prove to the German workers that they should not oppose the war, and called his sophistry dialectics.

In Russia the majority of the Social Democrats enthusiastically supported this 'war of defence against Prussian militarism and despotism'. Plekhanov used the same arguments as Kautsky to show why *Russians* should not oppose their government.

In the middle of July the national conference of the Socialist Party of France had passed a resolution calling for a general strike in the event of war. But as soon as war was declared, all the socialists, from the extreme right to the extreme left, united with the government in a loyal defence of 'their' country against the brutal invasion of the Huns! Vaillant, who had sponsored the general strike resolution, Marcel Sembat, one of the strongest socialists in France and Jules Guesde, who had delivered fiery speeches about turning the war into civil war, entered the French cabinet. They all became even more violently imperialist than Hyndman.

In Britain the socialist movement on the whole responded 'gallantly' to the Liberal government's appeal to protect 'poor little Belgium' and to 'fight for democracy' against the threatening Prussian despotism. The TUC, the co-operative movement and the Labour Party unreservedly gave their services in the cause of the Allies, the TUC promising complete industrial peace for the duration of the war. The leaders of the ILP, with their customary 'statesmanship', carefully sat on the fence. At first they took a fairly strong pacifist line, and Ramsay MacDonald resigned his chairmanship of the Parliamentary Labour Party to Arthur Henderson because of its pro-war line.

As it became evident, however, that the mass of the working-class movement was being carried away with war enthusiasm, Ramsay and his friends changed their tune.

Robert Blatchford, Hyndman, and the 'old guard' leaders of the British Socialist Party, were rabidly jingoist. *Justice* was used, as Maclean had so much feared, for both blatant and subtle war propaganda.

The war had not long begun before it was obvious that the centre of working-class struggle was to be the Clyde. London and even militant South Wales refused semi-pacifists like Macdonald a hearing; anti-war speakers were howled down and violently attacked. The Clyde was different. Willie Gallacher gave the reason in his book *Revolt on the Clyde*:

> The Clyde was not altogether taken by surprise when war broke out. Apart from the general propaganda for socialism which had for long been conducted throughout the West of Scotland by the SDP, the ILP, and the SLP, there had been carried on for a number of years an intense anti-war and anti-militarist propaganda which continually exposed the war intrigues of the British Government. In the forefront of the campaign was that indomitable and irrepressible revolutionary fighter, John Maclean.

It was no accident that the figures which stood out in the working-class of war-time were James Connolly and John Maclean, an Irishman and a Scotsman.

The Clyde, with its Highland and Irish population with no great love either for the 'Sassenachs' or for capitalism, was never completely submerged in the wave of patriotic enthusiasm which drowned the rest of the country. At first it looked on the anti-war men with hostility and scorn, but it tolerated them. Then as hunger and war-weariness crept on, it began to listen, and then to act. Thus the Clyde became the 'Red Clyde', Britain's symbol of revolt.

The Second International had failed its first test, and failed dismally. The advanced workers of the world learned their first hard lesson. The war revealed to them what had previously been obvious only to the clear understanding of a few revolutionaries. It revealed the rotten decay that had been growing up within the Labour movement during these long years of adaptation to capitalism, and which was now threatening to choke its very existence. Happily it revealed more than that. It revealed ultimately a strong, resolute, revolutionary movement which had been growing alongside rotten opportunism, a tiny movement which swelled in the struggle against the war and became symbolized to future generations by Lenin and Trotsky in Russia, Liebknecht and Luxemburg in Germany, Adler in Austria, and Connolly and Maclean in Britain.

16/In Glasgow

When war was declared John Maclean never flinched, never hesitated for one minute. 'From the first moment', wrote Gallacher, 'he declared his Marxian faith—war against the war-makers'. When, after the first wave of protest, the ILP and the large body of unattached socialists on the Clyde area became paralysed with doubt, Maclean stood firm and gave the example that ultimately rallied all the rest. As MacDougall has put it:

> When, under the shock of the terrible news and in fear of the widespread spontaneous patriotism, we will not say enthusiasm, of the great majority of the people, the ILP retreated from the street-corners, stopped their big Sunday night meeting in the Metropole Theatre, and took refuge in their local halls, where they could reach nobody but the converted, John Maclean decided to continue his work among the masses.

Although Maclean carried the majority of the Glasgow BSP members with him in his strong stand against the war, they were, on the whole, the younger, less experienced men. Most of the old-timers remained faithful to Hyndman, and this was true of Scotland as a whole; older men like Tom Kennedy, Alex Anderson and even John F Armour, went pro-war. Although there were now about 500 members in Glasgow, there were only a few practised public speakers and the burden of the work fell on the shoulders of Maclean and MacDougall.

They spoke again and again in every part of Glasgow, and began to hold a regular Sunday night meeting at Bath Street, which was later to become the central rallying ground of Glasgow's rebels. One of Maclean's first actions was to send MacDougall to speak at the workgates of such great munition factories as Weir's of Cathcart, Hyde Park, and Atlas of Springburn.

It is difficult for those who have never experienced an atmosphere of jingoism to realize the amount of courage required for this work. The temper of the Glasgow workers had not yet been tested. If violent hostility were to be shown it would come from the munition workers who would be the last members of the working-class to be asked to fight. MacDougall was then a young man of twenty-five, highly-strung, not blessed with Maclean's extraordinary vitality and self-confidence. Yet, inspired with the deep conviction which had led him to devote the best years of his youth to the workers' movement, he went completely alone and unsupported to give his anti-war message to the munition workers, and it is to their honour that he was able to hold large and fairly orderly meetings—with plenty of interruptions and opposition, but with no violence.

The work of the BSP was by no means confined to propaganda. In the confusion at the beginning of the war, the dependents of the soldiers were left without resources at all. 'The dependents of soldiers and sailors are receiving insults instead of sustenance' reported Maclean in *Justice* :

> Parkhead men, at a large meeting, shouted out to me that two women were going to the fighters' wives, advising them to sell their household goods, to go to smaller houses, and to go out and wash the clothes of the young men of their 'betters' (who stay at home to steal German trade, I suppose).

Pollokshaws Branch instructed Blair and MacDougall to propose to Eastwood School Board that they should provide free meals for necessitous children, in particular the children of the fighting soldiers and sailors. After a big struggle by the reactionary members, this was carried.

It was no surprise to Maclean when the Executive Committee in London issued a statement in *Justice* on 17 September recommending their members to take part in recruiting. Indignant protests began to pour in from branches all over the country. Eventually the EC was forced to give in. They had purposely made the recruiting manifesto ambiguous to test the feeling of the party, and now issued another statement saying it was not an instruction to members to advocate recruiting, but merely a recommendation to members to take advantage of opportunities for advocating the BSP proposals of socialization of industry and adequate provision for women and children. This was the first defeat for the jingoists.

Almost comical was the difference between the Executive Committee's manifesto and the letter which appeared in the same issue of *Justice*—the last contribution from Maclean which ever appeared in the paper:

> In last week's *Justice* Belfort Bax exhorts us to 'hate the present Prussian military and bureaucratic state-system'. Our first business is to hate the British capitalist system that, with 'business as usual',

means the continued robbery of the workers. After that I, for one, will transfer the larger portion of my hate to Russian soil against the devilish autocracy that prevents the peaceful development of the workers' organizations by organized murder, torture and scientific cruelty, with a regularity and on a scale that would make the Kaiser with all his evils intensified a thousand-fold blush with shame.

So far as I can see, it will be impossible to tell whether Russia or Germany is immediately responsible for the war. . . . Even supposing Germany is to blame, the motive force is not the ambitions of the Kaiser, nor the brute philosophy of the Prussian militarists, but the profit of the plundering class of Germany. Colonial expansion was denied the Germans because the British, the Russians, and the French had picked up most of the available ports of the world. What could the Germans do but build up an army and a navy that would hold its own against all comers? This it has done steadily for the last generation. It is mere cant to talk of German militarism when Britain has led the world in the navy business. It is merely the 'struggle for existence' on a capitalist, national scale. The inspiration of German militarism comes as much from Darwin and Huxley, as applied by British economists and sociologists against us socialists, as from Bernhardt or any other German apologist of organized murder. Capitalism has neither conscience nor morality when it is brought to bay.

Every interested person knew that Germany's easiest road of entry into France was by Belgium. Sir Edward Grey had only to wait until Belgium's neutrality had been broken to seize the 'moral' excuse for Britain taking up arms. The real reason was, and is, that he and his class knew that war between Britain and German capitalism had to come sooner or later. Now was the day, and Britain struck. Plunderers versus plunderers, with the workers as pawns taking the murdering with right good will. The working-class at home is beginning to be starved, and is being buoyed up with the assertion that this is the last great war. . . .

It is our business as socialists to develop 'class patriotism', refusing to murder one another for a sordid world capitalism. The absurdity of the present situation is surely apparent when we see British socialists going out to murder German socialists with the object of crushing Kaiserism and Prussian militarism. The only real enemy of Kaiserism and Prussian militarism, I assert against the world, was and is German social democracy. Let the propertied class, old and young alike, go out and defend their blessed property. When they have been disposed of, we of the working-class will have something to defend, and we shall do it.

Justice was now of no use to the Glasgow BSP, *Vanguard* had been discontinued, so the Glasgow District Council was forced to pay tribute to *Forward* (in spite of the jingoistic articles regularly contributed by Maclean's old adversary 'Rob Roy'):

> At the usual fortnightly meeting of the above council held today I was instructed to send you their congratulations on the bold stand being taken by you in *Forward*, and also on the general tone of the paper regarding the war. At a time like this it is indeed refreshing to find at least one paper with an Editor* and contributors who are carrying out the true Socialist International policy, and who remember that all socialists should be against all war and in favour of arbitration on the causes of dispute.

As time wore on, the anti-war members of all the three socialist parties were forced to work together more and more, and a new spirit of solidarity took form in the common struggle against the war-mongers.

17/Bath street meeting

Towards the end of 1914, the BSP decided to concentrate all its forces on one central Sunday-night meeting in Bath Street. MacDougall described it to me:

> From the very first the meeting attracted large numbers of Socialists. Sunday by Sunday it grew, as the seriousness of the war situation became plain even to the meanest intelligence, and after a number of weeks it had grown so large that the casual passers-by in Renfield Street were attracted. . . . It is a broad street. It was packed from side to side so that a child could have walked on the heads of the people, and that condition extended a long distance down the street. Week after week there was to be seen a vast body of men and women, standing in tense silence, their attention riveted on the speakers for two or three hours on end, while a succession of speakers kept the meeting going. . . . Maclean's principal assistants were MacDougall, George Pettigrew, Mrs Helen Crawford of the ILP and a famous suffragette, and William Gallacher. . . .
>
> At the conclusion of the meeting, the pure formality of taking a collection which had been such a farce in pre-war socialist meetings now had become sufficient of a reality to show the change

---

*   still Tom Johnston.

in the situation. £20 and £30 in coppers was the sum often yielded ...

Men who had never in their lives before taken any interest in Socialism ... flocked to Bath Street to hear what Maclean had to say, for by this time his name was a household word in the city ... All who attended remember it to this day as one of the most significant experiences of their lives. How can one describe the scene? At the foot of the street across on the opposite side of Renfield Street stood the Tramway Office, brilliantly lit, plastered with poster appeals to men to join the army.

Up the street, standing on a table in the midst of a dense crowd of the proletariat, stood John Maclean exhorting men in explicit terms under no circumstances to join the army! The war, he told them, was not an accident. It was the continuation of the peace competition for trade and for markets already carried on between the powers before hostilities broke out . . . It was in the very nature of capitalism to engender warfare, just as the class conflicts within the capitalist nations were the inevitable result of the antagonism of interests between workers and exploiters . . .

The men they were asked to shoot were their brothers, with the same difficulty on Saturdays to find a rent for their miserable dwellings, who had to suffer the same insults and impertinence from their gaffers and foremen. . . . What did it matter if they looked a little different? and spoke a different language? The Scottish miners when on strike had often received financial help from the German miners. The international solidarity of the working-class was not only the highest moral sentiment that existed in the world, it had already found expression in many ways.

He told them that the main thing for them to know was that their real enemy was the employers, and that as long as turning lathes, ploughs, coal-cutters, looms, ships—all the tools of wealth production—were possessed by a small class of privileged people, then so long they would be slaves. To get free from this slavery was their real concern, and that victory could only be won with the assistance of his brothers in other lands, for socialism could not triumph in one country alone. The victory of socialism must be world-wide.

MacDougall's description of Maclean addressing the Bath Street meeting was so vivid and striking that I include it:

Who that ever saw can forget the tense, drawn face of the orator, his broad features, high prominent cheekbones, his heavy, bushy eyebrows, firm, cleanshaven mouth, his glowing eyes, and the stream of natural eloquence that fell from his lips? As he drove on, his prematurely grey hair shone in the reflected light of the street-lamps, and his forehead became covered with sweat. The soul of the man leapt out of his eyes and took possession of that vast audience. Not a man, woman or child but knew that they saw a David before them casting defiance against the capitalist Goliath. They knew that all the organized power of the British state was against him, ready to crush him whenever the ruling parties in London might say that it would further their cause. His hearers knew that for these precious words of exhortation and of hope the man would have to pay, and pay dearly. Would he be shot? Would the traditions of British Liberalism stand the strain of this unprecedented test when the British Empire was standing with its back to the wall? Nobody knew. Would he be drafted into the army like Karl Liebknecht? It was at least certain that he would have to suffer imprisonment, and everybody was aware that the rigours of imprisonment would not be tempered for a man who, in the rotten capitalist jargon, was a traitor.

That was why the people of Glasgow listened as they listened to no other man, as he told them how men like Lord Northcliffe and Lloyd George were pressing for conscription while at the same time insulting as shirkers and traitors the workers who in 1915 began to ask for higher wages to meet the tremendously increased cost of living.

That was why they listened when he told them how the British Junkers, through the Defence of the Realm Act and the Munitions Act, were trying to seize from them the partial freedom which radical, Chartist, trade union and co-operative working-men had fought for, often at terrible cost.

That was why they listened as he exhorted them to teach a lesson to those greedy capitalists who imagined that the workers were going to be forced not only to fight their battle but to pay the cost as well; as he exhorted them to kick their hardest against increased rents and rising prices, against military slavery through conscription and against industrial slavery through the Munitions Act; as he exhorted them to press onwards, war or no war, and, as part of the international workers, organize to overthrow the organized capitalist class of the world. That was why people left Bath Street on Sunday nights inspired and fortified, and why Bath Street became the centre of the revolutionary movement on the Clyde.

18/The turn of the tide

Before the end of 1914 murmurings of discontent were to be heard in Glasgow. Not only at the front but also at home the workers were bearing the burden of this war to defend the profits of their bosses. Capitalists were taking advantage of the abnormal conditions to raise prices of coal, food, and other necessities, and making huge profits out of the deprivation of the ordinary people. As the private fortunes swelled to enormous proportions, the more violent grew the abuse of the 'Huns', and the more exalted grew the language in which 'our brave boys at the front' were lauded and the people at home exhorted to make greater and greater sacrifices. But not all the Glaswegians were taken in.

Just before the outbreak of war the engineers had been negotiating for an increase of two pence per hour. Rising prices made it doubly necessary, and negotiations were renewed in November, when the employers offered three farthings an hour. Most of the trade union officials wished to accept a compromise of a penny an hour, but the men stood firm.

The engineers gained their knowledge, both directly and indirectly, mainly from the BSP Sunday afternoon class held in Central Glasgow. Many of them had attended for years, and more had enrolled for the 1914-15 session than had ever done before.

Gallacher, who was now working in the Albion Motor Works in Glasgow, tells in *Revolt on the Clyde* how Maclean through his class was supplying a continuous stream of material for the agitation:

> Maclean never dealt in 'abstract' Marxism of the Kautsky variety. He applied his Marxist knowledge to the events round him and used all that was happening to show the truth of Marxism. He demonstrated in the clearest manner that the war was a war for trade and brought out into full relief the sinister robber forces behind it. He gave example after example of the financiers and big employers pointing a gun at the head of the Government and demanding increased profits, and of other firms selling war material to neutrals with the full knowledge that they were being resold to Germany. These examples, with instances of increased prices for ordinary commodities and higher rents, were carried day by day into the factories.

Matters came to a head in February 1915, when some American workers were imported into Weir's Works and paid ten shillings a week more than their own men. The fat was in the fire after that. Weir's men were, in any case, very militant. Some of them had been members of the Pollokshaws SDF/BSP for years, and most of the leading shop stewards, including the convener Jack Smith, attended the Central Class.* They defied their union, came out on strike, and soon the other factories followed.

The strike was, of course, unofficial, because of the TUC's pledge of industrial peace for the duration of the war. A committee to conduct the strike was formed and called the Labour Withholding Committee, in order to circumvent the Defence of the Realm Act which made strikes illegal. Willie Gallacher, of the BSP, was elected chairman, and J W Messer, a leading shop steward at Weir's, and also a 'Maclean man', was elected secretary.

In spite of fierce opposition from trade union officials, government, and employers alike, the strike was one of the best organized the Clyde had ever seen, and was the beginning of the rank and file movement that sprang up in defiance of the TUC. The drawback was that there was no strike pay and the men were eventually starved back, but that was by no means the end of the struggle. It had just begun.

In February also came six coincident conferences of the BSP. The jingoists had been making desperate efforts to bring the party round to their position. A letter was published in *Justice* at the end of January stating their case in detail, and was signed by thirty of the oldest and best-known members including Hyndman, Lee, Irving, Jones, Belfort Bax, A S Headingley, Ben Tillet, and others. Their steady propaganda and possession of *Justice* had its effect. The conferences showed that the party was divided into two fairly equal sections, one led by Maclean and E C Fairchild, the other by Hyndman and his friends. But Hyndman still had *Justice*. Voting for the executive members showed that Scottish branches were about equally divided between Maclean and Anderson, who supported the war; but Anderson was elected, once again.

For some time now Maclean's employers, the Govan School Board, had been looking round for some excuse to dismiss him. He had been teaching at Lambhill Street School for a few years, and when he became involved in a minor disciplinary matter in which many other teachers were involved as well, the headmaster

---

* One of the younger shop stewards was Harry McShane, a member of the BSP, who afterwards became one of Maclean's closest colleagues.

took the chance to suspend him. There was immediately an outcry from Maclean's supporters, and a large number of workers crowded into the board room on the night Maclean's case was to be discussed. The members were afraid, and eventually Maclean was censured and transferred to Lorne Street School. Further than that they dared not go, as yet.

Socialists have always been misrepresented and slandered by the enemies of the working-class, but no abuse they receive from that quarter is ever so venomous as the abuse of traitors to the movement. All decent socialists were shocked when they heard that Hyndman was accusing the ILP of being paid German agents, and Maclean wrote a long letter to *Forward*, in response to the editor's challenge to the BSP rank and file:

> I must confess that I have not read the ILP pamphlets on the war which gave Hyndman the excuse to write to *L'Homme Enchaîné*, although I have read extracts from the criticisms of them appearing in socialist and capitalist papers. Nor do I know exactly the position of Ramsay MacDonald and Keir Hardie; for whilst on occasions these worthy gentlemen have criticized the usual excuses for Britain's entry into the war, and have on others explained the bloodshed as a sacrifice on the altar of capitalism, yet they are credited with the position that we must now see the war through. That position to many of us inside and outside the ILP is not quite satisfactory, although somewhat excusable in view of the jingo-mad attitude of Hyndman, Blatchford and others, yet the last man who should dwell on it seems to me to be the veteran H M Hyndman. . . . It is just a stretch or two beyond the limit for our 'cultured' comrade to go to France, aye, and to the rag of Clemenceau—the detestable crusher and murderer of French wage-slaves—and there to suggest with the subtlety of the serpent that MacDonald, Hardie & Co. have stooped to the basest treachery any socialist could be guilty of—acting as paid agents in the interests of German Imperialistic Capitalism.

He went on to say that he would rather cut his tongue out than support Hyndman, continued to denounce the latter in a more outspoken fashion than ever before, and concluded:

> Hyndman was defeated on the 'big navy' question, after the Coventry Conference in 1911; the BSP since its conception has stood against jingoism and militarism in all their manifestations; in fact, it has gone against even the citizen army. It was therefore a shameful attempt at betrayal to slip into the capitalist press a manifesto absolutely repugnant to the old SDF and the new BSP position without the consent of the Party as a whole.

Hyndman may be anxious to free Europe from the 'tyranny of

the last military caste left on the planet', but he appears to me to be anxious to put in its place a 'British Socialist Autocracy' with himself as the lead, autocrat-in-chief, and *Justice* at his right hand as his public organ.

All Socialists are anxious to see German and British militarism and capitalism laid low; but is Hyndman taking the wisest course to accomplish his ends? Hyndman, with his fight to a finish, helps to prevent revolt in Germany, the only sure and permanent way to dispose of militarism there, and helps to stifle revolt here when genuine concessions might be obtained from our unscrupulous capitalist Liberal Government.

Meantime as a member of the BSP I consider it Hyndman's duty to withdraw his 'infamous letter'.

Thus Hyndman prepared the way for the vile insinuations made against Maclean and the militant Clyde workers by the government and its agents.

19/Rent strikes

Since the beginning of the war, house factors* in most of the working-class districts had been raising rents. Thousands of workers had flooded into Glasgow to make munitions, had caused the demand for houses in certain districts to be much greater than the supply, and the factors thought they could take advantage of this situation without opposition. The munition workers were all working long hours of overtime and making good money, and, in spite of the fact that the rise in prices had made this increase practically worthless, the factors were demanding quite bluntly a share in the 'plunder'.

But munition workers weren't the only tenants. Many of them were the wives and families of soldiers and sailors fighting overseas, and could not manage to pay the increased rents. Fortunately there was a militant anti-war socialist in Glasgow who knew what to do and had the courage to do it. This was Andrew McBride, an ILP town councillor, who was secretary of the Labour Party Housing Committee. He tried constitutional methods initially. He appealed to Labour leaders George Barnes and Arthur Henderson, who had

---

*   A Scottish term for landlords, agents, land-stewards.

become members of the recently-formed Coalition government, to get the increases in rent forbidden by law. They did nothing. He appealed to the Parliamentary Labour Party to put forward resolutions. They did nothing. Only one course was now open—direct action by the people involved.

The unrest in Govan was particularly great, and when one factor demanded his second increase, McBride seized the opportunity. A joint meeting of the Housing Committee and the Women's Housing Association was held in the middle of May, and decided to call a rent strike. That is, each tenant was to pay the ordinary rent, but refuse to pay the increase. McBride, with the help of other anti-war socialists like Maclean and MacDougall, set about rousing the men. Mid-day and evening workgate meetings outside, and the shop stewards inside, stimulated all the active workers in the large shipyards and engineering shops.

But it was the women who were chiefly concerned, and here McBride showed his ability. He organized committees in each tenement affected, with two women from each close. He trained Mrs Barbour, an ordinary Govan housewife, as a speaker and organizer, and soon she was leading a women's revolt of a kind never before seen in Glasgow. Every method was used to rouse the interest of the housewives. Meetings were held in the streets and in the back courts, bells were rung, drums were beaten, and trumpets were blown, all to draw the women out. By the middle of June the factors in Govan had to give in and the increases were withdrawn.

This victory stimulated the agitation in other districts, and soon the fever had spread far and wide. In Partick one factor who had received postal orders from his tenants for the ordinary rent had the nerve to come round next morning to return the postal orders and demand his increase. 'The women turned out in full force' reported *Forward*, 'and plastered the poor man with flour and pease-meal, and by the time the police arrived he looked like a grain store in disorder. Unkind observers said if the factor did not get his increase he got its worth in pease-meal.'

Large demonstrations were held all over the city. At the beginning of October a large number of women marched from St Enoch's Square to the Municipal Chambers at George Square, with banners flying. 'While my Father is a prisoner in Germany, the landlord is breaking up our home', said one. 'My Father is fighting in France; we are fighting Huns at home', another read. Delegates were sent to ask the town council to intervene with the government on their behalf. But the council, composed as it was of property owners, factors, and their friends, refused even to suspend standing orders to discuss the women's appeal. This only added fresh fuel to the fire, and finally the government was compelled to intervene. It set up a Committee of Enquiry.

By this time the Glasgow District Council of the BSP had re-issued the *Vanguard*, with Maclean as editor, and in the October number he commented on the Committee of Enquiry:

> The factors, knowing the game, immediately gave notice of rent increases all round, as soon as they heard what the Government had done. Why? It is quite clear to us. We are certain that the factors and landlords are calculating on a 'compromise'. If they demand an increase of £3 per tenant per annum—and that is even less than some are asking now that the 'enquiry' is in progress—they expect the committee to suggest to the Government that they be entitled to 30/-.

He went on to urge that the large and enthusiastic meetings that were being held to frighten the government were not enough. 'They must be backed by action' he insisted. 'The people ought now to refuse to pay any rent at all.' His prophecy came true. The members of the Committee of Enquiry were influenced by the united front of the factors, and were preparing a compromise. But they all reckoned without the awakened anger of the whole working class. People in the previously unaffected areas saw no objection to munition workers paying more, but when they themselves became liable to increased rent, that was different! Encouraged by the widespread working-class support and by the exhortations of the members of the BSP and ILP (who were now prepared to turn, as a last resort, to direct action), the Clyde munition workers were ready to strike.

The factors could not collect the rents, nor could the sheriff's officers manage to evict the tenants who refused to pay. Before they got near, the officer and his men were met with an army of angry women who drove them back.

'We are not paying increased rent!' was Glasgow's slogan.

20/The Munitions of War Act

While the women were drawn into the fight against higher rents, the men were being organized to fight the Munitions Act, which was passed in July 1915, and the growing menace of conscription.

The heavy losses of the allies on both fronts during the early months of 1915 created a panic in the British ruling class, the result of which was the formation of the Coalition government whose prime object was to increase the output of munitions. The militant spirit of trade unionism shown by the Clyde engineers in February must be crushed. The initiative came from William Weir, owner of Weir's Works, as described by Maclean in *Vanguard*:

> The Munitions Act, better known as the Industrial Slavery Act, since it was meant to tighten the chains of economic slavery on the workers, was the outcome of the suggestions of Mr William Weir, of Cathcart, whose usual arrogance forced his men to stop work and precipitate the Clyde engineers' strike, the first great workers' revolt since the Great Slaughter Match commenced. He demanded that the Government ought to prevent the workers' unions from being used to force up wages or improve conditions during the war. The Government has not only practically adopted his ideas, but it has appointed him supreme controller of munition supplies in Scotland.

The workers lost with one blow all the small freedoms and privileges which years of hard fighting had won for them—the right to organize, the right to strike, and the right to move from workshop to workshop. 'The workers of the Clyde' wrote Maclean 'have found themselves bullied and ordered about by foremen and managers as never before. . . . Silly, irritating impositions in the interests of greedy capitalism have ruthlessly cut across use and wont, or definite trade union regulations, to the utter disgust of even "patriotic" workmen with sons and other relatives at the front.'

After the February strike the revolutionaries inside the

factories had been listened to as never before. They had won the respect of the workers by their determined action, and the workers were now prepared to read their literature and discuss matters with them. More and more were beginning to attend Maclean's meetings and classes, and growing crowds were listening to MacDougall at the workgates with intense interest. Members of both SLP and BSP were taking the lead in the factories, and the syndicalist propaganda of the SLP in particular was taking root.

But the Munitions Act roused anger as no amount of agitation could have done. Previously when Maclean and the others had told the workers they were wage-slaves, they had laughed in scorn. Now their illusory sense of freedom was gone. Some of them were comforted by the thought that the slavery would last only during the war, but at every meeting Maclean was telling them what was going to happen if they did not fight for their freedom now:

> Here are the employers, finding year by year the political liberties of the working-class more and more of an obstacle in the way of the development of capitalism into the 'servile state'. In ordinary times they would find themselves faced with the unanimous opposition of the working class if they attempted to interfere with the workers' liberty of moving from one firm to another. In fact, they dare not make the attempt. But the war, the glorious war, gives them the opportunity, the excuse, the pretext they desire. Because then the workers are divided, many are so chloroformed by the existence of a state of war as to have lost that healthy class instinct by means of which the Labour Movement of this country, despite the lack of theoretical knowledge, has moved forward. This large body repeat parrot-like the ideas current in the capitalist press, and allow their actions to be determined by the shallow talk of ministerial demagogues. And so the capitalists fancy that now, when the workers are weak because disunited, they can rivet the chains more firmly upon the producing class.

In actual fact, the Munitions Act helped to produce the unity which the war had smashed. Under the influence of the SLP and BSP, works committees in the different factories were being set up, and the Central Committee which had organized the February strike, the Labour Withholding Committee, began to meet again. The famous case of the three Fairfield shipwrights speeded up this process.

In the autumn of 1915, 400 shipwrights at Fairfield's stopped work. Seventeen of them were hauled before a Munitions Tribunal and each was fined £10 with the alternative of thirty days' imprisonment. The BSP exhorted the men not to pay the fine. Maclean explained in the *Vanguard*:

> That would make them criminals, and acknowledged criminals at that. As other workers see the drift of the Act now, all are afraid that they will sooner or later be trapped and likewise made criminals at the request of the masters who rob them. Every worker who recognizes the infamy of the Act must be ready to down tools and follow the example of the Welsh miners* if these ship-wrights are sent to prison. The Clyde is ripe for a blow at the infamous audacity of the masters. Let them have it, comrades. Remember that you shall have the backing of many of our Lanarkshire comrades of the mining villages. These men have assured us that they are prepared to do their bit in the great conflict, if one is needed.

Only three men followed Maclean's advice, but when they were sent to prison the Clyde was in an uproar. Preparations were being made by the Fairfield and Govan workers for a strike, when the union officials took matters into their own hands. Thinking that the officials were going to call a strike the Labour Withholding Committee sat back, but instead the officials, as part of a delaying tactic, called for a government enquiry. This was, of course, a farce, but was protracted so long that in the end it was hardly worth striking to release the men.

While it was still hanging on, the conduct of the officials was strikingly shown up by rank and file action at Weir's. Robert Bridges, a shop steward and a member of Maclean's class, was charged with 'molesting' a worker because he had asked him to show his union card in accordance with the custom of the shop stewards at Weir's. The workers in Weir's did not issue a manifesto or pass a single resolution. They took action. They decided that the 200 men employed in Bridges's department should accompany him to the Munition Court, and that in the event of conviction no fine should be paid. They also decided that if Bridges went to prison 'drastic action' and not an enquiry would be employed to secure his release. The charge was dropped entirely.

Meanwhile the enquiry into the case of the shipwrights was dragging on, and the feeling was growing everywhere that the Labour Withholding Committee should take action. Then the men were released after a fortnight in prison, and it was generally agreed that fear of the new unofficial committee had forced the 'powers that be' into action.

---

* There was a mass strike of miners in South Wales in July 1915.

It was now obvious, wrote MacDougall in the *Vanguard* (October 1915) that the union officials were discredited and counted for little, and that the real leaders were to be found in the workshops. He went on:

> Over and above that the exceptional circumstances at present existing are producing something very like the beginning of a real industrial union movement. The need for solidarity is breaking down the old craft jealousies, the spread of socialism is showing to workers their essential unity as a class, in spite of all superficial differences of occupation. In many shops on the Clyde vigilance committees, composed of delegates from each of the trades in the shop, have been formed, and have already many times demonstrated their usefulness. It should be the duty of militant socialists and trade unionists in shops where such committees do not exist, or where they have been only partially formed, as in Beardmore's (Clydebank), to see that a complete organization is set up. Then the vigilance committees are linked up in a central committee, which contains the most trusted men of the labour movement in Glasgow.

Maclean described some of these developments in a letter to Hugh Hinshelwood of Greenock:

> We did very well with the *Vanguard* last month. We sold about 3,000 and cleared a slight profit. Our Economics Class enrolled 227 members the first day. . . .
> We are building up a vigilance organization on the basis of the Glasgow District ASE shop stewards. I've tried to get the miners in S Lanark to take similar steps and link up.
> I think the time has come when the shop, railway and mine workers in the Clyde basin ought to be directly linked together.
> I fancy you would do yourself the best favour—in the end—by trying to get the Greenock district built up on similar lines and linked up with Glasgow. Messer of Weir's, Cathcart, is the General Secretary . . .

Maclean also, in the columns of the *Vanguard*, exhorted the unofficial committee to forge ahead 'refusing to recognize officials who have betrayed the workers (as Highland chiefs and Indian princes have betrayed their people in the past to the English) and are equally ready to do the trick again.'

And so the Labour Withholding Committee began to organize in earnest, and issued a manifesto:

> Our purpose must not be misconstrued. We are out for unity and closer organization of all trades in the industry, one Union being the ultimate aim. We will support the officials just so long as they

rightly represent the workers, but we will act independently immediately they misrepresent them. Being composed of delegates from every shop, and untrammelled by obsolete rule or law, we claim to represent the true feeling of the workers.

From that time onwards the committee was called the Clyde Workers' Committee. A detailed constitution was drawn up and its main objectives stated, the most important of which was,

To organize the workers upon a class basis and to maintain the class struggle until the overthrow of the wages system, the freedom of the workers, and the establishment of industrial democracy have been attained.

It has often been assumed that the members of the SLP took the initiative in forming the Clyde Workers' Committee and dominated it throughout, but MacDougall told me that this was not the case. The majority of the members belonged to the BSP. According to Tom Anderson's pamphlet, *John Maclean*, the Committee came into being 'largely as the result of Comrade John's effort.'

21/The struggle begins

By October 1915, the unrest among the Glasgow workers was becoming intense. The growing fear of conscription, the slavery of the Munitions Act, the rising cost of living, the demands of the landlords and their factors, the unceasing agitation and propaganda of Maclean and the BSP at Bath Street and at the shipyard and factory gates, the springing up of the workers' committees—all these developments were fast bringing about a crisis that demanded correct leadership if the workers were to be guided along revolutionary channels.

The members of the Independent Labour Party were incapable of giving that leadership, although they were playing an important part with their pacifist, anti-war propaganda, their exposure of secret diplomacy, and their fight against the factors. However, although in Glasgow many of them had been much influenced by Marxist teaching and were prepared to support direct action as a last resort, their eyes in the pre-war days had

D

been turned constantly to representation in parliament and town councils as the road to socialism.

The members of the Socialist Labour Party were helping to lead the fight in the factories for unofficial workers' committees, but many of them had not yet rid themselves of their academic, ultra-left sectarianism, which inclined them to the view that strikes could not be justified except for the establishment of socialism, and taking part in the fight for immediate demands could not be justified under any circumstances. They were typical representatives of that left-wing communism which Lenin described, rather unfairly in my opinion, as 'an infantile disorder'.

The task of welding together the different sections of the movement and the different phases of the struggle fell inevitably to the BSP with Maclean at the head. The *Vanguard*, with Maclean as editor, gave an excellent Marxist analysis of every situation as it arose, and a concrete militant lead. It gave hope and courage to the revolutionaries, telling them the truth about the growing international movement abroad, news which had been denied them because the delegates appointed by the ILP and BSP to the International Socialist Conference in Switzerland had been refused passports by the Foreign Office and were unable to attend.

In his first editorial, called 'Our Prospects and Policy', Maclean gave the views of the Glasgow BSP on the present situation:

> Nothing but world socialism will do. This monstrous war shows that the day of social pottering or reform is past. . . . The 'social reformer' must be absolutely crushed, for intolerance to him is but justice to humanity . . . Capitalism, that is the right to rob the creators of wealth, must be killed, and it can be done in twelve solid months, starting any time, if but the workers are ready.

He went on to analyse the different roles of the three sections of the working-class movement, the trade unions, the co-operatives and the socialist parties:

> Trade Unionism, up to the present, has been a defensive movement. The workers' position has been slightly bettered, whilst the capitalists' has been immensely improved. While from this point of view it has failed, trade unionism has kept the workers together and enabled socialists to vastly swell its numbers.
>
> Our policy will be the advocacy of Unions by industry, and unions of these Unions on a world basis with a world cord system—keeping pace with the trustification of the money power, and the using of these unions towards a complete control of the organization and running of the workshops, mines, and land of the world. We

are not for the absolute control of each industry by workers engaged, for that would be trustified caste control . . . the final control and destiny of the products of an industry must be in the hands of humanity as a whole.

He went on further to describe co-operation as an attempt by the workers to get full control of their means of life and education, and that it was socialists who had largely helped to develop it,

We intend to urge that the co-operative movement should supply jobs to workers victimized for their fight against the capitalists; that a portion of its funds should be used to help in the social and political struggle against capitalism and that world co-operation should be established to bind the workers of all races more firmly together.

Dealing with the socialist movement, he attacked the ideas of anarcho-syndicalism so prevalent in the shop stewards' movement:

in view of the mighty forces the various States have summoned to their aid in the struggle of the nationally organized capitalists, it is sheer blind madness to talk of the uselessness of the State and of politics. . . . As socialists, we contend that the workers can use their existing and rapidly expanding State machinery for the fundamental re-organizing and unifying of the whole of the processes of production and exchange. We, therefore, shall advocate the getting of the vote for all adults, the full democratization of all public machinery of government, and the united use of the vote by the workers for the capture of all public bodies towards the attainment of the grand goal of a World Co-operative Industrial Democracy.

Regarding the immediate issue of the war he concluded:

We do not think national wars are of benefit to the workers so we shall oppose all national wars as we oppose this one. *The only war that is worth waging is the Class War*, the workers against the world exploiters, until we have obtained industrial freedom.

While the police had not yet attacked Maclean openly, they had been trying since the beginning to stop the Bath Street meeting indirectly. They tried to use the blocking of the pavements as an excuse to break it up, but failed. They brought along two well-known Glasgow characters, the 'Clincher' and the 'Tipster Parson' to hold meetings nearby and draw away Maclean's crowd. That failed.

The first open trouble took place, not at Bath Street, but at the Fountain in Shawlands, which was one of his regular stances.

On the evening of 2 September he was addressing quite a large meeting, and happened to refer to the war as 'this murder business'. Whereupon, a drunk soldier in the audience became obstreperous and accused Maclean of calling him a murderer. Maclean managed to quiet him, but after the public-houses came out at 9 pm, the soldier and some local 'patriots' who had also been refreshing themselves came together and tried to break up the meeting. They got hold of two policemen who asked Maclean to stop speaking. Maclean refused, but he got no chance to appeal to the meeting, as he had done before on similar occasions. He was marched straightaway down to Queen's Park Police Station and charged with using language likely to cause a breach of the peace. Soon wild stories spread around the district: that he had been detained under the Defence of the Realm Act; that he was going to be shot, and so on. As a matter of fact he was released and heard nothing further for some time.

The following Sunday, Maclean told the Bath Street meeting about this occurance, got the nucleus of a Free Speech Committee formed and a Free Speech Demonstration was held the next week at the very spot where he had been arrested. The chair was taken by Arthur McManus of the SLP, and Maclean, MacDougall, Milligan (SLP), and Harry Hopkins (ILP) spoke to a crowd of over two thousand—easily the largest gathering ever held in this middle-class locality.

Meanwhile the police tried another device at Bath Street. A gang of 'patriots' called the Federation of Labour was brought along to steal the stance. However, the BSP just started up behind them, and not only did not lose any of their usual crowd, but actually gained more. Their collections rose and they gained new members. On 19 September the crowd, instead of being fired by the 'patriots' to attack Maclean, turned round and rushed them off their platform. Maclean reported in *Vanguard*:

> The rushing of anti-socialists, brought to a Socialist meeting place by the police to break the Socialist gathering during a war is a tremendously significant fact. If the authorities do not comprehend its full import, we do. If men are dying for a country which is not theirs, then we are prepared to suffer any penalty for a country we mean to make the people's. It is the duty of every *Man* of the slave class to rally round us in this bitter fight to retain the freedom won by our fathers from the fathers of the Junkers who today ask us to die for them. Let them die for themselves, and we will look after ourselves against German and all other Junkers who crash up against us. The 'punch-like' notions of our Junkers seem to infer

that because we are not anxious to throw away our lives for them we are anxious to have the German Junkers as our masters! No, we are not anxious to swap masters; we are out to get rid of all masters. No man has the right to be any other man's master. It is because we object to the slavery implied in mastery, the mastery over land and the capital of the world, that we are socialists, and nothing but socialists. It is in our estimation a base myth to think that we shall win our freedom more easily from British than from German capitalists.

The war has brought out the fact that Germans own, and will own after the war, property in this country, and we are convinced that if we attempted to take our land and means of production, we would have to face not only the 'loyal' section of the British Army, but a contingent sent over by our 'beloved' enemy, the Kaiser. Remember how the Germans released French soldiers to shoot down 30,000 men, women and children in the streets of Paris, simply because the workers dared to establish a Commune in 1871 at the close of the Franco-Prussian War.

A desperate fight for freedom was beginning in Glasgow.

22/The dangerous man

By the end of October 1915, the Bath Street Sunday night meeting had grown to tremendous proportions and had become a magnet for all the light and intelligence in the city. The Central Economics and Industrial History Class had also swollen to an unprecedented size, attracting about 400 students. The authorities were beginning to realize just how dangerous this upsurge of the workers was becoming when led by revolutionaries like Maclean. 'John's ability and fearlessness' wrote John Wheatley in 'Catholic Notes' in *Forward* 'have singled him out as one of the great rebel leaders of our time, and consequently one of the first subjects of persecution. Our rulers fear Maclean more than they do the whole Labour Party.'

It was no surprise, therefore, when he was summonsed under the Defence of the Realm Act, charged with making statements likely to prejudice recruiting by stating at Bath Street, 'I have been enlisted in the Socialist Army for 15 years. God damn all other armies!', and by saying at the Fountain, Langside, that any soldier who shot another soldier in the war was a murderer, or words to that effect. Maclean appeared at the Sheriff Court on 27 October, pleaded not guilty, and his trial was fixed for 10 November.

His defence was organized by the Free Speech Committee which he himself had initiated, and which was linked up with various unions, the Glasgow Trades Council, the Govan Trades Council, the ILP, the BSP, and the SLP. Long before the trial a large crowd of working-men—munition workers, co-operators, trade unionists, and socialists—had gathered outside the court buildings. As soon as the proceedings began they swarmed into court and the galleries until it was packed to the door. A Glasgow Sheriff had never before had such an audience.

Detective followed detective, all repeating like gramophones 'God damn the army' or 'God damn the other armies'—the only part of Maclean's speech at Bath Street they could remember. Only one remembered that the speech had actually been about the Welsh miners' strike. During his cross-examination, the lawyer for the defence, Mr Cassels, several times indignantly raised his voice in protest against the disgraceful methods of the police in this case.

After the witnesses, for and against, came Maclean:

> I said 'I have been enlisted in the Socialist Army for fifteen years, the only army worth fighting for. God damn all other armies.' Take out of that what meaning you like.

He went on to point out that in his speech at the Langside meeting he did not desire to injure the feelings of any soldier:

> The major portion of the Army is drawn from the working class, and I certainly did not say that the soldiers were murderers. The soldiers belonging to the working-class are those who will not get any benefit from this war. I say here and now that the soldiers themselves are not murderers, but those who sent them and are sending them to the war are murderers.

The trial was nothing but a farce, and it was obvious that the Sheriff himself realized it. In his summing up he stated that Maclean had had a certain amount of provocation in that on both occasions his meeting had been interfered with in an irrelevant and impertinent way, and that on neither occasion had he sought to elaborate on what he had probably said on the spur of the moment. His concluding remarks, announcing the sentence of £5 or five days' imprisonment, were made in an atmosphere tense with excitement.

'Three cheers for Maclean! Three cheers for the Revolution!' someone called out, and hundreds of people in the court, galleries, and in the corridors, responded enthusiastically, and the sacred precincts rang with the strains of *The Red Flag*. When Maclean appeared outside he received a tremendous ovation from the large crowd which had been unable to obtain admission, and which had been waiting patiently to hear the result.

On 16 November the farce was continued at the offices of the Govan School Board. Ever since his transfer to Lorne Street School, Maclean had been having trouble with the Board. He had refused to take what he considered injustice lying down, and had written an indignant letter of protest. He was asked to withdraw the letter, but refused to do so until the Board should re-instate him in Lambhill Street School. This was the chance the Board were waiting for, and he was asked to attend a meeting of the Board on 16 November, when a motion for his dismissal was to be discussed.

The meeting resembled the May one. Once more the Board members had to face a 'gallery', and once more they were afraid to discuss Maclean's case openly. Only Harry Hopkins (ILP) and Stewart, a co-operative member, opposed a private discussion of a matter which, as Hopkins said, 'deeply concerned the working class movement in Glasgow'. At first the visitors refused to leave the room, insisting on remaining to see that justice was done. Hopkins eventually persuaded them to leave, but no sooner was the room cleared than another crowd rushed in, and a shop steward from Beardmore's made a strong speech to the applause of his fellow-workers. The Board members lost their heads, the chairman deserted his post, and a brawny riveter from Fairfield's occupied the vacant chair. The Board members fled to the committee rooms, while a tremendous meeting was organized outside.

The news that Maclean was to be dismissed met with intense indignation in the audience and created consternation in Govan and indeed in the entire Glasgow working-class movement. The feeling was so great that in many of the large factories and works a strike of protest was suggested. Many unions sent protests against both his trial and his dismissal. One letter to the Govan School Board from Emmanuel Shinwell, then secretary of the Glasgow Branch of the Seafarers' Union, was published in the *Vanguard* in December:

> I am desired on behalf of the above Society to write you with reference to the recent dismissal of Mr John Maclean from his position as teacher in one of the schools under your jurisdiction. I may mention that this Society has over 3,000 members in the

district, about 1,000 of whom are estimated to reside in the Plantation and adjacent districts, so that you can understand the matter is one in which we are deeply interested.

We hold the view that Mr Maclean's dismissal without any definite charge being formulated is manifestly unfair, and in our judgment he should be immediately reinstated in the service of the Board.

A very characteristic resolution was received from the shop stewards at Weir's:

that we immediately get into touch with all Convenors of Shop Stewards or representatives of the Kindred Trades with a view to levying ourself 1d, 2d, or such a sum as would be sufficient to employ our victimized fellow-worker, John Maclean, as an independent organizer, at a salary equivalent to what he was in receipt of from the Govan School Board. Furthermore that we henceforth labour unceasingly until Comrade Maclean is reinstated in his former position.

23/The political strike

Two days later the scene of the drama changed back to the Sheriff Court.

Confounded by the refusal of tenants to pay the increased rents, and by their inability to secure evictions because of the militancy of the working-class women, the landlords and factors hit on what they considered to be a winning plan. They decided to sue the householders at the Small Debt Court, where the factors would be able to get their extra rent money deducted from the wages of the householders. But they reckoned without the Glasgow workers. When eighteen men were summoned to appear at the Small Debt Court on 18 November, they were roused in an unprecedented manner.

When the big day dawned, large sections of the population were keyed up and ready for action. From early morning Mrs Barbour was organizing her women for a great march to the Sheriff Court. Many of the Govan shipyards and factories came out on strike. From early morning McBride was organizing the strikers to take part in an orderly demonstration, together with large deputations of men from Parkhead in the east, Cathcart in the south, Dalmuir in the west, and Hydepark in the north. The workers were on the march!

The different sections met in the town and the huge procession, preceded by a band of improvised instruments including tin whistles, hooters, and dilapidated big drums, aroused tremendous interest as it marched through the typical Glasgow November fog, the marchers carrying lighted candles to see the way.

One contingent marched to Lorne Street School where Maclean was teaching under notice of dismissal. They called him out, and carried him shoulder high through the streets till they reached their goal at the Sheriff Court. That was to be Maclean's last day as a teacher.

A crowd of about 10,000 people had now gathered outside the Court. The streets were packed and traffic was completely stopped. Platforms consisting of long poster boards picked up from the front of newspaper shops were improvised, placed on the shoulders of half a dozen husky men, and the speakers lifted on to them. Maclean was right in front of the court addressing the crowd as far as his voice would reach. In other streets, Gallacher, McBride, MacDougall, and other leaders were also speaking. Roars of rage surged from the masses as each speaker told of the robbery and injustice of the factors.

Maclean was instructed to forward the following resolution to Prime Minister Asquith:

> That this meeting of Clyde munition workers requests the Government to definitely state, not later than Saturday first, that it forbids any increases of rent during the period of the war; and that, this failing, a general strike will be declared on Monday, 22 November.

Meanwhile the deputation sent by the crowd was waiting inside the Court along with deputations from Beardmore's of Dalmuir and other factories and yards; once more the Court was crowded to overflowing. The Sheriff and his clerks were white with anxiety. Inside the deputations were demanding to be heard; outside the roars of the crowd were making the windows rattle. The Sheriff consented to hear the deputations. Each man's declaration was the same. The workers were going to down tools unless the landlords were prevented from using the present extraordinary demand for houses to raise rents. The Sheriff realized that the situation was too desperate for a compromise, and telephoned Lloyd George, Minister of Munitions. His panic communicated itself to the Minister, who told him to stop the case immediately, and that a Rent Restriction Act would be introduced as soon as possible. That night working-class Glasgow celebrated its victory.

The BSP Glasgow District Council was also triumphant. They had been advocating direct action in the form of the political strike for some time.

Maclean commented in the December *Vanguard*:

It should be noted that the rent strike on the Clyde is the first step towards the Political Strike, so frequently resorted to on the Continent in times past. We rest assured that our comrades in the various works will incessantly urge this aspect on their shop-mates, and so prepare the ground for the next great counter-move of our class in the raging class warfare—raging more than ever during the Great Unrest period of three or four years ago.

On 19 November Maclean went to prison to serve his five days, having refused on principle to pay the fine. Early on the morning of his release a crowd gathered outside the prison gate to welcome him, but they had to go home frustrated. The authorities, fearing a demonstration, had let him out earlier than usual.

Another kind of demonstration, however, did take place. A deputation from South Lanark—forty miners who had struck work for the day—arrived in Central Station at 9 o'clock, wearing their pit clothes and with their lamps burning. They caused a great sensation in the station and in the streets through which they marched. 'Where is the strike?' people shouted. 'Is it a rent strike?' the women asked. 'No' they replied. 'We are here to protest against the imprisonment and dismissal of John Maclean.' 'Good luck to you, brave fellows!' came the reply.

They marched to the prison, and after finding they were too late, marched right out to Newlands to Maclean's house in order to be sure that their friend was alive and hearty after his ordeal. A meeting was held in Pollokshaws, then they made their way to the gates of Fairfield Shipbuilding Yard in Govan. A monster meeting was held at the dinner hour, the miners with their lamps burning scattered here and there among the huge mass of workers. Strong resolutions against the government, the Govan School Board, the Munitions Act, and also against conscription were carried. Then the deputation of miners went home, carrying with them the greetings of the shipyard workers to the Lanarkshire miners.

24/Threat of conscription

The Munitions Act did not achieve its objective on the Clyde. Instead of speeding up the production of munitions and cowing the workers into obedience and subjection, it had produced more fertile ground for revolutionary propaganda than ever before. After the case of the Fairfield Shipwrights, the government realized this, and made tentative suggestions towards amending that part of the Act which bound every worker to his master, but there was not one whisper about amending the one great grievance, the loss of trade union rights. All through October and November of 1915 the unrest was growing and spreading in wider and wider circles. The government was desperate. The loss of both men and munitions on both fronts had been tremendous during 1915, and it was now forced to play its trump card—conscription. The revolutionary socialists knew exactly what it meant and they were prepared to fight it tooth and nail. Maclean warned non-socialist trade unionists:

> that conscription means the bringing of all young men under the control of the military authorities, whether they be in the field of battle or in the factory or workshop. Every controlled factory comes directly under military discipline as well, and thus the old as well as the young will be bound hand and foot to Mr William Weir and his capitalist friends. Military conscription implies industrial conscription, the most abject form of slavery the world has ever known. . . . The only way to retain our freedom—the small shred of it we now possess—is by solid combination as a class. The only weapon we can use today is the strike. We urge our comrades to be ready to use that weapon to prevent the coming of absolute chattel slavery.

It was soon demonstrated that the Glasgow workers were going to put up a stern resistance to conscription. At the end of November, the Free Speech Committee joined with the Herald League,* whose representative in Glasgow was Maclean's old friend Willie McGill, the anarchist, in organizing anti-conscription meetings. They engaged the City Hall for 29 November, and brought George Lansbury and Sylvia Pankhurst, the famous

---

* This was connected with the *Daily Herald,* edited by George Lansbury.

suffragette and revolutionary socialist, up from London to speak along with Maclean. At the last moment, Lord Provost Dunlop, with the support of the majority of the city council, broke the contract letting the hall and prohibited any demonstrations, on the grounds that they would be detrimental to recruiting.

However, this piece of arrogant tyranny was twice as detrimental to recruiting as any demonstration could have been. Thousands of leaflets were distributed all over Glasgow. Huge meetings were addressed by the three speakers in the Panopticon, the Metropole and the Pavilion. Maclean and Pankhurst were fully prepared to lead the workers in breaking down the City Hall doors. In his autobiography, Lansbury tells how he spent practically a whole day trying to persuade the two militants to abandon their idea of violence. He went to the chief constable and promised that if they were allowed to hold a demonstration outside the Hall all would go quietly and peaceably. The Chief Constable gave in, but by that time so much feeling had been roused that Lansbury attributes the lack of more militant action simply to the fact that the outside meeting took place in a drenching downpour of rain.

The next move came quickly. The authorities refused to let halls to the socialist organization for anti-conscription meetings, and cancelled all existing licences. The BSP, however, managed to obtain the small International Hall in Stockwell Street for their Sunday night indoor meetings. It was let to the Lithuanian Colony in Glasgow, many of whom had fought in the 1905 Revolution, and were members of the BSP. One member of the BSP in Glasgow told me how, in pre-war days, some of the new immigrants would lift up their shirts during branch meetings to show the whip marks on their backs.

This attack closed the Socialist ranks. Even the 'patriots' could not stomach conscription, and were beginning to realize just how they had been led up the garden path. A great united meeting was held in the centre of the City in George Square, and emphatic resolutions against conscription were carried unanimously. All the speakers, who were drawn from the three Socialist parties, were 'booked', the excuse being that they were obstructing the pavements. It is interesting to note their names, because some of them became well-known national figures. They were P J Dollan (afterwards Lord Provost of Glasgow and a 'Sir'), John S Taylor, Emmanuel Shinwell (Minister of Mines in the first Labour government, and Minister of Defence in the 1945 Labour government), Harry Hopkins, James Maxton (leader of the Clyde group of ILP-ers in the House of Commons, and best-known of all the 'Red

Clydesiders'), Arthur McManus, T Milligan, John Maclean, Willie Gallacher (Communist MP for West Fife from 1935-50), and Malcolm McColl. However, the police eventually dropped the charge—they were afraid.

Meantime the Clyde Workers' Committee had been developing until it had become one of the most influential working-class organizations in the Clyde area. It developed, however, by conflict and struggle, like everything else in this world. The great mass of the members—delegates from the workshops, factories and shipyards—were militant trade unionists only and not conscious revolutionaries. Most of the leading members of the Central Committee were revolutionary socialists, but there, also, an ideological struggle went on between 'patriots' and anti-war men and between 'Maclean' men and SLP men. Maclean and his followers were orthodox Marxists, but many of the SLP men had not yet advanced beyond the narrow sectarianism of pre-war days and their objection to strikes for immediate demands. A few even objected to Maclean and MacDougall being members because they were not industrial workers. But while they disagreed on tactics, they all were united in their endeavours to make the Clyde Workers' Committee not only an organization fighting for trade union rights, but also a conscious revolutionary force.

Among the SLP-ers who afterwards became prominent were John Muir (afterwards Under-Secretary for Health in the first Labour government); Arthur McManus, who became not only first president of the British CP, but also a member of the Executive Committee of the Third International; Tom Bell, who became president of the Scottish Ironmoulders' Union and leader of the 1920 Moulders' Strike; Tom Clark, who became an executive member of the AEU; Jock McBain, who became Scottish organizer of the British Ironfounders' Union; and David Kirkwood, who eventually became Lord Kirkwood.

While Maclean participated enthusiastically in every meeting of the Committee, he was not convinced, like the syndicalist SLP-ers, that committees drawn from the factories, like the Clyde Workers' Committee were all that was necessary to lead the workers to victory. As I have previously tried to make clear, he believed in the well-organized political party as the essential leadership, as all orthodox Marxists did, and set out his doubts in the *Vanguard*:

Whether the Clyde Workers' Committee as constituted today is able or willing to cope with the situation is doubtful; but it is just as well to give it a further chance with the added support of miners and railwaymen. However, just as this unofficial committee views with suspicion the official committees of the various unions, and attempts to act as a driving force, we warn our comrades that they ought to adopt the same attitude towards the unofficial committee and see that it pushes ahead. If it still clings on to academic discussion and futile proposals, it is their business to take the initiative into their own hands as they did in the case of the rent strike.

Remember that the only way to fight the class war is by accepting every challenge of the master class and throwing down more challenges ourselves. Every determined fight binds the workers together more and more, and so prepares for the final conflict.

Another bone of contention in the Clyde Workers' Committee was the presence of Peter Petroff.

25/Peter Petroff

In October Petroff was invited to Glasgow by the Glasgow District Council to address a meeting in the Panopticon, where the BSP held regular Sunday night meetings on the Russian Revolution of 1905. Before he arrived, however, Maclean had been summoned under the Defence of the Realm Act and was expecting at least six months' imprisonment. Wishing to ensure that this would involve no hitch in the conduct of the Glasgow Economic Class, the publication of the *Vanguard* and 'the other activities that are helping to make the Clyde valley a danger spot to capitalism', he suggested to the Glasgow District Committee that Petroff should be kept in Glasgow as a second organizer. This was agreed to, and after the meeting in the Panopticon, to which Petroff drew a crowd of over a thousand, Petroff and his wife Irma remained in Glasgow as guests of Maclean at our home at Auldhouse Road.

Petroff had married Irma, a German girl, then a London correspondent of one of the many German social-democratic daily papers, some years before the war. I cannot remember either of them, but my older sister Jean was charmed with Irma. She was still with us at Christmas and was horrified because we had no Christmas tree. At that time, New Year was the great festival in Scotland, and very few people celebrated Christmas as they did in Germany. However, Irma bought us a tree and decorated it herself to our great delight.

To make Petroff safe, Maclean took him to meetings of the Free Speech Committee, the Clyde Workers' Committee, and other working-class organizations. He had no status on the Clyde Workers' Committee (CWC), but was allowed to speak.

Willie Gallacher, chairman of the CWC, complained in his book *Revolt on the Clyde* about an attack by Petroff on Johnnie Muir, but failed to explain that Muir, although an SLP-er at that time, was not anti-war. Moreover, the tendency had grown strongly in the CWC to concentrate solely on purely trade union, economic issues, to the exclusion of political issues like the war and conscription. MacDougall told me about this tendency, which was confirmed many years later by Harry McShane, then a shop steward at Weir's, a foundation member of the BSP, and a member of the CWC.

Peter Petroff was a very courageous man, as well as a very able one. He was desperately anxious to accompany Maclean and MacDougall to workgate meetings, but they decided it was too dangerous for him, a foreigner, with a German wife, to risk the severe punishment that could be meted out to him if he came up against the law. He was forbidden, therefore, to take part in the outdoor agitation.

He was, however, a first-class contributor to the *Vanguard*. He was in constant touch with revolutionaries abroad, especially with Trotsky in Paris, and he was able to give information from the continent which would have been otherwise unobtainable.

Already Maclean had been able to give a report in the October *Vanguard* of the famous Zimmerwald Conference in Switzerland, because of information from Petroff, who was the London agent for *Vanguard*. He had outlined the proceedings, giving an account of the delegates from the various countries, mentioning particularly that:

Both sections of the Russian Social Democrats at the conference are internationalists and are fighting the Russian Government with all their might. . . . We learn that a gigantic political strike has already been declared in Petrograd and other important centres. We wish our comrades every success.

He concluded with a warning:

Even should those controlling the International Socialist Bureau continue the policy of keeping the respective parties apart, this conference clearly indicates that the International itself will go on. The traitors to the International will have to be treated later on. . . .

We draw attention to the fact that Hyndman's paper *Justice* which boasts its international information, was totally innocent of the

International conference. At least, it said so. 'None so blind', etc. Faithful Social Democrats here have been led a sorry dance by the bourgeois members of the Central Branch of the BSP. Our business is to trust ourselves and our cause and line up with our world comrades as quickly as we can.

We assure our comrades that we in Glasgow are internationalists first, last, and all the time.

In the November *Vanguard*, Petroff contributed a long article on 'The Breakdown of the International', analysing the past and present condition of the Second International and concluding:

The war has revealed all that was bad in the Labour and Socialist movement. The progress of the war, with all that is accompanying it, is strengthening those elements who will build a new International on a more sound basis.

Petroff followed this up with another long article in the December issue 'Rebuilding the International':

Words and illusions vanish; facts remain.

The realities of the war are being understood, the glamour and romance is passing away. Events are teaching in a few months more than they could have learned from years of propaganda. How weak and pitiful are now the words of those Labour and Socialist 'leaders' who, at the very outbreak of the war, deserted the Socialist and Labour banner and rushed to the assistance of the enemy.

He went on to relate facts concerning the Zimmerwald Conference, quoted its Manifesto, and, while calling on all comrades to affiliate to its committee, urged that it was only one step in the right direction. It did not call for positive revolutionary action, probably because there were only one or two delegates who came from countries where the workers were actually carrying on a revolutionary struggle.

He attacked the Executive Committee of the BSP for adopting a resolution expressing pious approval of the Conference, and in the same breath announcing that the Belgian Minister of State, Vandervelde, required money for the rebuilding of the International. He called again for the building of a new International, on a different, more democratic basis.

Petroff was venomously attacked in *Justice* (23 December), in an article entitled 'Who and What is Peter Petroff?', which described Petroff as a sinister and shady character, leading the Clyde workers by the nose for his own ends! Maclean immediately sprang to his defence (*Justice*, 6 January 1916), and wrote:

It just happens that Petroff was arrested in Bowhill, Fife, on Wednesday, 22 December, for entering a prohibited area. He went to Lochgelly, as he had done before, and registered as he had done before. Yet he was jailed before he had a chance to speak for the BSP branch in Bowhill. He was rushed off to Dunfermline next morning and sentenced to £3 or 15 days.

I had arranged to go to Bowhill and speak against conscription, but by mistake the Anderston Branch had ticketed MacDougall and myself for the same night. MacDougall had to go to Lesmehagow and my choice fell on the Anderston meeting to prime the comrades up for Lloyd George. We were one of the factors delaying that gentleman's meeting. His instigation to the employers in his Commons' speech on Monday gave us a chance, and we took it, and will continue to take it.

I consequently asked Petroff to go to Fife. I am responsible and shoulder the blame. The police knew I was on the road to Fife on Thursday morning, yet condemned Petroff without a witness in his defence. The matter does not rest there, I assure you. Some of us in Glasgow have been asking 'Who and what are Messrs Hyndman, Bax, Fisher, Hunter Watts, Gorle, etc?'

An indignant letter was also sent to the Executive Committee by G Chicherin (a future Foreign Minister in the Soviet government):

A few years ago, when from an unknown source, damaging rumours were put into circulation against comrade Peter Petroff, I wrote, as Secretary of our Central Bureau of the groups abroad of the Social Democratic Labour Party of Russia, acting on its behalf, to H W Lee, the then Secretary of the BSP and now editor of *Justice*, stating the stainless revolutionary past of comrade Petroff, and also the excellent reputation of wholehearted loyalty to the cause that he is enjoying in our party. Today I read in *Justice*—'Who and What is Peter Petroff?' Who and what he is is excellently known to us, his fellow-revolutionaries, and, as stated above, has been authoritatively communicated to the BSP. The editor of Justice must be aware of the exceedingly difficult position of Russian political refugees and of the dangers to which they are exposed by the present unbounded domination of reaction in all countries, including Great Britain, where, as even *Justice* pointed out, liberties become more and more curtailed.

As we shall see, Maclean kept in close contact with the Petroffs throughout the war years, and Petroff regularly sent articles to Trotsky's paper *Nashe Slovo* in Paris. MacDougall told me that the articles were translated into German and re-published in Robert Grimm's *Berlin Tagwacht*, copies of which were smuggled over the Swiss border into Germany and sent to leaders such as Liebknecht so that they became informed of events in Britain.

Chicherin and the Petroffs were deported to Russia at the beginning of 1918, being exchanged for minor British diplomats. Petroff received a minor appointment in the Soviet Foreign Office, and MacDougall told me of the part he played in the negotiations at Brest Litovsk. Alone he walked out to meet and halt the German Army, waving a white flag, while Trotsky and others waited in the rear. MacDougall considered he was the most courageous man he had ever known. Later both the Petroffs had positions in the Soviet Embassy in Berlin. After Lenin's death, they became increasingly perturbed about the situation in Russia, and eventually broke off all connection with the Communist Party, gave up their Embassy jobs, and began to work for the German Trade Union movement. Both were Jewish. Before Hitler came to power, they escaped by night along with their two young daughters, leaving all their possessions behind, and fled back to Britain. In 1934 they published a brilliant book *The Secret of Hitler's Victory*, a first-rate Marxist analysis of the failure of the Social Democratic Government of the Weimar Republic to cope with capitalism, and of the failure of the Communist leaders who, under the influence of the Stalinist bureaucrats in Russia, gave half-hearted support to Hitler, coining the infamous phrase 'After Hitler our turn!' The Petroffs, however, were full of praise for the heroic conduct of the rank and file of the German Communist Party.

It was not long after the appearance of this book that Willie Gallacher published his *Revolt on the Clyde*. The reason for his attempts to discredit Petroff is obvious, as Gallacher was a faithful Stalinist. The same pattern was repeated in Tom Bell's book on Maclean.

26/Imprisonment

While the socialist parties were waging a strenuous battle against the menace of conscription, the men in the factories were fighting against the government's proposed introduction of female, unskilled labour into the munition works.

The withdrawal of millions of men from production into the army meant that many occupations hitherto closed to women were now open, much to the delight of the employers, because women could be bought more cheaply than men. 'And so', said MacDougall at a Co-operative Women's Conference, 'the war will strengthen the normal tendency of capitalism towards replacing men by women, and, unfortunately, the standard of life of the working-class seems likely to continue to fall for this reason. The only way in which this tendency could be counteracted would be by women demanding and enforcing the same wages as were obtained by men.'

MacDougall's speech 'Position of Women after the War' was published in the November *Vanguard*, and is important because it reflected the socialist attitude to women at that time. He concluded:

> As women enter out into production in huger and huger numbers, as they take their place alongside the men, their importance to society will come to be more fully realized, not merely as producers of wealth, but as producers of men. Women themselves will become more conscious of the decisive part that they play in human development, and will no longer be content to sit at the feet of the male sex, or should we say, remain under the heel? They will arise in their power and demand their rightful position as equal friends and comrades of men. Then there will be no question of treating women as inferiors by refusing them the vote or in any other way. For woman with practice will acquire just as great an influence over society in the future as she has today in the home. That influence will, I am convinced, be used for the humanizing of this mankind which is today wallowing in filth and beastliness.

The whole trade union movement, official and unofficial, joined together in opposing 'dilution' of labour: the official side because the trade unions had always been hostile to the introduction of women into male-dominated occupations, and the unofficial side because they realized that the government's move towards dilution was part of the drive towards military conscription.

It was the task of Lloyd George, then Minister of Munitions, to go round the country getting the men to agree to dilution. Probably the best demagogue in the country, he was cocksure of his ability to tame the 'wild men' of the Clyde. He arranged to address a delegate meeting of shop stewards on Thursday, 22 December, at St Andrew's Hall. At the last minute, however, his confidence deserted him. He had a conference in Newcastle with some of the union officials concerned, and decided to have a tour of the workshops first, and postpone the big meeting until Saturday,

25 December. He also promised the officials to have nothing to do with the Clyde Workers' Committee.

So Lloyd George, described pawkily in *Forward* as 'the best paid munition worker in Britain' came to Glasgow on Thursday morning, prepared to make a triumphal tour of the Glasgow munition works. He visited Parkhead Forge first. David Kirkwood, who was Convener of Shop Stewards, introduced the Minister to the others. 'This is Mr Lloyd George', he said. 'He has come specially to speak to you, and no doubt you will give him a patient hearing. I can assure him that every word he says will be carefully weighed. We regard him with suspicion, because every Act with which his name is associated has a taint of slavery about it. . . .' He went on to say that if the Minister was prepared to give the workers a share in the management, they were prepared to co-operate with him in speeding up production. Lloyd George was completely flabbergasted. But worse was to come. The men at Weir's, under the leadership of Convener Jack Smith, flatly refused to hear him at all. Next day he sidled into one or two of the smaller and less militant factories. That was his conquering tour.

On Thursday night the Clyde Workers' Committee, engineering union officials and the Committee of Trades Representatives responsible for calling the first meeting, met to decide if they would have anything to do with the Saturday morning one. The latter two groups decided to boycott it, much to the alarm of Lloyd George and his friends. When the officials reached home that night they found telegrams waiting for them inviting them to come to the Central Station Hotel next morning for a discussion, in the course of which it transpired, much to Lloyd George's consternation, that the Clyde Workers' Committee had agreed to support the meeting and had commandeered the tickets given to the officials to distribute. Thus the Minister was forced to negotiate with the committee. On Friday night the leaders came round to see him. He flattered them, he argued with them, he tried to bribe them—but it was no use.

Meanwhile Maclean and the BSP spokesmen had been busy. They distributed thousands of leaflets all over the munition works exposing the real purpose of 'dilution' and explaining exactly what it would mean for the munition workers.

On Saturday morning the Hall was packed and the atmosphere was tense. As Lloyd George, 'traitor Arthur Henderson' and the rest, walked on to the platform, the whole audience rose to its feet singing the *Red Flag*, and the platform party had to stand to the finish. When Henderson tried to make his Chairman's remarks, he was drowned in a hurricane of hissing and booing. When it died down he tried desperately to make himself heard in spite of constant interruptions. 'I am delighted', he said, 'to have the opportunity of appearing in this hall with the Minister of Munitions (interruption—what about the hall for the workers?) to lay before you the great issue of the present moment so far as the war is concerned (aye! profits!). You are all aware of the fact that we are engaged in probably the greatest war (at hame!) that ever the old country has been concerned with. . . .' And so it went on until Lloyd George was introduced. As the 'great man' came forward to speak, wave after wave of jeers, catcalls, and boos greeted him. The audience rose spontaneously and sang two verses of the *Red Flag* before he could say one word. Then he went on, hardly able to make himself heard in face of the constant interruptions. Eventually Kirkwood appealed to the audience to give him a hearing, but it was no use. Then Johnny Muir stood up on a bench to address the meeting. There was instant silence. The platform party walked off in disgust and the meeting was left in the hands of the workers.

Inspired by this victory, the socialists redoubled their fight against the war and against conscription. 'Maclean was everywhere', wrote Gallacher. 'His indoor meetings were packed out; until he was forced to run two meetings a night. He was the centre of the anti-war movement; and all the other movements, whatever their tendencies, supported the general line he was taking. He demanded an immediate armistice, with no annexations and no indemnities; along with this went his drive for the revolutionary overthrow of the capitalist class.' Nevertheless, a Conscription Bill was brought before the House of Commons on 5 January.

The campaign against conscription drew in all sorts of people and was growing to a tremendous strength. In England the pacifist bodies such as the No Conscription Fellowship and the ILP were looking to the Clyde for a lead. Inside the factories the Clyde Workers' Committee carried on the agitation, while the BSP and ILP with Maclean at the head conducted it outside. 'Every day he spoke at the factory gates', Gallacher recounted. 'From one end of the Clyde to another he travelled. Every night he spoke on the streets, in the halls or lecture rooms. He was turning out scores of new agitators and distributing them to all parts of the area. All over the Clyde the atmosphere was becoming electrical.'

On Sunday afternoons the Economics Class had reached the magnificent total of 481 students. On Sunday nights the Bath Street meeting spread far and wide, the numbers every week reaching many thousands. With this kind of support, Maclean now saw the realization within sight of his most cherished dream, the formation of a Scottish Labour College. A Labour College Committee was formed from the class, with Maclean at its head. Plans were going well, and an Inaugural Conference arranged for 12 February 1916. There was an enthusiastic response from the hundreds of working-class organizations and branches approached, and Bob Smillie, for whom Maclean had a great admiration, consented to preside over the conference.

By this time, Maclean had been appointed Secretary of the National Scottish Labour Housing Association which had been recently formed to promote the fight against the factors all over the country. During January 1916, it indeed appeared as if the Clyde workers were lining up behind Maclean and social revolution.

The government soon began to realize how dangerous the situation on the Clyde was. The iron heel began to come down, ever so gently at first. *Forward* was banned for three weeks for daring to print a correct account of the Lloyd George meeting. On 8 January the *Vanguard* was banned, and every copy of the January number confiscated. Undaunted, the Clyde Workers' Committee started another paper *The Worker*.

Meanwhile public opinion was being prepared for the next blows that were to fall. In October some of the capitalist papers had made veiled insinuations about the Clyde socialists being agents of the Kaiser. Now they were quite blatant. Maclean and the Clyde workers were being financed by German gold; there was no doubt about it. 'German gold' became their war-cry.

The next blow fell on Petroff who, as an unprotected alien, was the weakest link in the Clyde chain. He was seized, removed to Edinburgh Castle, and confined under the military authorities for an indefinite period. No reason was given, but it was obvious that his crime had been revolutionary propaganda among the workers of the Clyde.

Late one night the police raided the Socialist Labour Press (owned by the SLP) in Renfrew Street, where *The Worker* was printed, seized the type and manuscripts, and closed down the premises.

Meanwhile the government, while amending the offensive penalty of imprisonment contained in the Munitions Act, passed an Order in Council which for the first time made it a criminal act under the Defence of the Realm Act, punishable by imprisonment with hard labour, for any person to impede, delay, or restrict the production, repair or transport of raw materials, or any other work necessary for the successful prosecution of the war. Maclean was the first victim of these new powers.

On Sunday, 6 February, he was speaking at the Bath Street meeting as usual. Before he could get home, he was seized by the police, and taken next day to Edinburgh Castle as a prisoner of war.

I was taken on Sunday night to the Central Police Station (he wrote to my mother from Edinburgh Castle) and there kept till Monday at 5.30 pm, when I was brought to Queen St and then to the Castle, a 'prisoner of war' till my trial under DORA. I can be tried by the High Court of Judiciary or by Court Martial. Naturally I'll select the High Court. . . . I have been well treated so far, so need not feel anxious.

I trust you got Jimmie to arrange for Saturday's Conference* —a report, the paper, and the purvey. He might be at the hall at 2 pm to meet the Committee, so that full arrangements can be made. . . .

You might write Mr Heenan, Landressy St, Bridgeton, to take over the Secretaryship of the National Housing Committee and come out for the circulars, envelopes, letters, minute book and the lists of addresses I was working from. . . . Tell him I intended to put an appeal, an agenda form, and a delegate form into those going to Renfrewshire, Lanarkshire and Fifeshire to save labour and expense. Sam Hynds gave two addresses of halls in Dunfermline. Perhaps Heenan might write these and fix up one of them. . . .

Tell Jimmie to be at the Sunday class at 2.30 pm. I was just beginning the Bills of Exchange and the Foreign Exchange . . .

I asked to see Petroff, but haven't got permission.

You might open all letters and you could bring through those needing my advice. Remember that you must first show them to the Commander here.

Next night Gallacher, Johnnie Muir (the editor), and Walter Bell, the printer of *The Worker*, were arrested for an article published on 29 January called 'Should the Workers Arm?' In actual fact, the article opposed armed insurrection as a tactic, maintaining that the workers' strength lay in their economic power when united as a class. However, it was supposed to be seditious.

Meantime Maclean was not alarmed. His sanguine temperament plus the fact that his inspiring personality had whipped up the masses to great heights of enthusiasm wherever he went, caused him to over-estimate the extent of his support—or more likely to over-estimate the courage of men who had not his burning convictions.

* The Labour College Conference.

27/The Scottish Labour College

John Maclean did not believe that it was altogether a co-incidence that he was arrested before he could take part in the Conference organized to form a Scottish Labour College. It had always been his contention that a successful revolution in Britain could be carried through only by workers thoroughly grounded in Marxist principles, and he was convinced that the chief reason he had been singled out for special punishment by the government, that the greatest 'crime' that he had committed in their eyes, was the teaching of Marxian economics to the Scottish workers.

The Committee had been busy. On 25 December 1915, the following letter, signed by all eleven members and written by Maclean appeared in *Forward*:

For some years an Economics and Industrial History Class has been conducted in Glasgow during the winter. . . . Out of the class has been formed a committee to promote a Labour College for Glasgow. It is intended to call a Conference of delegates from all working-class organizations early in 1916 to discuss the question of establishing a representative provisional committee for the realization of a Labour College.

The Universities and other institutions for higher education have for their objective the training of men and women to run capitalist society in the interests of the wealthy. We think the time has come for an independent College, financed and controlled by the working class, in which workers might be trained for the battle against the masters. Such a College could be conveniently established in Glasgow.

Students might attend the College each day for three months. The College might be run for three terms a year—October till December, January till March, and April till June. Such subjects as Economics; General and Industrial History; History, Structure and Problems of Trade Unions; History, etc of Co-operation; Laws affecting Labour; Business Methods applied to Labour

Organizations; English Composition and Literature; Arithmetic and Algebra, etc, might be studied.

The only sound method of financing the scheme would be by the raising of a compulsory levy of 1d. a month (say). . . . £100 would thus be obtained from 2,000 workers in a year. Students brought from the work shops might require maintenance bursaries rising to as much as £2 a week. A student per term at £2 a week, or three students a year, would cost £72. Out of the £100 would thus be left at least £28 for staffing and other expenses. The less the bursary the more the students could avail themselves of the College privileges. A hundred thousand workers at ¼d a week levy could in this way maintain a College of 50 students a term or 150 a year.

This need not prevent organizations other than Trade Unions, or individuals interested in education, giving grants for the support of the institution. . . .

Students sent by contributing bodies would have to be selected by these bodies, by ballot and from one work or district per man preferably, so that each work or district would have its just number of students. Students ought to be selected for both enthusiasm for knowledge, and activities in the workers' movement.

This need not preclude private students from attending the College on payment of a fixed fee.

The lecturers would be at the disposal of those willing to form evening and week-end classes, so that all might have the chance of benefiting by their support of the College.

The Board of Directors might be composed of representatives of contributing bodies, one per £100 (say). The Directors ought to be selected in the same way as the students, the same qualifications being expected.

Remember that the Ruskin College at Oxford has been maintained by several Trade Unions and Co-operative organizations, and that the Plebs College in London is maintained by the Welsh miners and railwaymen. . . . Agitate! Educate! Organize!

The committee decided to hold the Conference on 12 February, and there was an enthusiastic response from the hundreds of working-class organizations and branches approached. Bob Smillie could not attend because of illness, and the president of Glasgow Trades Council, B Shanks, took his place.

Shanks presided over a great gathering of 496 delegates, representing, according to a report in *Justice* (17 February):

412 organizations and branches of organizations, including Co-operative Societies, Trade Unions, Trades Councils, BSP, ILP, Women's Labour League, etc.

The first item on the programme should have been an address by Maclean on the proposed Labour College, but he was still in prison. After protests by the Glasgow Trades Council and other working-class bodies, the authorities had agreed to release him on bail of £100 until his trial, but my mother was not able to collect that sum on such short notice, and he was not released until two days later, 14 February.

He had not managed to finish the preparation of this address, which was published later as a pamphlet, *A Plea for a Labour College for Scotland*, but it was completed by MacDougall and read by him. This, as it turned out, was a very suitable arrangement, for the first part dealt with the necessity of Marxian economics being the basis of the College's curriculum, and the second part, by MacDougall, dealt with the teaching of industrial history, his speciality, and other parts of the proposed curriculum.

After a valuable and interesting discussion, according to the foreword of the pamphlet, the following resolution was moved by Thomas Scott, Kinning Park Co-operative Educational Committee, and seconded by William McCreath, District Committee of the Amalgamated Society of Engineers, and was unanimously accepted:

> That this Conference of Delegates from Labour Organizations in Scotland approves of the establishment of a Scottish Labour College, and agrees to the appointment of a Provisional Committee with full powers to act until the First Annual Conference of the Scottish Labour College.

Thirty-two members were elected, including the original Class Committee. The most notable were Bob Smillie (Scottish Mine Workers), James Maxton (Scottish Divisional Council ILP, of which he was Chairman), Helen Crawford (Women's International League), and John McClure (Plebs League).

The notable absentees, both from the Conference and from the Committee, were official representatives of the SLP, although John McClure was present representing the Plebs League which was associated with the SLP. This was typical of the sectarianism of the SLP at this period.

The work of the Provisional Committee of the Scottish Labour College was to be inhibited by the impending imprisonment of Maclean, MacDougall and Maxton, but in the meantime it made arrangements for a new class to begin on 2 April, on trade union history and industrial organization (past, present, and future); very relevant indeed in the circumstances prevailing at the time. The lecturers were advertized as being John F Armour, Neil MacLean, MacDougall and John Maclean.

28/The iron heel

During March Maclean worked furiously to bring all his various activities up-to-date before his trial, which had been fixed for 11 April. Successful conferences were held by the Labour Housing Association in Renfrewshire, Lanarkshire and Fifeshire, plans for which he had been making when he was arrested. He kept up his propaganda meetings and classes until the last minute. The BSP announced that it would look after the Maclean family (mother, myself and Jean), but *Forward* made an urgent appeal for funds for the dependents of Muir, Bell, and Gallacher.

Meanwhile, at the beginning of March, trouble had arisen in Parkhead Forge when Kirkwood was refused permission to carry out his duties as Convener of Shop Stewards. He resigned in protest, and the engineers went on strike. Workers in another factory were asked to do the work of the strikers, but refused. At the same time the workers at Dalmuir struck in sympathy. The authorities pretended to see in these occurrences a plot to sabotage the production of munitions. The *Glasgow Herald* began talking about a 'vile conspiracy against the State' and about 'plots hatched in impenetrable secrecy'.

This was, of course, ridiculous. Undoubtedly most of the leaders of the unofficial movement were militant socialists, concerned primarily with the fight against the government rather than questions of hours and wages. But even among them, by no means all were anti-war and they would not have supported the kind of 'ca-canny' policy being advocated by, for example, the BSP.

These kind of accusations were merely used as an excuse for seizing the principal leaders of the Clyde Workers' Committee. In the course of a few days Kirkwood, McManus, Shields, Messer, Clark, Wainwright, Bridges and Glass, were seized, deported to Edinburgh (an environment in which the government considered they could do no harm), and ordered to report to the police thrice a day.

The Clyde was in a ferment. Next day a huge demonstration took place in Glasgow Green. Among the speakers were Emmanuel Shinwell, Pat Dollan, Helen Crawford, Maxton, and MacDougall. The two latter made rousing speeches, urging the workers to strike, the only weapon now left to them. But the removal of the 'ringleaders' certainly resulted in the fear and confusion which the government had hoped to create.

On 31 March the next blow fell. Maxton and MacDougall were arrested for sedition because of the speeches made at the Glasgow Green demonstration, and held in Duke Street Prison without bail. Soon after, Jack Smith, the Convener of Stewards at Weir's, was also arrested on a sedition charge.

Meantime Maclean was preparing for his trial. While the BSP had undertaken to look after his family, the Glasgow Class had undertaken to provide his defence. Whatever the legal advice might be, he was determined to put up a big fight. Our house at Auldhouse Road was constantly crowded with people wishing him luck.

It was an excited group of people who took the train to Edinburgh on the morning of 11 April. Maclean, on his way to face his trial at the High Court, was accompanied by his wife, sister, and a whole crowd of young miners and engineers who had taken the day off work for one of the most significant events of their lives. Every now and then the strains of a violin rose above the steady chug-chug of the train, and fervent young voices joined to sing the *Red Flag*. Those who were there found it difficult to forget the expression in Maclean's eyes as he sang the last verse, 'Come dungeons dark or gallows grim'—those words, so often sung lightly and thoughtlessly, had become full of painful meaning. For it was the very simple truth that he was absolutely prepared to make any sacrifice to keep the red flag flying.

The court was full and many hundreds had been turned away, for the trial had aroused tremendous interest and excitement. The audience, representative of aristocratic and conservative Edinburgh, was bitterly opposed to the man in the dock and the hostile atmosphere was sufficient to daunt all but the most forceful of personalities. However, his keen consciousness of the symbolic part he was playing rendered him quite unaffected by the enmity surrounding him. Outwardly he was alone facing overwhelming odds, but in his mind's eye he could see ranged on his side the powerful historical forces which would one day sweep aside all this awe-inspiring pomp as so much worthless junk. In his ears he could hear the encouraging voices of the rebels of past ages, once as despised and rejected as he was himself, but now looked up to as saints and heroes. Most important of all, he knew that hundreds of workers were looking to him, were supporting him, and that although they might be ineffectual just now, their day was coming.

The six counts of the indictment were read with all due

solemnity, each connected with statements he was alleged to have made at different meetings in January 1916, all likely to prejudice recruiting, to cause mutiny, sedition and disaffection amongst the civil population, and to impede the production, repair and transport of war material. He was alleged to have said:

1 that conscription was unnecessary, as the government had plenty of soldiers and munitions; that after the war conscription would be used to secure cheap labour; that should the government enforce the Military Service Act and Munitions Act the workers should 'down tools'; that if the British soldiers laid down their arms the Germans would do the same, as all were tired of the war
2 that the workers should strike in order to attend a meeting
3 that the workers should 'down tools' and resist conscription
4 that if conscription became law the workers would become conscripts to industrial labour—the real aim of the government
5 that the workers should strike and those who had guns should use them
6 that the workers should sell or pawn their alarm clocks, sleep in in the morning and not go to work.

He pleaded 'Not Guilty'.

Evidence for the prosecution was given by eighteen policemen, but not one civilian. At the conclusion the Chief Detective-Inspector said that he had arrested Maclean on an order from the Military. During the month of January there had been a somewhat anxious situation on the Clyde.

Twenty-eight witnesses, some socialists and some not, testified for Maclean. They included James Maxton, Emmanuel Shinwell, and Helen Crawford.

The climax of the trial was reached next morning as Maclean, quite confident and sure of himself, took his place in the witness box. He described his activities in general in the socialist movement, and denied the charges made in the indictment. He had certainly taken an active part in the struggle against conscription. He was an out and out opponent of compulsory military service, and believed that the present war was a war of capitalist aggression and defence. If he were asked if, having been attacked by Germany we were bound to defend ourselves, his answer would be that the matter of defence is the business of the capitalists whose interests were more immediately concerned. If there were conscription of property and capital he would instantly concede it to be the duty of the workers to defend. That had been his attitude all along. He had not, however, used the expressions at the time and places attributed.

It was ridiculous to charge him with having advised the

workers to use guns. The workers had no guns. Moreover he had always been against the use of arms for the purpose of securing redress. He had pointed out again and again that that type of thing might be good enough for men in Dublin but that it was no good whatever for the Clyde workers who, even if they had the inclination to use guns, had not got them.

He went on to deal with every charge in detail, enlarging on the evidence previously given. Cross-examined by the Lord Advocate he stated that he had been devoting his time to the most important thing in the world, the establishment of a Labour College. He had started his class in economics at the beginning of October, and he could not say how many of his pupils were witnesses; there were about 500 altogether, and he did not know them. He was not holding a class for conscientious objectors; he did not know what a conscientious objector was. There was a class on trade unionism which had been in existence for about a fortnight. He was in favour of industrial unionism, but was a socialist not a syndicalist. He had been speaking lately almost every day on the Labour College. He had spoken on conscription and had addressed meetings of munition workers at Beardmore's and Weir's.

Lord Advocate I suggest to you that your purpose was to strike in order to compel the government to withdraw the Conscription Bill?

Maclean That is not so.

Lord Advocate What was your object in addressing munition workers on the subject?

Maclean To explain to them the danger of it.

Lord Advocate Are you against strikes or in favour of strikes in order to achieve particular objects?

Maclean I am in favour of strikes.

Lord Advocate Even at this particular juncture of the nation's affairs?

Maclean That depends.

Coming to the counts of the indictment, the Lord Advocate asked:

'Is it your suggestion that the whole thing was a conspiracy by the police against you?'

Maclean Conspiracy is a strong word.

Lord Advocate How otherwise do you explain the circumstances to which I have referred?

Maclean I am puzzled to know.

After his cross-examination was concluded, the Lord Advocate addressed the jury. He contended that it had been proved up to the hilt that Maclean had committed a felony punishable by penal servitude or even by death. Any man who at the present state of affairs interfered with the procuring of men for the army or with the production of munitions was a traitor to his country. The charges had been proved by the evidence of eighteen members of the police force, and the jury could return a verdict for the accused only on the view that the police witnesses had perjured themselves, and had engaged in a gigantic conspiracy to defeat the ends of justice, and ruin the prisoner.

After the defiant attitude of Maclean, his counsel's plea for the defence was somewhat weak and tinged with defeatism. He hoped that the jury would not allow different political tenets to influence them against the accused. He also pointed out that the Crown had been unable to obtain any civilian witnesses, and had founded their charges on isolated sentences supplied by the police. It was not, however, necessary to assert that the police had invented a conspiracy; what he did say was that they had misinterpreted the accused's statements.

In his summing-up the Judge said that the case was undoubtedly a difficult one. There was a definite conflict of evidence. He was, however, obviously in favour of the police evidence, and pointed out that a verdict against the Crown would amount to a charge of conspiracy against the police.

In spite of these explicit directions, the jury nevertheless took over an hour to decide on their verdict. It was not altogether a vote of confidence in the police. They found Maclean guilty on the first four charges, not proven on the fifth, and not guilty on the sixth. A verdict of guilty had been expected by Maclean and his friends, but as the Judge read out the sentence they were stunned. Three years penal servitude—that is, imprisonment with hard labour! It was hardly believable!

Maclean, however, was unperturbed. As he made his way out of the court, he turned and waved his hat to his wife and friends, sitting overwhelmed by the severity of the sentence.

'Ta, ta, Johnnie! Good old Johnnie!' came the answering cries, and then they all stood up spontaneously with their heads uncovered, and sang the *Red Flag* as they had never sung it before. One scene of the great drama of human struggle against evil was ended, as John Maclean left the stage, branded as a traitor to his country, an enemy of the people.

But the drama was not ended; it had scarcely begun.

29/In prison

On 13 April 1916, John Maclean lost his identity and became Convict 2652; the torture that the prison system of those days meant to any sensitive person began. Scottish patriots who pride themselves on the superiority of Scots law should note the fact that at that time the Scottish system was probably one of the most inhuman in Europe. Even in Czarist Russia political prisoners were allowed books, writing materials, cigarettes, their own food and clothes, but in bourgeois Scotland they were allowed none of these privileges. They were criminals, and nothing else.

Maclean spent the first month of his sentence in the Calton Jail in Edinburgh, notorious as probably the worst prison in the country. MacDougall described it as a gloomy, tomb-like building run under the rigorous 'separate and silent' system. The food was unappetizing and insufficient and the prisoners suffered from chronic hunger. The warders were specially chosen from the army, the police force and from mental hospitals, for their hardness and brutality. No doubt some of them were human and tried to ease conditions for their unfortunate charges; these were only a small minority. Sanitary arrangements were inadequate and bunks were hard and comfortless.

Yet bad as these physical hardships were to bear, these were not the penalties which degraded men, sent them mad, and killed them. It was the absence of all that makes the animal human—speech, social intercourse, literature, newspapers—that was brutalizing and degrading. It was the isolation, monotonous drabness and nerve-racking silence that provided the torture that only those people especially gifted with sympathetic imagination could grasp without experience. The prisoners were confined to their cells except for one half-hour's exercise in the sunless courtyard and even then silence was rigidly enforced. The cells were tiny so that there was scarcely room to move about. They were bare save for a stool to sit on and boards and a mattress to sleep on. The blank walls were painted a dull cream unbroken by any kind of decoration. The painful monotony was completed by the fact that the window, situated high up on the wall, was of dulled glass, so that even a glimpse of the sky, the sun, or the stars, was denied.

During his stay at what jocularly became known as 'The Calton Hotel', Maclean's half-hour of exercise was enlivened by glimpses of his comrades, Gallacher, Muir, and Bell, who had been tried immediately after himself. *The Worker* trial created as much interest as Maclean's. But the defence put up by the accused was notable only in its lack of militancy. For instance, the first witness for the defence was the secretary (also a director) of the firm of Barr & Stroud where Muir worked. He testified that Muir was an industrious workman and a good timekeeper, and had given every satisfaction as a maker of munitions. As Convener of Shop Stewards, a position in which he could have created trouble had he wished, he had always done his best to smooth over any differences with employees. He had always found that Muir, far from being antagonistic to the dilution of labour, had done his best to carry it out. The evidence was corroborated by the Works Manager. It was also testified that he had been in favour of the war from the very beginning and had resigned his position as editor of *The Socialist* for this reason.

While giving evidence, Gallacher stated that right from the beginning it had been laid down that the Clyde Workers' Committee could not call a strike. He had been a munition worker all through the war and had no desire to impede production; there had been no trouble in the shop in which he was engaged; both he and Muir had always strenuously opposed the use of the strike.

All three were found guilty. Muir and Gallacher were sentenced to one year's imprisonment and Bell to three months.

Just before Maclean's transfer to Peterhead Convict Prison in May, the ranks of the political prisoners in Calton Jail were further augmented by James Maxton, Jimmie MacDougall, and Jack Smith. At the last minute, intimidated by the heavy sentences passed during the previous trials, they changed their pleas to guilty, on legal advice, and their trial is therefore of no interest here. In spite of this, however, Maxton and MacDougall were sentenced to one year's imprisonment and Smith to eighteen months.

The change to Peterhead was a change for the better for Maclean. The 'separate and silent' system was to an extent harder to bear than the hard labour of the penal prisons where the convicts worked in gangs, and where, although silence was strictly enjoined, a certain amount of furtive communication did take place. Nevertheless, the hard work outside in all kinds of weather did have an effect on Maclean's health, which had never been perfect. He had suffered all his life from chronic sinus trouble,

E

which had been aggravated, especially since the war began, by constant open-air speaking all through the year regardless of the weather. Both my mother and MacDougall told me that he often suffered torture, which he endured without complaint.

30/The Easter Rising

To those 'practical' men in the socialist movement who claimed that the men in jail should have been more cautious, that they would have been of much more use to the socialist cause outside jail, and indeed, that their sacrifice was a futile one, there are two answers. First, if socialists had the courage to do their duty and so become a menace to the establishment, some excuse would have been found to silence them, no matter how circumspect they tried to be. Second, the so-called practical men betrayed an outlook narrow, limited and completely without vision. Maclean was an internationalist to the core. He was concerned not only with his little corner of the globe. He knew that, temporarily defeated though the Clyde workers might be, their fight had been an inspiration to the socialists in Russia, in Italy, in France, in Germany, in Austria and in Ireland, just as Karl Liebknecht's 'noble conduct', as he called it, had helped to inspire the socialists in Scotland.

There is no doubt that events in Scotland had their effect on Maclean's old friend, James Connolly. Connolly, whom Maclean described later as 'the brain centre of the Irish working class', was brought up in Edinburgh, his parents being Irish immigrants. He early came under the influence of his uncle, John Leslie, a prominent member of the SDF, and an able propagandist. He became a Marxist, joined the SDF, and stood as a socialist municipal candidate. After suffering the usual victimization for socialist activities, he went to Dublin, where he founded the Irish Socialist Republican Party in 1896.

Connolly still kept close ties with Scotland, and although I have not been able to discover when his friendship with Maclean began, it was probably during this period, before the end of 1903 when Connolly went to America. Before this, however, Connolly seemed to have been the moving spirit behind the secession of the

Scottish branches of the SDF in 1903 to form the SLP and he is recorded as having been its first Chairman.

He came back to Ireland in 1910, became closely associated with Larkin and the Irish Transport and General Workers' Union, and when Larkin went to America in 1914, assumed command at Liberty Hall, the headquarters of the union.

By the end of 1915 he was preparing the Irish Citizen Army for the role which it was to play as the spearhead of the anti-war, anti-imperialist insurrection in Dublin, Easter 1916, the Easter Rising. By this time, Connolly was prepared to join with the non-socialist but revolutionary forces of the Irish Volunteers and the Irish Republican Brotherhood (IRB) as the only course of action in an under-developed, oppressed, colonial country where the industrial working-class was only a minority of the population. In 1922, Maclean was to declare 'when Jim Connolly saw how things were going on the Clyde, he determined on the Easter Rising'.

This claim was confirmed in a letter to me from Seamus Reader, who was one of the many Scotsmen who became actively involved in the Easter Rising and the subsequent revolutionary struggle. He organized and fought with the Scottish Brigade of the IRA, and was one of the founders of the abortive Scottish Republican Army. He wrote from Dublin in 1968:

> Your father was right in his remarks about James Connolly, because anti-conscription and the intended revolt on the Clyde did influence Countess MarKievicz, James Connolly and Sean MacDiarmid. They were determined that at least the Liffey would assert itself.

Reader was arrested in May, after the Rising, and taken to Edinburgh Castle as a prisoner of war where, he told me 'one of the Argyll and Sutherland Highlanders told me that John Maclean had also been a prisoner there. Some of the soldiers had admiration for your father and James Connolly'.

Reader also told me that Maclean had association with the Irish Republican Movement in Scotland, that he often carried reports to Dublin concerning him and that 'after the 1916 Rising and his release from prison he had contacts with some members of the Scottish Divisional Board of the IRB'.

Meanwhile the Easter rebellion was, as expected, a failure, and Connolly and most of the other leaders were murdered by the British government. But it achieved something no amount of 'cautious' action could have done. As John Wheatley described in *Forward* (7 June):

Connolly's death has removed a mountain of prejudice against Socialism. 'He was a socialist and he died for Ireland'. This is a common remark among the Irish population. They are now interested in Connolly, and in Connolly's views.

But the official ILP attitude to the Rising was different, as expressed in the *Socialist Review* of September 1916:

In no degree do we approve of the Sinn Fein rebellion. We do not approve of armed rebellion at all, any more than any other form of militarism and war.

Lenin saw it as the first great blow against the might of the British Empire, and of the greatest importance:

The struggle of the oppressed nations of Europe, a struggle capable of going to the length of insurrection and street fighting, of breaking down the iron discipline in the army and martial law, will sharpen the revolutionary crisis in Europe more than a much more developed rebellion in a remote colony. A blow delivered against the British imperialist bourgeois rule by a rebellion in Ireland is of a hundred times greater political significance than a blow of equal weight in Asia or Africa. (*Berlin Tagwacht*, 9 May 1916.)

Later John Maclean was to agree with Lenin.

I have no doubt at all that the anti-war activities on the Clyde and in Ireland encouraged the Social Democratic minority in Germany who had also stood out against the war. During March 1916, Liebknecht delivered a passionate speech in the Prussian Assembly proving that German soldiers had been shot down by cannons sold by Krupps to Belgium, and in another speech a fortnight later demanded that workers in the trenches and at home should turn against the common enemy, the great German landed proprietors, the German capitalists and their executive committee. He put out a manifesto along the same lines on May Day and was eventually arrested and sentenced to thirty months' penal servitude.

In 1916, the writings of Lenin showed that he also was encouraged by the events in Britain and Germany:

In all the countries during the war there has been observed—notwithstanding the gagging of mouths and the ruthless persecution by the bourgeoisie—a trend of revolutionary internationalism. This trend has remained loyal to Socialism. . . . To this trend belong, for example, Maclean in England, who has been sentenced to eighteen months' imprisonment with hard labour for fighting against the predatory British Bourgeoisie, Karl Liebknecht in Germany, who has been condemned to hard labour by the German imperialist pirates for the crime of calling for a revolution in Germany and for exposing the predatory character of the war pursued by Germany. To this trend belong the Bolsheviks of Russia who are persecuted by the agents of Russian republican-democratic imperialism for the same crimes as that for which Maclean and Karl Liebknecht are being persecuted.

31/The fight for Maclean

The pith seemed to have been taken out of the movement with the removal of its most militant leaders. The storm of agitation for their release which Maclean had expected failed to materialize, and calm apparently settled down on the troubled waters of the Clyde—at least on the surface.

One reason for the lack of more militant action was the struggle going on inside the British Socialist Party itself. The contest between the pro-war and anti-war factions which had been so evenly balanced at the 1915 conference was now beginning to favour the internationalists. A referendum of the branches had endorsed a resolution expressing the adherence of the BSP to the Zimmerwald platform, yet Hyndman and his clique still had control of *Justice,* and were using it to express their own views. By the beginning of 1916 the crisis was coming to a head. The trustees of the paper refused to accept party control, and in February E C Fairchild was forced to begin a new paper, *The Call,* which expressed more truly the internationalist view of the majority.

The annual conference at Easter was a stormy affair. A resolution to secure proper control of *Justice* was carried by 70 votes to 14, but in the middle of the conference the whole of the Hyndman clique, numbering 22, marched out, left the party, and took *Justice* with them. If only Maclean's 1913 warning had been taken!

The withdrawal of the older men, although they had the well-known names and reputations, had the effect of strengthening the virile elements of the left, and from the Salford conference onward the BSP was definitely ranged with the left wing of the International. The party emerged from the ordeal with new life and new purpose. Lesser-known men stepped into the places so long held by Hyndman's friends, and for the first time Maclean himself was elected a member of the National Executive. This was a step forward that he must have been overjoyed to hear about when my mother paid her first visit to him, in July 1916.

Under the guidance of the solicitor, John Cassells, who had defended Maclean at his trial, the Glasgow District Council had been getting ready a big petition for Maclean's release, but were finding it no easy matter. To be effective it was discovered that it would have to take the form of an appeal for leniency or an appeal for the quashing of the sentence on the grounds of the contradictory character of the evidence. As regards the first, Maclean at his trial had very emphatically refused to permit anything in the nature of an appeal for leniency to be made. When it was put to him before his sentence that it was either a matter of sacrificing principles or liberty, he had instantly, and with his eyes open, sacrificed liberty. So it was felt that before going ahead Maclean would have to be consulted.

Mother was not due a visit until November, but in view of this position, she arranged to have her visit in July instead. As expected he made it quite clear that he did not want a begging petition of any kind. He was not sorry, he had nothing to apologize for and what he had said he would say again. What he did suggest was that the agitation might take the form of a struggle for political rights for political prisoners in Scotland. She immediately wrote to John Mackay, secretary of the Glasgow District Council:

> I saw John for twenty minutes last Saturday. He is looking well and seemed in good spirits. He was very disappointed so little is being done to get him political treatment. He says we must keep petitioning the Home Secretary and other MPs to let them know Scotland is far behind Germany, Russia and England in this matter . . . He gets absolutely no privileges. This visit was instead of November and he will get seeing no one until one year is in. He will get writing a letter in November.

He also sent best wishes to all his comrades, assured them he would be keener than ever when he was free and urged them not to go to any more expense with the solicitor as it was quite unnecessary.

She also wrote to Albert Inkpin, the General Secretary of the British Socialist Party, along the same lines, emphasizing again that the party should realize 'Scotland is the most backward country in their treatment of political prisoners. England has second division, and Germany and even Russia is the same. . . . I don't know if the Executive realize that he is a *convict* and is having no privileges whatever. I saw him for twenty minutes . . . with two warders present. We did not even get shaking hands—we were separated by bars. . . . He gets reading no newspapers, and he has to work out of doors all day'.

It was decided in both Glasgow and London, therefore, to go ahead as Maclean suggested, concentrating in the meantime on his treatment as a political prisoner and ultimately on his release. Demonstrations throughout the country were immediately organized. The one in Glasgow Green on 3 September 1916 was very successful.

A letter was circulated to all progressive MPs pointing out the unsatisfactory nature of the evidence and drawing comparison between Maclean's heavy sentence and that of three months in the second division passed on Captain White in South Wales, who was on a charge under the Defence of the Realm Act of a much more serious character. They were asked to raise the matter in parliament and bring pressure to bear on the Home Secretary. The fight in parliament was begun by King, the Liberal member for Somerset, who had played a very noteworthy part in defending the Clyde Workers' Committee at the time of the deportations.

A circular of the same nature was also sent to every working-class organization, asking them to pass resolutions to be forwarded the Home Secretary and finally an appeal was sent to internationalist socialists abroad, asking them to bring pressure to bear on their ambassadors to approach the British government on Maclean's behalf. 'Remember, however, John Maclean does not ask for mercy, but merely demands Justice.' That was the spirit behind it all.

In August the severe nervous breakdown of MacDougall, along with a temporary loss of memory, shocked the movement into a more serious realization of the terrible ordeal being endured by these men of high character and sensibility. MacDougall's was probably an exceptional case. Scarcely yet mature, his exceptional idealism had led him to strain his strength for years in the service of the movement, and he was therefore less able to stand the strain than older and more stolid men. Yet each and every one had to suffer acutely, and each and every one had to bear the marks of that suffering for many a day to come. MacDougall's collapse naturally gave an impetus to the release agitation, for all were convinced that he would never regain his health until away from his present surroundings.

Cheering news came for Maclean from my mother in his first letter (14 November), after the July visit:

> The Trades Council and others are urging the Labour Party to get something done for political prisoners. . . . When I saw you in July I never thought for one minute you would still be in jail. Don't get downhearted. Your cause is more alive today than ever it was, and although there is nothing but silence for you meantime, your day is coming. It would take pages to tell you of the people who are always asking about you and thinking of you. Our fund for maintenance is being closed already. There is enough to keep us although you are away the whole time, and enough to keep you for some time until you are in good condition to take up your life work again.
>
> A John Maclean Sale of Work was held on 14 October in the Central Halls which realized £180. This Sale originated at the Women's Guild, so don't say it has been of no use! The women were aiming at about £100, and of course they were delighted when the sale was such a success. They could have got double the money if the hall had been larger. Crowds of people could not get near the stalls at all. It would have done your heart good to have had a peep in that day. The enthusiasm was great. Tom Kerr and the Glee Party ran a splendid concert upstairs.
>
> Your College speech is to be printed this winter. J F Armour tells me he will send it round the Trades Unions and Co-operative Societies, and will send out the prospectus of the College with it. The Class is going on well. They enrolled upwards of 300 and the attendance is excellent.

The remainder of the letter dealt with news about various comrades—not so cheerful—including MacDougall's illness, Maxton's dismissal by his School Board (only two of the Board members voting against it), and news that Johnnie Lennox, one of the most active members of Pollokshaws BSP, had been killed in France.

His first letter from Peterhead (18 November), was also a cheerful one:

> On no account worry about me. I am keeping the promise I gave you on 12 April. I have no reason to feel depressed even if kept here three years. If all goes well here I get out in less than 20 mths, as 9 mths counts a year here. More than 2 mths ago I heard rumours that a good fight was being made for me. Supposing I knew there wouldn't be a Soc. in Scot. when I came out I would not let that worry me, but resolve to come out and begin the good work again. Believe no one who should hint or suggest that I can

be depressed. . . . Glad to know you are secure. Thank the Guild for me . . . Tell Armour that Jimmie wrote part of the speech and that this must be stated. Send my greetings to the class and say that they must beat last year's record when they can send a telegram to Ll. George! A re-instatement com. ought to be formed for Houston, Maxton, myself etc. Thank all working for me. . . . As my throat was a bit worse I got inside for good to patch shirts, etc. I'm much better. . . . I read steadily a book a week, and having no distractions enjoy the books better than I did all my reading for years. . . . The bye-word here is 'Cheer up'! Apply it!

In January Maclean was granted a 'very special privilege'. I had succumbed to the scarlet fever epidemic which was sweeping the country, and was very seriously ill, so mother was actually allowed to write and let him know about my progress, and he was allowed to reply—on condition that no mention was made on any other subject! But, although I was at one stage at the point of death, there would have been no question of him being allowed to see me. No compassion in the Scottish prison service! Eventually both mother and Jean took fever, and were removed to an isolation hospital, while my Aunt Lizzie (Maclean's younger sister), looked after me.

Meantime his own health deteriorated, and mother received an official letter from Perth Prison at the beginning of March stating that he had been transferred there, apparently to the prison hospital. He wrote to Aunt Lizzie on 18 April, mostly about family matters, but also adding:

I wish to know what the Housing Assoc. of which I was secy. is doing at present. You can assure the Labour College Committee that I have been revolving many schemes since my incarceration and will try to further them vigorously on release. Armour might meantime consider the advisability of a meeting of the Com. with the Parliamentary Com. of the Scot. TU Congress for the more firmly establishing our object. My greetings to all comrades, especially those of the 'Shaws branch—the fail-me-nevers. You might find out all about Petroff and his wife, as I've often thought of them.

I conclude with heartiest wishes to all and will sing the *Red Flag* as a bond between me and the outside world.

Yours for the Social Revolution and Human Freedom, Johnnie.

He was allowed to write another letter next month, this time to mother, mostly about personal matters, and concluded by obviously trying to cheer and reassure her:

I have nothing to add to what I said to you re my health on your last visit. I am the same as then and will be the same till I am free. Draw no conclusions from hair or tongue. . . . I am glad to hear that you yourself are feeling stronger and I trust you will continue improving until my release when we could do no better than spend a good holiday at Perth and Peterhead—outside His Majesty's Hotel, however! Remember me to all relatives, friends and comrades.

Your *living* husband, Johnnie.

32/New horizons

At the beginning of 1917, the position in the Labour Party with regard to the war still seemed pretty hopeless. A motion of confidence in those leaders who had joined the Coalition Cabinet was carried by a majority of 1,542,000, only 307,000 voting against. The anti-war propaganda of the BSP, which had been granted affiliation to the Labour Party in 1916 (having applied in 1914), was swamped by the constant flood of patriotic sentimentality churned out by press and pulpit.

Moreover, many of the socialists had now been conscripted into the army. The large majority of the revolutionaries, of course, were in jail or concentration camps as conscientious objectors, but others again, like some of the young, zealous lads of Pollokshaws BSP, had been forced, reluctantly, to obey the call. These were the lads who belonged to small towns and villages where everybody knew everybody else, and where to have a conscientious objector in the family was an overwhelming disgrace. Mother used to describe how clothes and money were collected for one well-loved young comrade, and arrangements made for him to escape to Ireland. Johnnie Lennox, however, decided that he could not inflict the lasting shame on his 'folks' of having a son a 'deserter' and joined the colours. He was killed one week after being drafted to France.

While he was in camp he wrote to mother describing the life and giving an insight into the quiet work being done by socialists in the army:

The first few weeks were the worst, and many times I felt like kicking out against the way they order you about . . . I have met all sorts of chaps in the Army, but so far haven't met one who has had any love for it. . . . The second night I was under canvas I got up an argument with the chaps in my tent about the war, introduced the class war and told them right off I was a socialist. The result was I soon found out how the rest of the chaps were thinking, and as luck would have it there was a socialist among them. He is a fine fellow and he and I have become great chums. At every opportunity after that I rubbed it in, and now I'm known all over the whole camp as an agitator. Even the sergeants purposely come down to my tent at night to argue the point with me. They are fine fellows but have to be more careful than me, and although they are generally against me, when I meet them on the quiet they don't forget to tell me I was quite right only it doesn't do for them to agree. . . .

The other night I was across at a picture show, and before it started I was having a look at the *Forward* when a young chap came up to me and asked me if it was the *Forward* I was reading. I got into conversation with him . . . He was a socialist and came from Glasgow. He pulled out a postcard photo of Mr Maclean and was surprised to learn that I knew more about Johnnie than he did.

Another soldier wrote from Aldershot about Maclean:

What a great game he has played! . . . No one seems to be able to take his place, but we have his prototype, Liebknecht, doing exactly the same in Germany. . . . One thing I am convinced of is that John is the biggest man in the country. His name is written large in the history of our movement and he is coming out a bigger and greater man than he went in.

The February Revolution in Russia came like an electric shock to Western Europe. The socialist movement seemed to spring to life again with the new hope that was surging up everywhere. MacDougall, Gallacher, Maxton, and Muir were now at liberty. A great welcome-home meeting packed St Mungo's Hall to the door. Enthusiasm was tremendous, and as each speaker emphasized that the big question was now the release of Maclean and urged the concentrating of all forces on that object, the room was nearly lifted off the building with applause.

The following message was sent to Russia by the Annual Conference of the BSP at Easter:

In the name of the International Socialists in Britain we send greetings to the revolutionary Russian working class and express our unity with them in their struggle for international labour solidarity.

E C Fairchild, now the recognized leader in England, was appointed to convey the greetings of the party to the Russian revolutionaries in Petrograd. This was the first conference since the secession of the Hyndman group, and it was apparent that the party had never before been so strong. Militant resolutions protesting against the imprisonment of Maclean and the other political prisoners were carried with great enthusiasm and it was obvious that the delegates were now thoroughly in earnest.

May Day 1917 was Glasgow's expression of solidarity with the Revolution in Russia and never had there been such a demonstration in the city. About seventy or eighty thousand people marched in the procession itself, while about a quarter of a million lined the streets. In Glasgow Green, MacDougall, Gallacher and the other revolutionaries were cheered again and again. Militant resolutions declaring solidarity with the Russian Soviets and for the overthrow of capitalism everywhere were rapturously received. The demonstration broke up with great cheers for the social revolution and for John Maclean.

Next Sunday a tremendous meeting to celebrate the Revolution was held in St Andrew's Hall, with Bob Smillie and George Lansbury among the principal speakers. Thousands couldn't get inside the hall, and a huge overflow meeting was held outside. The spirit was tremendous, and the suggestion that Russia's example should be emulated here and that Workers' and Soldiers' Committees should be set up was applauded vociferously, the audience standing to cheer and wave their caps. No less enthusiastic was the response to Lansbury's fervent appeal that immediate and definite action should be taken for Maclean's release.

A wave of protest swept the movement when it was heard that Glasgow Corporation had invited Lloyd George to come north on 29 June to receive the Freedom of the City and loud demands were made that John Maclean, Davy Kirkwood and their comrades should receive that honour instead. A great protest demonstration took place at the end of May, when about 100,000 people crowded into Glasgow Green to show their resentment and to call for Maclean's release. The outstanding feature of this demonstration was the participation of about two hundred Russian sailors from a warship lying in the harbour. Their primary purpose in attending, they declared, was to protest in the name of the international solidarity of labour against the continued imprisonment of John Maclean and their fellow-countryman, Peter Petroff. 'The funny little Welshman', reported The Call, 'would be well advised to stay in a dug-out instead of going north for honours as he proposes to do.'

The passionate desire for unity which was sweeping the movement was expressed by the Conference of United Socialists held at Leeds on 3 June to declare solidarity with the Russian Revolution. About 1,500 delegates from trade unions, Labour Parties, Trades Councils, the Shop Stewards' Movement, and the BSP, ILP, and SLP, took part. The Convention, however, was dominated by reformists of the Ramsay MacDonald type, who were quite content, if not anxious, that the Russian Revolution should go no further than the overthrow of Czarist autocracy and who were lyrical in their praises of capitalist democracy. Those who dared to suggest that the Revolution was not completed and that the workers must go forward to seize power were pooh-poohed and laughed at. This emptiness behind the bold front was obvious to only a few far-sighted revolutionaries, and the Convention sent a flood of new hope coursing through the movement. The National Committee which was elected went ahead with the organization of Workers' and Soldiers' Councils throughout the country.

Events were moving fast. Lloyd George, anxious for a safe passage on 29 June, tried to pour oil on the troubled waters of the Clyde and on 4 June, Kirkwood, Messer and the others were allowed to return to Glasgow.

By this time the agitation for Maclean's release was going forward fast and furious. A Committee representing the whole socialist and labour movement had been formed with Harry Hopkins as secretary. *The Call* for the first time began to devote leading articles to his case, and his name was becoming the rallying cry of the anti-war socialists, not only on the Clyde, but all over Britain.

On 21 June Johnnie Muir published a letter telling about his own desperate ill health resulting from his imprisonment, and saying that Maclean's health was gradually deteriorating in the same way. 'It will be a standing disgrace and shame on the workers with whom he has so long been associated and on whose behalf he has devoted his life's work if the ruling class is thus permitted to wreak its vengeance on John Maclean and remove him permanently from its path', was the comment in *The Call*.

But Maclean was now not only a national figure. To revolutionaries abroad his militancy stood out like a beacon of hope amidst the blackness of traditional British reaction. Money to help his family and messages of encouragement came from all parts of the globe, and especially from Russia.

In June the All Russian Congress of Workmen's and Soldiers' Delegates in Petrograd enthusiastically adopted a resolution of fraternal greetings:

Convention of All Russian Councils of Workmen's and Soldiers'

Deputies (they telegraphed) send their greetings to the brave fighter for the International, Comrade Maclean, and express their hopes that the new rise of international solidarity will bring him liberty.

With the prisoners and the deportees back in the workshops once more the shop steward movement, which had been failing to function properly, began to revive and soon the government could not fail to observe the gathering unrest.

In spite of this situation, Lloyd George came to Glasgow on 29 June, as planned, to receive the 'Freedom' of the City. The workers came out on to the streets in their thousands, but it was impossible to get anywhere near him; he was surrounded by soldiers and policemen. As he drove up to St Andrew's Hall, he was met by a huge mass of threatening men and women, and a great red flag flying from an adjacent building. As described by Gallacher in *Revolt on the Clyde*:

All round the centre of the city, the workers were gathering and shouting for the release of Maclean. Given a start there was no saying what might have happened.

Then the genius of the British ruling class for compromise was once more demonstrated, as word was given out that Maclean would be released next day, and was now at Duke Street Prison in Glasgow. Immediately the whole crowd marched to the prison, where they raised lusty cheers for the prisoner inside. That evening mother received a telegram from the Secretary for Scotland: 'Have directed the release of your husband as soon as possible.'

33/Release

Those who met Maclean as he came out of the gates of Duke Street Prison were struck with the vital intensity of his devotion to the socialist cause after an experience which would have made most men rather more lukewarm and calculating in future. But the old eager enthusiasm was still there, and the abounding vitality which seemed to warm all those near him. 'My encounter with Maclean after an interval of nearly one-and-a-half years', wrote one of his comrades, 'resembled the sensation one would feel after a closing door shuts out the sound of music. There is a momentary silence, and then the door re-opens as the notes are swelling to a crescendo and a burst of sound greets the ear.'

It was the opinion of many in Glasgow that the reception given to welcome him home was the most inspiring meeting they had ever attended, transcending even the welcome-home to the other prisoners earlier in the year. Again thousands could not get into the crammed hall and an overflow meeting was held outside. On the platform, as chairman Tom Johnston pointed out, were all the men most fit to welcome home a 'convict', for they were all men who had been in prison, men who would probably be in prison and some who ought to be in prison! There was great cheering when the telegram sent from the Petrograd Soviet was read out. After speeches from MacDougall, Gallacher, Jack Smith, Kirkwood and E C Fairchild, each one emphasizing that the one great need at the present moment was socialist unity, the climax of the evening came when Maclean rose to speak.

Never before had an audience listened to him so keenly as he described the tortures of prison life and made an impassioned appeal for a great agitation to release the conscientious objectors and other political prisoners still suffering jail. When he went on to deal with the war situation in general and expose the Allies' real war aims, when he urged the immeasurable importance of the revolution going on in Russia and declared for a workers' Russia as the only 'free' Russia, and when he finished up by declaring that all the forces of the workers' movement must be thrown into the fight against the war and for the overthrow of capitalism, the audience was stirred to the depth. 'The next day', recorded Gallacher in *Revolt on the Clyde,* 'the message of this great demonstration was carried into every factory and supplied the drive for meal-hour meetings and discussions all over the Clyde.'

Maclean had made up his mind that his first duty was to do all he possibly could to gain the freedom of the conscientious objectors, especially those detained in ordinary prisons, and of political prisoners like Peter and Irma Petroff. He made appeals to the press and asked the Russians to cease negotiations with the British government till these three internees were set free.

George Lansbury, who had probably done more than any other of the socialist leaders to get Maclean released, also persuaded him to take a holiday in Hastings, and booked rooms for all the family. But we had barely settled down before the old fever began to stir in his blood. He could not remain away voluntarily from the fight and he made his way to London to attend a conference for the setting up of Workers' and Soldiers' Committees, in imitation of the Russians. However, ever since the Leeds Convention the authorities had been growing increasingly anxious about this new development, and so the London conference was cleverly sabotaged. At the very last moment the let of the hall was cancelled and it was only with great difficulty that another meeting place was found. When Maclean arrived there, he found a 'howling mob of male and female dervishes' skirmishing round the place and the meeting was completely broken up. Similar conferences arranged to take place in Swansea and Newcastle were also riotously broken up—the work, Maclean was convinced, of the usual *agents provocateurs*.

It was Glasgow that once again renewed hope. Banned though their conference had been by the authorities, a demonstration was held outside the hall. 'Patriots' were not in evidence, and the only scenes were ones of wild enthusiasm. Workers' and Soldiers' Councils! Well might the government fear their success, for unrest was growing almost hourly. An old school pupil wrote to Maclean from France telling about the feeling among the soldiers:

> I am one of those misguided people who joined the Army believing in Britain as a righteous angel, and in the terrible wickedness of Germany. . . . After two years in France, I can definitely state from wide observation that 90 per cent of our army have turned socialist or republican, and the present feeling is 'let the war end somehow —never mind the terms; it makes no difference to us'.

Although, under the stimulus of the Russian Revolution and the return of their leaders, the old militancy of the Glasgow munition workers had been rapidly reviving, the Clyde Workers' Committee was not re-constituted until September 1917. Before this, however, the scene of the struggle had changed to Lanarkshire and the miners. Even before the war Maclean and Mac-Dougall had had a very considerable influence among the miners of Lanarkshire and Fife. As disgust with the war grew stronger, their influence had grown proportionately. During the stormy months of the fight against conscription, Maclean had by no means neglected the miners. The critical month of January 1916, had seen him conducting a strenuous campaign against conscription not only at the pit-heads, but also at the street-corners of the mining towns and villages. Even if he did not obtain all the support he expected, his seed did not fall on stony ground.

After his release from prison MacDougall went to Blantyre in Lanarkshire to do work 'of national importance' in the mines. There he lived with George Russell, for years a faithful member of the Central Economics Class and an important member of the

Lanarkshire Miners' Union. MacDougall's health was still poor and it had been his intention to take Maclean's advice and keep away from politics in the meantime. Events willed otherwise.

By this time all the mines were under government control (the railways also) because the miners' leaders had not knuckled under like the engineers' officials, and the government had been forced to step in to ensure the industrial peace necessary for the conduct of the war. Both the miners and railwaymen had achieved a reasonable national wage and up to the present the miners had been immune from conscription. Now, however, prices had been rising so steeply that their real wages had decreased spectacularly, and the 'comb out' of younger men was now taking place even in 'industries of national importance'.

It was just at this time also that the agitation for the Peace Conference at Stockholm was reaching its height and the Blantyre District Committee had arranged a big demonstration in its support, with Bob Smillie as speaker. At the last minute Smillie failed to turn up and in desperation the organizers turned to MacDougall to fill the breach. It must be understood that this request was very natural. MacDougall was recognized to be the best orator in Scotland by this time and some thought he was even better than Lloyd George and Ramsay MacDonald. But it was only natural for MacDougall to hesitate. Only a few months out of jail, here he was being asked virtually to repeat his offence and run the risk of another dose of prison. Regard for personal safety is not a characteristic of revolutionaries—and MacDougall spoke. A fortnight later Smillie again failed to turn up to speak at a big demonstration, and again MacDougall took his place. Thus he was launched, willy-nilly, into the turbulent sea of working-class struggle once again.

Just one week after the second meeting, MacDougall was dismissed from his work at the pit-head, the reason given being that he was not fit for the work. It seemed very strange to the Blantyre miners that MacDougall's incompetence had been so long in being discovered and they drew their own conclusions. Obviously it was the manager's answer to the eruption of a new agitator among 'his' men. By this time MacDougall had become something of a hero to the men, partly because of his victimization and imprisonment, partly because of his association with Maclean, and most of all because of his courage in entering the fight once more.

The District Committee therefore met immediately and decided that unless MacDougall was back on the 'dirthill' next morning every pit in the district would be idle. What agitated discussions went on between union and management! But Mac-Dougall went back to the pit-head—and without a strike. Now, every morning on his way to work as he passed the hundreds of others on their way to the different pits, at least one would say pawkily—'Ye're aye there yit, sir!' After that it took only a rumour that MacDougall was sacked for one pit or another to stop work. Such was his prestige.

MacDougall was rapidly becoming a well-known and popular figure, and when he decided that the time was ripe to organize a Miners' Reform Committee after the pattern of the South Wales one formed before the war, he obtained considerable support. Several hundred men attended the Inaugural Conference held in Hamilton in July, and although as yet they had no mandate from their respective organizations, they were all outstanding and representative men. Once the Committee was formed and the Manifesto, written by MacDougall, distributed in thousands all over Lanarkshire, the mandates were not long in coming. The Manifesto was an excellent piece of work which combined in true Marxian manner the abstract with the concrete, theory with practice, and revealed that MacDougall had imbibed the syndicalist ideas of the SLP much more than Maclean had done. It recommended the formation of a British Miners' Industrial Union with pooled resources, centralized direction, and a wide enough scope to embrace every worker in the industry.

MacDougall was, however, more concerned with the ultimate purpose of the union:

> So far as is compatible with majority rule in society and final power being exercised by the delegates of all the industries, we desire that the workers in each industry shall have autonomous control over their own work. Only in that way can economic freedom be realized. . . . We want an industrial democracy in which the means of production shall be owned by the community and largely controlled by the workers in each industry . . .
>
> We conceive of our Union as the embryo of the future society.

The Manifesto was distributed at every pit-head, and every night MacDougall cycled to the different towns and villages, carrying on a ceaseless agitation. It was not long before his work began to have its effect. The first sign of conscious militancy was an 'idle day' called by Blantyre District Committee to protest against the rising cost of living and to call for peace. This was followed by the whole body of Lanarkshire miners, 50,000 strong, downing tools for one day with a similar object. That day, with Smillie at their head, mass demonstrations and meetings were held all over the county, and socialist and anti-war speeches were vociferously applauded.

Maclean compared this strike with the Rent Strike that had forced the Rent Restriction Act in 1915. That had been the first time in British history that the workers had struck for a political object of a class nature, and now here again the workers were striking for a political objective, and on a much grander scale. He maintained that the organized miners had raised themselves to the highest of levels as champions of the working-class and not merely champions of miners as miners. At this period Maclean considered Bob Smillie to be the mightiest fighter for the workers that Scotland had ever known, his reputation being only enhanced by his refusal to accept the Food Controllers' job offered to him as a bribe by the government—and which was later accepted by the Rt Hon George Barnes.

In an article in *The Call* (2 August), describing the strike, he declared it to be 'the most important in the whole history of the working-class in Scotland . . . I am confident, at any rate, that my comrades in the engineering and shipbuilding industries of the Clyde will fully appreciate the significance of Thursday's great event in Lanarkshire. This preliminary swipe at the profiteers must lead to a general battle. These worse-than-Junker scoundrels, who exploit the patriotism of the people to rob them, are united and are represented by their Grand Committee, the House of Commons, and their executive, the two Cabinets. Now is the time for the whole working-class to line up alongside Smillie and his merry men, for the time is on us when events will require the united efforts of the organized workers of the world'.

34/Back in the struggle

While MacDougall was thus stirring up the fires among the Lanarkshire miners and the workshop committee movement was being revived among the heavy industries on the Clyde, Maclean was beginning his work once more. One of his first actions in Glasgow was typical. He set about planning an ambitious educational programme for the winter and at least a dozen classes in Lanarkshire, Glasgow and Clydeside were organized by the Labour

College Committee, supported by the ILP and BSP. 'Marxian education', he wrote, 'that is, independent working-class education, must be the supreme effort of workers this winter'.

Maclean made no apologies for harping on this educational work, so neglected and despised by the major part of the socialist movement today. As I have said, he was convinced that he had been singled out for persecution because of the success of his Economics Classes. This was the opinion of others as well. In September the *Glasgow Herald* published a series of articles on the Clyde movement, attributing the serious unrest to the teaching of Marxism. This, naturally, was an added incentive to Maclean and his colleagues.

There was absolutely nothing mean or egotistical in Maclean's nature. He was delighted when the SLP also decided to set up classes throughout the city. As Tom Bell, then a leading member, said in his book on Maclean:

> The initiative towards the formation of groups of 'Plebs' came from the SLP, which since the beginning of the war had been striving to break away from its former narrow moorings in other directions, and now turned to working-class Education. A Glasgow 'Plebs League' was formed and classes in Independent Working-Class Education were organized mostly with members of the SLP as tutors.

This endeavour by the SLP to supplant the existing Labour College Committee was another indication of their continuing sectarianism and underlying antagonism to the BSP and to Maclean. However, the latter accepted it with enthusiasm and in an article in *The Call* advertised both the work of the Labour College Committee and the Plebs League:

> Everyone now admits that Germany's marvellous resistance to overwhelming odds is due to her mighty powers of organization, and that her ability to organize follows from her superior education. Everyone as readily admits that the remarkable output of the workshops of the USA depends on minute and thorough organization, and that this results from widespread technical education . . .
>
> Just as the Boer War revealed in the clearest manner the economic hostility of the German and the American capitalist class to the British capitalist class, and led to the Education Act of 1902, and the raising of scientific and commercial education to a position above that of the old classical education, so the economic antagonisms that led to the present war, and will revive fiercer than ever after the conclusion of 'peace', is fundamentally responsible for these so-called 'educational reconstruction' schemes already commenced or mooted.

The underlying motive in all the reorganization and development of education is 'increased efficiency', and this capitalist phrase simply means better wage-slaves or better producers of commodities. . . . Yet we would be foolish reactionaries to oppose schemes over which we as voters have a slight control—just as foolish as those who resist improved machinery and methods in the workshop. We, as socialists, must be intensely interested in improved education along technical and commercial lines, and it is our special business to see that all public, educational institutions be used for the creation of intelligent, class-conscious workers.

In this respect we differ from the WEA, which simply has for its object the creation of intelligent workers. Personally, I wish to see all opportunities for self-development opened up to the working-class. But I am specially interested in such education as will make revolutionists . . .

The very antagonisms in society that called into being the Co-operative organization in production and distribution, the Trade Union movement, Socialist parties, and the Labour Party, make it equally urgent that the workers should forge their own educational machine for their own class ends. It was for this supposed end that Ruskin College was for a time supported by the working-class; it was explicitly for this end that the Central Labour College was established. The war has closed down both these institutions. Fortunately, their temporary cessation did not mean the demise of independent working-class education (assuming that Ruskin College was independent). Marxian classes increased in number and members in South Wales, Glasgow, Sheffield and elsewhere, as a very consequence of the war. It was in these centres that the greatest resistance was put up against the profiteering patriots.

In August a Plebs League was formed in London, and various agencies are at work to establish an organized network of classes in our benighted imperial capital. Yorkshire will soon outstrip Lancashire if Fred Shaw and others carry out their ambitious plans.

The Scottish Labour College Committee, supported by the BSP and ILP, will be responsible for at least a dozen large classes in Lanarkshire, Glasgow and Clydeside.

The SLP are holding a conference in Glasgow for the establishment of further classes in the West of Scotland. Where classes cannot be held it is to be hoped that groups will be formed in workshops, at meal-times and in houses or halls after work-time, to read together and discuss the smaller works of Marx and Engels, and those of well-known Marxian scholars. The Russian revolution was buttressed by city workers thoroughly educated in Marxism. Marxian education, that is, independent working-class education, must be the supreme effort of workers this winter.

The greatest 'crime' I have committed in the eyes of the British Government and the Scottish capitalist class has been the teaching of Marxian economics to Scottish workers. That was evident at my 'trial'; that dictated Lord Strathclyde's sentence of three years. Nevertheless I mean to spend every evening this winter in teaching economics. And every reader should push ahead as a teacher or as a student, and in the active organizing of classes.

Maclean attended the SLP conference as a BSP representative and while agreeing with and endorsing two of the three resolutions to be discussed, that is, the ones dealing with the desirability of 'adequate independent working-class education in the subjects of Economics, History and Philosophy' and the setting up of a committee to organize educational classes, he strongly objected to the third resolution:

> That this conference . . . endorses the aims and methods of the Plebs League, and establishes the Glasgow Branch of that organization.

He maintained that the conference was not taking into account the existing Scottish Labour College Committee, which although its work had been undermined by the imprisonment of the two main tutors, had continued since its formation in 1916. He moved an amendment to delay the formation of a branch of the Plebs League, but although he did not receive a majority of the votes, his support was so considerable that it was agreed that a committee should meet the SLC Committee with a view to a united movement. Eventually the two organizations merged, but the tendency remained that the SLP-ers did not support the SLC, but preferred to support the English organization.

The Call had this to say:

> Friendly rivalry in the business of educating the workers is to be welcomed, provided everything is done with one object, the true education of the workers. A multiplicity of classes for the spread of socialist economics even to the ideal extent of every individual Marxist doing his bit as a teacher, is a desirable thing, but it should not interfere with the truth of Maclean's statement in support of big classes—'Mass Education means Mass Action!'

Maclean's main concern was still therefore the Central Class at Bath Street, the largest class of its kind in the world. A great campaign was carried on to advertise its opening on 7 October 1917. Thousands of leaflets were distributed at the work-gates, open-air meetings were held, occasion was taken of every disturbance among the workers to point out their pressing need to understand their slavish status in society. The following is an extract from the leaflet advertisement:

J D MacDougall will this winter address classes for miners in Lanarkshire every evening of the week, and John Maclean will do the same in smelting, engineering and shipbuilding centres if individuals or committees in those places are prepared to avail themselves of his services as well as of those of others who are willing to assist. The capitalists are making a big move for efficiency in production; let us educate for the socialist revolution.

By 8 November, *The Call* was able to report that the Glasgow Class had attracted over 500 students, the Greenock one about 125 and that as a direct result of a visit by Maclean to several centres in London, similar classes had sprung up there, including one at Stratford numbering 90.

35/The Bolshevik Revolution

For months now the revolutionary socialists had been becoming more and more anxious about the development of the Russian Revolution. The July days had come and gone, and the Bolsheviks and their revolutionary slogan 'All Power to the Soviets' seemed to have been completely suppressed. The Mensheviks and Social Revolutionaries, with their lack of faith in the working-class and their faith in a 'popular front' with the liberal capitalists, seemed to be all-powerful.

The news from Russia is appalling (wrote *The Call*). The Government turned into a Directory with Kerensky as First Consul, capital punishment restored by the very hands which abolished it in the first days of the revolution; Trotsky and other 'extremists' thrown into prison; severe censorship established over all speeches and writings opposing the war.

The reality of the situation, however, was very different from the appearance. The reality was that the Bolsheviks, far from being crushed, were stronger than ever and that the real struggle, the fight for working-class power, was only just beginning.

The great majority of the British socialists, however, were

not revolutionaries, and they, like the British and French governments, were delighted with the Kerensky government. They agreed
with the Mensheviks that all that socialists could wish for in un-
developed Russia was capitalist democracy. To think of carrying
through the democratic revolution of February to a working-class
revolution, as Lenin and Trotsky were demanding, was sheer
lunacy.

Just because the majority of the socialists did not fully
comprehend the situation in Russia, it was inevitable that, in spite
of the great enthusiasm for Workers' and Soldiers' 'Soviets' in
Britain, in emulation of the Russians, the whole movement was
a failure. The first full meeting of the National Council in London
betrayed the fundamental lack of understanding of the Russian
Councils or Soviets. There was no conception of the Soviet as an
executive committee of the working-class in its struggle for power,
no conception of it as the embryo organ of government in a
workers' state. 'The Workers' and Soldiers' Council has been
formed primarily as a propagandist body, not as a rival to, or to
supplant any of the existing working-class organizations, but to
infuse into them a more active spirit of liberty' was the first
clause of the statement issued by the Council, showing clearly
its whole weakness. No, the nearest parallel to the Russian Soviets
was not this artificial mock Soviet, but the workshop committee
movement which was springing up stronger than ever in all the
industrial centres of the country.

There was one bright spot about the Council, however. Of
the two delegates elected to represent Scotland, one was John
Maclean, an out-and-out supporter of the Bolsheviks. That was
one straw to show the way the wind was blowing in Scotland.
Another straw was the resurrection of the Clyde Workers' Committee with Gallacher again as chairman and Messer as secretary.
Another was the growing unrest in the factories. As prices soared
food became more and more scarce and all workers were being
threatened with a 'comb-out'. Strikes and disturbances had been
almost everyday occurrences for some time now, and it was the
aim now of the Clyde Workers' Committee to consolidate these
isolated and sporadic outbreaks into centralized action and use it
not only to gain better conditions, but also to arouse feeling against
the war and the war-makers. A big strike of moulders in September
was led by Tom Bell and Jock McBain, both of whom were
prominent members of the SLP and CWC, and was successful in
obtaining a wage increase not only for the moulders but for the
whole of the engineering industry.

Another straw was the resolution passed at a meeting of the Scottish Advisory Council of the Labour Party which now demanded an immediate peace with no annexations and no indemnities.

Still another straw was the tremendous success of the Marxian classes throughout the West of Scotland. As we have noted, 500 students had been enrolled in the Glasgow Class before the end of October, and as many as 125 in at least one provincial one, in Greenock. It is difficult to convey just how much Maclean and the Glasgow Class meant to the socialist movement in Glasgow. Just as in every other industrial centre in the country, all the ingredients for militant working-class action were present, but in Glasgow Maclean was the catalyst which set them in motion—Maclean the agitator, rousing indignation, sweeping aside doubts and hesitations, inspiring courage and confidence; Maclean the educator, clear-headed and deliberate, patiently explaining the truth about society, and uncovering the reality lying beneath the illusions carefully cultivated by the bosses, patiently explaining the truth about the war, patiently explaining the truth about Russia; and Maclean the organizer, energetic and practical, organizing opposition to capitalism at every possible point, trying to link up every phase of the struggle into the fight against the war and the struggle for power, trying to form the BSP into the effective spearhead of attack.

The class was the brain centre of the movement and the rallying ground for the most militant shop stewards. It was like a large stone thrown into the centre of a pond. The ripples and eddies of its ideas reached out far and wide. It had an influence far disproportionate to its size. It was like no other class. The great mass of students, the electrical sympathy between teacher and pupils, the suppressed excitement produced by the critical condition of world affairs, Maclean's expert handling of his difficult and intricate subject and his ability to link up the dry, abstract theories with the practical problems burning the minds of his listeners, created an atmosphere of tense interest akin to that of a revivalist meeting rather than that of a lecture hall. After the lecture the men would bring him the latest news of events in the factories to serve as fresh material for lectures and illustrations of Marxist principles. They sought his advice on every important action. They argued with him and fought him. They carried his opinions and arguments back to their mates in the factories. Thus his influence spread quietly but effectively to every corner of the city.

Then came the world-shattering event longed for by Maclean and his comrades on the Clyde and all over the world. To the rest of the world it might come like a bolt from the blue, but, although they had scarcely dared hope for it, it came as no surprise to the Glasgow revolutionaries. They knew that capitalism was bound to break first at its weakest link, in Russia. And now it was broken. The Bolsheviks and the Soviets were taking control of Russia. The excitement became almost unbearable, not only because the Russian workers had seized power and were going to run Russia for themselves, not only because a section of the proletariat had come into their own for the first time in history, but also because they thought that the Bolshevik Revolution was only the first step in the great world revolution. That was its greatest significance to the Clyde socialists. It changed the outlook of the whole world movement. 'The Revolution' was no longer a distant dream; it had begun!

Right from the very beginning, even when the majority of socialists in Britain regarded the new revolution with suspicion and misgiving, the 'Red Clyde' knew better. News had scarcely come through before a great meeting was held to demand the release of the Petroffs and of Chicherin (all of whom were now interned without trial in Brixton Jail). The meeting had been organized by the Russian Political Refugees Defence Committee which had grown out of Maclean's campaign for the release of political prisoners, and of which Maclean himself was chairman. Louis Shammes, a Russian refugee, was the secretary. All the most important representatives of the left wing were speakers—Maclean, McManus, Maxton, Helen Crawford, and Davy Kirkwood.

This meeting was doubly significant. It testified to the growing support for the revolutionary elements of the movement, and it testified to the fact that a large section of the Glasgow workers could interpret the events in Russia in their own way. When Maclean referred to Russia and to the supreme efforts of Lenin and Trotsky in the cause of socialism, the hall thundered with fervent applause. And that was before reliable information about events could be obtained, and before the publication of the Bolshevik statement that they were going to declare an immediate peace with no annexations and no indemnities. Some of the Glasgow workers had certainly learned to think for themselves. The Bolshevik Revolution was as sound a proof as the Great War of the tremendous value of a thorough grounding in the principles of Marxism.

As more and more information about the revolution filtered

through, hope and enthusiasm rose, and the fight against the war received a tremendous impetus. All over the city Helen Crawford and the Women's Peace Crusade, launched in June 1917, were holding meetings and demonstrations. The women, embittered by the loss of husbands and sons, suffering deprivation and starvation, standing for hours shivering in food queues, were angry and resentful about the war, and it was beginning to be comparatively easy to turn their bitterness against those who had made the war and who were reaping vast profits from it. By the middle of December a more intense fervour was flooding the Clyde than in the days of the fight against conscription. The Bolshevik Revolution had set the movement on fire. Excitement and tension grew. Nobody knew what was going to happen, but everybody expected great events.

The authorities were once more becoming anxious. The Corporation passed an order forbidding the publication of any printed matter unless it could pass the censorship of its Press Bureau. This itself provoked a storm of protest. The women put out streams of leaflets, marched to the City Chambers and forced their way inside in spite of bands of police. 'Illegal' literature was distributed right and left. The Council had succeeded only in rousing greater anger.

The BSP's application for the St Andrew's Hall so that Maclean might deliver a lecture to the people of Glasgow on 'How to Achieve Industrial Harmony' was refused. As *The Call* remarked, 'It is not the subject they object to, but the man. Were Maclean to lecture on the composition of stellar bodies, the reply would be the same.'

Discontent with the official Labour movement and its spokesmen also swelled. When a demonstration to protest against the high price of food and other necessities was held by the Trades Council, the Labour Party and co-operative movement jointly, this discontent showed strongly. When John Wheatley, now a Baillie, tried to tell the crowd what the socialists would have done if they had had power, he was received with angry shouts. 'You're a fine socialist!' 'Too much talk, Wheatley!' 'It's the revolution we want!' And so the 'Red Clyde' was born.

36/Russian Consul

Thus the new year of 1918 was borne in on a wave of revolt stronger even than that of 1916, and with that growth in quantity had come a qualitative change.

The revolt of two years ago had been roused in the fight against high rents and a lowered standard of living, against the loss of trade union rights, and against conscription. Only a comparatively small minority had been consciously in opposition to the war and the warmakers. Now a change had taken place. Intense hardship at home and callous slaughter at the front had produced a savage discontent which was expressing itself more and more in open opposition to the war.

The government's endeavours to obtain fresh supplies for the slaughterhouse at the front by its new Manpower Bill for the conscription of young boys of eighteen, roused the Clyde to fury. Even the trade union officials passed a resolution threatening the government with a strike unless the Bill was withdrawn by the end of the month and demanding an international conference to discuss peace terms.

It was obvious that the Clyde must be pacified, and so Lloyd George sent Sir Auckland Geddes to do what the great man had failed to do in 1915, to charm the shop stewards into subjection. A meeting was arranged for 28 January. But the shop stewards, once more well-organized in the Clyde Workers' Committee, and well-primed by Maclean's Economics Classes, were in no mood for charm.

After a great deal of disturbance, Geddes was allowed to speak for half an hour. He was heard in hostile silence. Then when Arthur McManus rose, what a difference! The audience listened eagerly as he spoke. He put forward the resolution drawn up by the CWC, pledging the meeting to oppose the government's call for more men to the very utmost, pledging them to take action for an immediate armistice, and pledging them to give no further support to the carrying on of the war. When the wild cheers had died down, Jimmy Maxton rose to second the resolution. Then the whole audience marched out of the hall, formed itself into a procession, marched to George Square and held a midnight meeting of protest against the war.

The news that Maclean had been elected an Honorary President of the First All Russian Congress of Soviets, along with Lenin, Trotsky, Liebknecht, Adler and Spiridonova, was hailed with delight on the Clyde, because the workers knew that they were being honoured. Maclean had been singled out, not in the first place because of any special greatness of his own, but because he represented the most revolutionary part of the whole British Empire. Maclean himself was naturally deeply gratified.

Still another honour was conferred on him by the Bolshevik government. In recognition of his continuous efforts through the Russian Political Refugees Defence Committee, of which he was chairman, for the release of Chicherin, the Petroffs, and other imprisoned Russians, he was appointed Bolshevik Consul in Glasgow, which meant that he was the first native representative of Soviet Russia in Britain. There was, however, more hard work and trouble than honour attached to this post. It brought Maclean into further conflict with the authorities.

Early in January, Maxim Litvinov, Russian Ambassador in Britain (and himself a member of the BSP), sent instructions to Maclean:

> I am writing to the Russian Consul in Glasgow informing him of your appointment and ordering him to hand over to you the Consulate. He may refuse to do so, in which case you will open a new consulate and make it public through the press. Your position may be difficult somehow, but you will have my full support. . . . It is most important to keep me informed (and through me the Russian Soviets) of the Labour Movement in North Britain.

As expected, there was some difficulty with the existing Consulate, and it was February before Maclean was able to open the new Consulate, at 12 South Portland Street and begin his work in earnest. Russia's withdrawal from the war produced a great deal of confusion. Maclean was assailed on all sides by Russians wanting to know about military service. Eventually word was received that Russians were no longer to be recruited and then he had to see about the release of those already called-up or in the army.

His main work, however, was in connection with the dependents of the men who had been deported the previous autumn to serve in the Russian Army. There had been large colonies of Russian and Lithuanian miners in the Lanarkshire coalfields, and now there were hundreds of women and children left destitute except for the pitifully small provision made for them by the government.

He was working under great difficulties, for he had not even enough money for the expenses of running the Consulate. There was difficulty in transferring money from Russia, partly because of the abnormal relations existing between the two countries and partly because of the nationalization of the banks in Russia. Kamenev had been sent as a courier to Litvinov, but he had been detained at Aberdeen and deprived of a £5,000 cheque intended for the maintenance of both the Glasgow Consulate and the London Embassy. In the meantime Maclean had to do what he could.

He appealed to all working-class organizations to support him, as his only hope of continuing the work of helping Russians in Scotland, emphasizing:

> The fact that the Central Powers and the Allies are at present united in the attempt to crush the Russian Revolution ought to suffice to spur on all class-conscious international workers to stand by our Russian comrades in this their darkest hour.

He organized the International Women's Protection League, with himself as honorary treasurer, in an endeavour to raise funds for the relief of the Russian women and children. As he said during his 1918 trial a few months hence:

> the British Government had sent Russian subjects back to Russia to fight, and had given their wives 12/6 per week and 2/6 for each child. Now, when I was functioning as Russian Consul, two deputations of Russian women came to me and they told me sorrowful tales of depression, disease and death. . . .
> The children ought not to suffer because their fathers have been taken, but those children suffered. There is not a Lithuanian family in the West of Scotland but has trouble today as a consequence of the starving of these people.

Difficulties faced him everywhere. The authorities refused to accept his signature on official documents, as his appointment had not been officially endorsed. Litvinov wrote to the Home Office early in February, but it was fully a month before he was told that 'HM Government cannot admit the right of the present authorities at Petrograd to appoint Consuls'. The government was showing itself to be unmistakably the avowed enemy of the Bolshevik government.

By the middle of March the money difficulty was partly overcome, as a cheque for £50 arrived from Litvinov, but more troubles cropped up. Relations between himself and Litvinov had been perfectly smooth until the middle of March. After that, Litvinov would write to Maclean asking for urgent information, and would receive no reply; Maclean in turn would write to Litvinov, and *he* would receive no reply. Then the mystery was solved. One day Litvinov received a batch of letters from the Returned Letters Branch of the Glasgow Post Office, each marked 'Consul not recognized by HM Government', in spite of the fact that each envelope bore Maclean's full name and address. That was an insult which Maclean could not brook. Straightaway he wrote a fiery letter to the Head Postmaster, who must have been thoroughly intimidated by this communication from the most notorious man in Glasgow, for thereafter all went smoothly.

As soon as this was settled there was another disturbance. On the afternoon of 22 March, two detectives raided the Consulate and arrested Louis Shammes, Maclean's secretary. He was taken to the Southern Police Station, where an order from Sir George Cave for his deportation to Russia was read out, and from there he was removed to Barlinnie Jail to await deportation. As a result, Maclean had not only to suffer the inconvenience of being deprived of an assistant who could speak and write Russian, but, as Shammes had been deported solely because of his revolutionary activity and his work in connection with the Consulate, the responsibility of maintaining his wife and children now lay with him.

The Petroffs and Chicherin had been deported to Russia early in January, much to Maclean's relief.

Maclean's greatest work for Russia, however, did not lie in the Consulate.

37/Crisis

Ever since the great news of the Bolshevik Revolution had reached the Clyde, Maclean had been carrying on an agitational campaign which surpassed anything he had done before. He knew that the British ruling class would unite wholeheartedly with the German ruling class to crush their common enemy, the Russian workers and peasants. There was only one thing to do now. The workers in every country must develop revolutions inside their own countries. Even where the revolutionary movement was so small and weak, as in Britain, that there was little hope of a successful revolution as yet, so much trouble must be created that the government dare not interfere in Russia.

So he set to work with feverish intensity to carry the message of the Russian Revolution to every working-class centre in Scotland. Wherever workers gathered, at the street corners, at the pit-heads, at the factory gates, even at football parks, he was there, and wherever he went he lit fires of revolt. According to Gallacher:

> The work done by Maclean during this winter of 1917-18 has never been equalled by anyone. His educational work would have been sufficient for half a dozen ordinary men, but on top of this, he was carrying on a truly terrific propaganda and agitational campaign. Every minute of his time was devoted to the revolutionary struggle, every ounce of his extraordinary energy was thrown into the fight.

It is unfortunate that no record of his speeches has been kept, but one thing above all he taught at this period. The workers must have faith in themselves. They must trust none of the Labour leaders, not even the best of them, for all idols, without exception, had feet of clay. They were to trust themselves and go forward in boldness and confidence. He knew they all wanted peace. The resolutions passed by the trade union officials and by the Geddes meeting were proof of that. But they must be prepared to fight for it. Striking alone was useless, because they would be starved back to work again. The government had already held up supplies in order to get food rationing passed and would do it again.

Under the abnormal conditions of the war the British government had thrown aside constitutional methods, and what was good enough for the government was good enough for the workers. Under similar circumstances in Russia, Soviets had been forced into existence, and similar organs would have to be evolved in this country. Of one thing, however, he was completely convinced. If the workers were going to take action for peace, they must also go out for revolution. They must take matters into their own hands, and take the land and means of production.

If they did down tools, they must first see to it that they did not go hungry. There was plenty of food in stores in Glasgow, and the farmers had food stored up in their farms. They had been making huge profits out of the food scarcity, whilst refusing to give their farm labourers a minimum wage of twenty-five to thirty shillings a week. If they refused to give the workers food, the farms and foodstores should be seized. Workers' Committees should be set up, and the City Chambers, the Post Offices, the banks and the newspaper offices should be seized. That was the kind of action that was necessary, but the workers would have to work out their own plans.

At this period, he began to devote a great deal of his time to the Gorbals division of Glasgow, for ever since his release from prison he had made up his mind that he was going to oppose the Rt Hon George Barnes, the only 'Labour' MP in Glasgow, at the next General Election. On 19 March he was formally adopted by the Gorbals constituency Labour Representation Committee as official Labour candidate, George Barnes having been disowned by the Labour Party because he continued to remain in the Cabinet in opposition to party policy. The BSP now being affiliated to the Labour Party, Maclean was officially a member of the Labour Party.

In Lanark and Fife the soil had been well prepared for his revolutionary propaganda by MacDougall. By this time over twenty collieries had affiliated to the Lanarkshire Miners' Reform Committee, and the formation of a Reform Committee in Fife was on the cards. The miners flocked in their thousands to hear MacDougall. Such was his influence that even Smillie was displeased about 'politicians interfering in the Miners' Movement'. In Fife Maclean spoke to large and attentive audiences.

The munition workers were being disturbed at this time by the 'ca' canny' question. In 1915 Davy Kirkwood had told the authorities that the Parkhead Forge workers were prepared to give a greater output of munitions and to accept dilution if they were given some control over their working conditions. Now he was boasting about the record output of the Parkhead workers, although they were still without any control over conditions. As he spoke at the work-gates, Maclean was beseiged with questions from angry and perplexed men wanting to know if that was consistent with the position of the working class.

Maclean was completely disgusted with Kirkwood. The business of the workers now should be to get right back to normal, to ca' canny so far as the general output was concerned. At the commencement of the war when the workers were asked to toil harder, they had been assured that when the war was over conditions would come back to normal. He had told them then that this would never happen, that circumstances would make such a return impossible. Now they had ample evidence to support his contention. The workers were being asked to toil harder and

F

harder. They were speeded up again and again and never allowed
to go back. They would have to work still harder after the war,
because there was going to be a 'war after the war', the economic
war that caused the present bloodshed.

This was the theme of a pamphlet called *The War after the
War in the Light of Working-Class Economics* which Maclean
wrote as 'Glasgow Economics Class Pamphlet No 1'.

This pamphlet is important, because it is the only available
record of his method of teaching economics. It gives only a
glimpse of the very basic principles, but it is sufficient to show his
ability to relate theory to all that was happening in the world at
the time.

He began by tracing the economic causes of the war, and
went on to claim that it was the growing knowledge of Marxian
economics which had enabled the workers to see through the 'Free
Trade' and other panaceas of the Liberals.

He pointed out that the government was also aware of its
importance:

> The Commissioners on Industrial Unrest have attributed the
> determination of the South Wales miners to their knowledge and
> teaching of Marxian Economics . . . They consequently have urged
> the establishment of WEA classes in South Wales as a counter-
> agent. A like attempt is being fostered in Scotland, but **in the
> Clyde area this has so far been a miserable failure owing to
> Marxism having too deep roots.** (My emphasis.)

He also warned his readers about the government's attempts
to:

> sidetrack the Revolutionary Shop Stewards' Movement by applying
> the suggestions of the Whitley Report to the establishment of
> Industrial Councils, Industrial Parliaments or Industrial Guilds,
> the main object being continuity of work or avoidance of strikes,
> increased output, with a show of partial shop control over trifling,
> though irritating, details, that nowise endangers the capitalist struc-
> ture of society. . . . The 'harmony' in theory means that for the
> complete abandonment of all trade union restrictions and taking
> an interest in the industry the masters may reduce hours and
> increase real, as well as money, wages. In other words, the govern-
> ment intends to use the Workshop Movement in the interests of
> the capitalist class.

His subsequent analysis of the basic facts of capitalist production included chapters on 'The Pilgrim Starts' (Selling Price),
the problem of value, labour and value, normal price, proofs of the
labour-time theory of value, the value of labour-power, and surplus

value. Perhaps the most significant paragraph was that which showed clearly the difference between labour and labour-power, one of the essential differences between Marxist theory and that of Adam Smith:

> The Labour-time theory of value applies to the worker's commodity, his Labour-power. Note carefully that the worker does not sell his Labour, but his ability, force, or power to labour—his Labour-power. To understand the difference let us take the case of the watch. The wound-up mainspring has a stored-up energy or power. This we may compare to Labour-power. The mainspring keeps the wheels and hands of the watch in motion; the energy stored up in the spring is being used up in keeping the mechanism in motion. This motion we may compare to Labour. The capitalist class is conscious that it purchases Labour-power, and not Labour, although its defenders in public would have the workers imagine it pays for every hour of labour worked or every commodity created.

He gave a variety of concrete proofs of the labour-time theory of value. He gave examples of the ways in which 'efficiency' or productive capacity was increased by cutting the time taken to do a job:

> Scientific Management (Taylorism)—the application of which brought on the great Sydney railway strike in the autumn of 1917— is . . . the resort to any and every expedient to increase output, or, to put it another way, to reduce the time taken to do a piece of work or turn out the completed commodity.

He gave many other examples of methods used to reduce labour-time—individual piecework, collective piecework, departmental contract, premium bonus, and profit-sharing systems:

> To make a higher wage than under the time system the worker toils harder under all these others; his 'efficiency' is increased. The piece rate or the time allowed may be broken, and under the profit-sharing system the books can be manipulated so as to show decreased profits or the capital may be watered to absorb more of the rate of profit on capital, in order to still further speed-up the output in a lower outlay in wages. It is the donkey and the carrot comedy applied to Mr Henry Dubb, the highly respectable working-man found everywhere. In *The Efficiency Magazine* for October 1917, the docile Henry is not even compared with the donkey, but with the cow. 'If cows can be developed so as to give three times as much milk, is it not possible to train employees so that the output will be multiplied by three?' But the artful writer, knowing his Henry, suggests to his fellow-capitalists to write these words over the doors of their shops and factories:

> Every man who enters here
> Must earn 'high wages' every year.

He pointed out, of course, that increased efficiency did not wholly depend on the 'human cows',

> but on increased sub-division of labour, the use of better machinery, applied science, use of waste material, trustification, improved office and business methods, etc. By their superiority in this respect the Americans could in 1909 turn out about three times as much per worker as we here in Britain . . . In the assembling of motor parts to form the completed motor-car the Ford Company fixes the chassis on a travelling platform, and in its journey of 3½ hours a succession of fitters put on and screw up the various parts needed to finish the car. The cinematograph film has been called into the service of the capitalists to enable them to analyse the workers' motions as an aid to the extremest possible division of labour.

He went on to anticipate automation:

> Along with division of labour goes adaptation of tools and specialized automatic machines. One feature of the revolution inside the munition factories is the introduction of American single purpose automatic machines enabling unskilled male and female labour to turn out twice or thrice as much as was formerly done by skilled artisans. . . . That there is no finality to the application of science or the invention of labour-saving machinery and appliances is now so well recognized by the capitalists that we find their Government organizing research and experimental departments, preparing for improved technical training of apprentices and journeymen. . . . The Government is also urging trustification of industries, as this unification is a prerequisite of improved output in every way. Its appeal is: 'Capitalists of the Empire, unite! You have nothing but a world to win!'

He concluded this section with an anticipation of the 'Welfare State:

> Some capitalists have found out, eg, Cadbury, Rowntree, and Lord Leverhulme, that a certain standard of comfort above the animal level increases efficiency, and is therefore advantageous to them. These are urging their class to adopt the policy of 'enlightened capitalism' to save capitalism from the establishment of a Socialist Republic.

In the final part of the pamphlet, he pointed out:

> The increased output of commodities, and especially of that part called capital, will necessitate larger markets abroad, and hence a

larger empire. The same will apply to other capitalist countries. This must develop a more intense economic war than led up to the present war, and so precipitate the world into a bloodier business than we are steeped in just now. The temporary advantage the workers may get in shorter hours and higher wages with higher purchasing power will then be swept away in the destruction of millions of good lives, and fabulous masses of wealth.

We see preparations for this economic war, this war after the war, in the establishment by the Government of a Commercial Intelligence Department, partly connected with the Board of Trade, and partly with the Foreign Office, which shall work hand in hand with the growing industrial trusts for the monopoly of markets outside the Empire. Every other capitalist country is doing the same, **especially the United States, which has now definitely passed from being a borrowing to being a lending country.** (My emphasis.)

During that winter of 1917–18, the Labour College Committee managed to organize seventeen classes in various districts, attended by about 1,500 students, and a further Conference was held on 16 March, attended by 417 delegates representing 271 organizations. A Constitution and curriculum were agreed on, and an Executive Committee and officials elected. John McLure (ILP) was appointed chairman, William Leonard (later a Co-operative MP) appointed secretary and F Rafther appointed treasurer. Maclean and J Thomson of the SLP were appointed tutors. Only Maclean and Leonard were to be paid for their work.

At the beginning of April, Maclean was invited down to speak by the members of the ILP at Durham and there he spent a week among the miners helping the Plebs League and the Central Labour College to organize classes throughout the district. It was significant of the change in public opinion that only a few months previously some anti-war socialists had asked the ILP to bring him down to speak and had been categorically refused. Now he spoke in every town and village, and as one of the local men said, set the whole place on fire.

He was asked to lecture at Chopwell Miners' Institute. The Institute was running a course of twelve lectures, and several very mild ones had been delivered. The local Catholic priest was inveigled into taking the chair for Maclean, the title of whose lecture was innocuous enough: 'Efficiency and Harmony'. The priest introduced Maclean with several polite remarks, and then the fun began. Without any introduction, Maclean plunged straight away into a panegyric of the Russian Revolution, and lashed out bitterly against the war. The priest sat dumbfounded while Maclean carried the whole excited audience with him.

The next day a huge crowd gathered to hear him at Annfield Plain. Knowing his record, they had come mainly out of curiosity about this notorious Bolshevik, but they stayed to listen. He spoke for two hours without an interruption.

After that his reputation spread like wildfire over the whole district, and wherever he went huge crowds assembled to give him an enthusiastic reception. He insisted on speaking even in Consett, where, until that time, a pacifist or ILP meeting had been a sheer impossibility. Maclean was the only socialist speaker who was not chased from Consett during the war.

The same change was taking place all over the country, with the Clyde leading the way. The situation was once more becoming dangerous to the fulfilment of the government's plans. Although now since the entry of America into the war, there was no danger of Germany winning, the Allies were determined to crush her so that she would never rise again to threaten British profits. But there was a large body of people in the country, whose numbers were increasing daily, who were growing more and more determined that the war should cease immediately. This rising tide of struggle must be stemmed. The Clyde was the danger spot, and John Maclean was the centre of the Clyde movement, so he must be crushed.

Maclean had just returned from his successful campaign in Durham. On the forenoon of 15 April, two detectives arrived at the Consulate, and carried him off to jail. He was charged with sedition, his trial fixed for 9 May at Edinburgh and he was refused bail.

38/'I object to the whole of them!'

While Maclean lay in Duke Street Prison awaiting his trial, Glasgow witnessed the most magnificent demonstration of working-class solidarity in its history.

For years socialists had urged that the Labour movement

should assert its independence by holding its May Day demonstration, not on the first Sunday of May to suit capitalist interests, but on the first day of May. It had been a pious wish until recently, for the Labour movement had been so small and weak that wholesale victimization would have been the only result of such a stand. Now, however, the situation was entirely different. The dwarf of pre-war years had grown into a giant, and was placed by the war in a position of economic power which might never again be equalled inside capitalism. If it failed to assert itself now, in these circumstances, there was little hope for its successful future.

Before his arrest, Maclean had been trying to rouse the movement round his call for a militant 1 May demonstration. This was their chance. Let them rally together, let them leave their factories and workshops empty, and make the demonstration a one-day strike for peace. Let them all come out on the streets, and strike the first blow for the revolution. The May Day Committee's decision to hold the demonstration for the first time on Wednesday, 1 May was received throughout the Clyde with triumphant jubilation.

The Tory press for weeks before strained every nerve to make it a failure. Every trick was used. They spoke of disloyalty to comrades in France, they threatened wholesale dismissal for the participants, they offered to see that those who did not respond to the May Day call were not combed out for military service. For years the capitalist press had sneered at the May Day demonstration, hoping to ridicule it out of existence. Now they pleaded that if only the workers would hold it on a Sunday, everybody would welcome it!

When their wiles did not succeed, they demanded its suppression, but it was obvious from the beginning that all their efforts were going to be futile. The workers had made up their minds; they were going to respond. To ban it would make no difference. 250 organizations, including sections and branches of the various bodies, decided to take part, and the Scottish Co-operative Society decided to give all its employees the day off with pay. But the capitalists had already done the one thing necessary to prevent real trouble and that was to see that John Maclean was safely behind lock and key.

When the great day dawned, the most sanguine hopes were justified. One hundred thousand Glasgow workers took the day off work to march in the procession, and thousands more lined the streets to cheer the demonstrators as they passed by. Glasgow was on fire with red banners, red ribbons, and red rosettes. The air was alive with the sound of revolutionary songs, and with the blare of bands. Socialist literature was showered everywhere, and eagerly purchased on all sides. On Glasgow Green orators spoke from twenty-two different platforms and every platform commanded a crowd. Sectarian bitterness was forgotten. There was plenty of friendly criticism but the common struggle united all in bonds of real solidarity.

This great celebration finished up with a huge crowd marching to Duke Street Prison. Three times a tremendous shout arose from thousands of lusty throats. 'John Maclean! John Maclean! John Maclean!' They hoped he would hear, and so capture some of the spirit that would have thrilled him so much. Special forces were organized on the prison side of the gates lest the crowd should attempt to force them.

This great demonstration was an inspiring prelude to Maclean's trial. It opened in a blaze of unprecedented publicity, and the whole socialist movement was agog with excitement. The great mass of the Clyde workers, whether they agreed totally with his 'extreme' views or not, looked to him as their champion. On the eve of the trial a band of fifty socialists set out from Glasgow to march to Edinburgh, hoping thus to draw more public attention to the infamous persecution of their comrade. For five miles of their journey they were accompanied by many hundreds of sympathizers, cheering and shouting protests. At Bargeddie, the procession was joined by miners and they all arrived in Edinburgh at 8 o'clock in the morning, making their way straight to the Court.

Long before the proceedings were due to begin the court was crowded and for the first time in the history of criminal trials in Edinburgh High Court the queue system of admission was introduced. Many who sought admission were turned away.

As he took his seat in the dock Maclean 'looked paler than usual', according to a newspaper report. And well might he be pale—not because in front of him loomed the dread prospect of prison, but because he knew that this was the greatest hour of his life. This was his great opportunity. Tomorrow millions of people all over the country would read a detailed report of the trial. Could he make the most of this great chance to transmit his message far and wide? Could he use the dock, revealed by history as the greatest propaganda platform of all time, to stir the people into consciousness that the real criminal was not the man in the dock but the hideous and bloody system represented by the man with the judge's wig?

Maclean had decided to conduct his own defence this time

and, unhampered by legal caution, raise a threatening fist in the face of authority. His very first words showed quite clearly that he was not there to defend, but to attack.

'Are you guilty or not guilty?' asked the Lord Justice-General.

'I refuse to plead!'

This reply having been taken as a plea of not guilty, His Lordship went on to remind him that he had the right to object to any member of the jury. Maclean replied like lightening:

'I object to the whole of them!'

That sentence will stand as the most powerful protest of his time against contemporary 'justice'. He objected to all the trappings of a legal system which had for its primary purpose the protection of that very system of private property-ownership which was poisoning the roots of society and driving millions of men to violent death.

The indictment, which took fully ten minutes to read, accused Maclean of addressing meetings in Glasgow, Lanarkshire and Fife between the dates of 20 January and 4 April 1918, and there making statements likely to prejudice recruiting and cause mutiny and sedition among the people. There were eleven charges in all, but in essence his main crime was his call to the workers to follow the example of their Russian comrades, go forward, and strike the first blow for revolution on 1 May.

There were 28 witnesses for the prosecution, 15 policemen, 8 special constables, 2 shorthand writers employed by the police, one newspaper reporter, one mining inspector, and one slater.

Evidence regarding meetings held in Glasgow was given by three special constables. One asserted that he heard Maclean call himself a 'Socialist Democrat'. He advocated the downing of tools and said that the socialists should break through all laws and establish their own rules and regulations; he stated that the Clyde district had helped to win the Russian revolution, and that the revolutionary spirit on the Clyde was at present ten times as strong as it was two years ago. At another meeting Maclean said that the workers should take control of the City Chambers and retain hostages, take control of the Post Office and the banks, compel the farmers to produce food and if they did not, burn the farms; he stated that this movement would have the support of French-Canadians and the workers in New York and that when it became known what the Clyde was doing, other districts would follow suit; he stated that the present House of Commons should be superseded by a Soviet and that he did not care whether it met in the usual place or in Buckingham Palace; and he advised the workers in Beardmore's munition works to 'ca' canny' and restrict their output of munitions.

The other two witnesses corroborated.

Maclean cross-examined them at considerable length, and it transpired that one had not taken a verbatim report of the speeches, but only a 'good note'. Another had taken no notes at all of the first meeting and only a 'few notes' of the second, while the third 'might have taken a word or two on a slip of paper' but went home and wrote his notes from memory. Yet, as Maclean pointed out, all three gave exactly the same evidence!

Several policemen testified that during a meeting at Shettles-ton Football Park, Maclean had said that the workers in Russia had caused a revolution and he wished to impress them that the workers here should be prepared for the same.

In the course of evidence one witness pointed out that he did not consider it wise to take notes at the meeting because of the attitude of the crowd. He went instead to the Police Office and made notes there. The other witnesses also chose the better part of valour and took 'nothing but mental notes'.

Further evidence was led regarding meetings in Fife. Maclean was accused of saying that the men of Fife should come out against the Manpower Bill as the government was simply waiting to drag more young men away to be slaughtered. An interesting point was raised by Maclean during the cross-examination of the Police Superintendent of Fife. This witness had notes supplied to him by a press reporter who was present at Maclean's meetings in the interests of the police and the press. The Superintendent admitted that he had paid little attention to what Maclean had said. Maclean protested against small portions being taken out of his speeches here and there:

> The consequences of any man's speech are always based upon what goes before. The main parts of my speech, in which my themes are developed, are omitted. I want to expose the trickery of the British government and their police and their lawyers.

One witness declared in the course of his evidence that Maclean had stated that he was quite prepared to run any risk if he thought he could bring about a social revolution in Glasgow.

Maclean Do you think it is a correct report of what I said at Hartshill to say that I talked about bringing about a social revolution in Glasgow?

Witness You did.

Maclean It seems to me a very bad slip, because a social revolution cannot be brought about in a city. It is either a slip on your part or a slip on my part.

Witness It is not a slip on my part. You spoke about seizing the Municipal Buildings in Glasgow, and it seems to me that you meant that the revolution would have its beginning in Glasgow.

Maclean There is a difference between a social revolution in Glasgow, and *beginning* a social revolution in Glasgow.

A mining inspector in the service of the Fife Coal Co gave evidence regarding a meeting at Crossgates in Fife. He considered the speech a dangerous one and made a report of it to his employers. He took no notes.

In the course of cross-examination, Maclean asked if he was not aware that in the past the land had been violently seized from the people, and did he not object to the present owners holding the land when they had got it violently?

Witness I might object to that, but it is a question of how you take it from them. For instance, in answer to a question as to how these things should be got, the question being 'Could we get these things by peaceful action?' you said, 'I am here to develop a revolution.'

Maclean Do you infer that revolution means violence?

Witness You could not have put any other construction on your words after you said that revolution here was to be on the same lines as in Russia. I understand that the Russian Revolution was a violent revolution.

Maclean It is the most peaceful revolution the world has ever seen, and it is the biggest. Don't you know that this war is the most bloody that has ever taken place, and that revolution and bloodshed do not go together?

Witness No.

Maclean You said it was a dangerous speech. Dangerous to whom? To the Fife Coal Co?

Witness I was a servant of the Fife Coal Company, and I was an official, and it was my duty to report to them.

A slater also gave evidence regarding this meeting. He took no notes, but remembered a few things said. The speech was a bit strong on revolution and was likely to unsettle the audience.

Cross-examined by Maclean, he said that the speech was likely to carry people away, especially the younger people, and was therefore unsettling.

Maclean A canny place, Fife?

Witness Yes.

Maclean I should say the last place in which a revolution would take place would be in Fife?

Witness It will take some working up for you.

Maclean Don't you think the war also has unsettled the people, that it has had an unsettling influence?

Evidence was given by a Glasgow Special Constable regarding a meeting which he attended in Glasgow on 13 March, and at which Maclean was alleged to have said that when peace was proclaimed the Army and Navy would rally to the Red Flag, and to have urged the audience to make the May Day demonstration a one-day strike for peace, to empty the workshops on that day, so that the first day of May might be the first blow for the revolution.

Maclean You were instructed not to take notes openly?

Witness Yes.

Maclean Why?

Witness I don't know. No reason was given.

Maclean You were not afraid to take notes openly?

Witness I was not afraid, but I did not think it was judicious.

Maclean You thought you would go there as a spy, and not let people know you were there?

Maclean called no witnesses, and in reply to the Lord Justice-General said he did not wish to go into the witness-box. He would reserve what he had to say until later.

The Lord Advocate addressed the jury. There was nothing in the law of the country as at present framed to prevent people getting up and talking about socialism, however inappropriate it might be, but there came a time when such discussion of social questions became seditious. They could not afford that—indeed the truth was that society could not afford that at any time. The prisoner had by a long and persistent series of violent, inflammatory, and revolutionary addresses done the best he could to create sedition and disaffection among the civilian population. He did not pretend to see into Maclean's heart, to understand the motives that had tempted him, but just because they could never know that, they must judge Maclean by what he did. It was their duty to protect themselves from men like Maclean unless they wanted to be overtaken by the same catastrophe as befell Russia.

39/Maclean stands in judgement

In an impassioned speech lasting seventy-five minutes, Maclean addressed the jury. Fifty-five years of world turmoil and upheaval have passed since then and another even more bloody world war has confirmed his darkest forebodings, but the years have added to the depth of his words. Today the 'Holy War' of 1914-18 has been stripped of its glamour. Maclean's statements and prophecies, regarded by many in 1918 as the ravings of an unbalanced fanatic, have been revealed in their historical truth.

There is not a socialist today who can fail to be moved by his efforts to unmask the real meaning of the war. There is not a socialist worthy of the name who can fail to be stirred by the revolutionary passion with which he, not as the accused but as the accuser, poured out fierce denunciations of his 'judges' and the State they represented.

The Lord Advocate had said he could not fathom his motives, he began. If they were not clean and genuine, would he have made his statements in the presence of shorthand reporters? He had simply been proceeding along the lines upon which he had proceeded for many years. For the full period of his active life he had been a teacher of economics to the working classes, and his contention had always been that capitalism was rotten to its foundations and must give place to a new society. He was out for the benefit of society, not for any individual human being, but he realized that justice and freedom could only be obtained when placed on a sound economic basis. He knew that in the reconstruction of society the class interests of those who were on top would resist the change and that the only factor that could make for a clean sweep was the working class.

In his economics classes he had pointed out for years that because of the inability of the workers to purchase the wealth they created, it was necessary to create markets abroad, and in order to have these markets it was necessary to have empire. The capitalist development of Germany since the Franco-Prussian War had forced on her also the need for empire and a clash must come between the two countries.

In one lecture which he had delivered regularly before the war, he had taken as his theme 'Thou shalt not steal! Thou shalt not kill!', and had pointed out that as a result of the robbery going on in all civilized countries they had to keep armies, but these armies must inevitably clash. In another called 'Edward the Peacemaker' he had pointed out that Edward VII's alliance with France and Russia was for the purpose of encircling Germany in preparation for the coming struggle.

He considered capitalism the most infamous, bloody and evil system that mankind had ever witnessed. He wished no harm to any human being, but he, as one man, was going to exercise his freedom of speech. 'No human being on the face of the earth', he challenged, 'no government, is going to take from me my right to speak, my right to protest against wrong, my right to do everything that is for the benefit of mankind. I AM NOT HERE, THEN, AS THE ACCUSED: I AM HERE AS THE ACCUSER OF CAPITALISM DRIPPING WITH BLOOD FROM HEAD TO FOOT.'

He poured ridicule on the self-righteous indignation displayed by the warmongers when the Germans killed women and children in this country, when not a voice was raised to protest against the deaths of women and children through terrible housing and factory conditions. The government was responsible for these deaths, just as they were responsible for the deaths of the Russian women who had been left without adequate means of life. He took this opportunity to advertise the plight of these women, in the hope that public opinion would press the government to see that they got paid at least as well as the dependants of British soldiers.

The Edinburgh press had been preparing public opinion for this trial by slanders against the Bolsheviks. The truth was that since the Bolsheviks came into power there had been fewer deaths in Russia than for the same period under any Czar for 300 years. The White Guards had been responsible for more deaths than the Soviets. Under the Bolsheviks the co-operative movement had grown more rapidly than ever before, the universities, theatres, picture houses, music halls, schools, were open day and night for the purpose of training the workers to manage the affairs of the country and to organize production. The Bolsheviks wanted peace throughout the world and had entered into negotiations with the

Germans at Brest Litovsk. A pause had been made in the negotiations to allow Great Britain and the Allies to have time to take part, but they had refused.

The Bolsheviks were accused of being in the pay of the Germans, but the truth was that while the peace meeting was being held Trotsky had been playing a very bold game. He had spread millions of leaflets amongst the German soldiers in the trenches urging them to stop fighting and to overthrow the Kaiser and the capitalist class of Germany.

Britain had been doing that same thing since the very beginning of the war. The learned gentleman for the prosecution had said that revolution inside Germany was good, but revolution inside Britain was bad. He could square it if he could. Maclean could not. The conditions of Germany, economically, were the same conditions as Britain; there was only a slight difference between the political super-structure of the two countries. And the workers were not concerned with the political super-structure, but with the economic foundation.

More serious strikes than in this country had been taking place in Germany. Soldiers and sailors had mutinied and been shot down by the German government. Revolution in Germany was near, but it would be a very bad thing for the workers of the world if a revolution were unsuccessful in Germany and no similar effort made here. The workers' enemy was the same in all countries, and if the German workers overthrew their autocratic government, it was our duty to see that they were not enslaved at the dictates of the capitalists of other parts of the world.

He was convinced that the problems of capitalism would not be solved by the war. With improved methods of speeding up, improved machinery and technique, the workers would be able to produce five times the amount of wealth that they did before the war and the problem of the disposal of surplus goods would be greater than ever. The new rush for empire had already begun. America had got hold of one or two islands in the West Indies, and had seized Dutch Guiana. She had prevented Japan getting control of North China and when Japan had been incited by the Allies to land at Vladivostok in order to crush the Bolsheviks, America began to back up the Bolsheviks because she was afraid that if Japan got half Siberian Russia it would give her strategic control of Siberia. Britain had taken the German colonies, and was taking control of Mesopotamia and Palestine. The secret treaties made public by the Bolsheviks had shown that all the nations had been making plans so that when Germany was crushed they would get this territory or that territory. 'THEY WERE ALL OUT FOR EMPIRE.'

> All the property destroyed during the war will be replaced. In the next five years there is going to be a great world trade depression and the respective Governments, to stave off trouble, must turn more and more into the markets of the world to get rid of their produce, and in fifteen years' time from the close of this war—I have pointed this out at all my meetings—we are into the next war if Capitalism lasts; we cannot escape it.

He had taken up constitutional action at this time because of the abnormal circumstances and because precedent had been given by the British government. If it was right for the government to throw aside law and order and adopt methods that mankind had never seen before, then it was equally right for members of the working class. They must take abnormal lines of action, and he urged them to follow the example of their comrades in Russia.

> The Lord Advocate pointed out here that I was probably a more dangerous enemy that you have got to face than the Germans. THE WORKING CLASS WHEN THEY RISE FOR THEIR OWN ARE MORE DANGEROUS TO CAPITALISTS THAN EVEN THE GERMAN ENEMIES AT YOUR GATES. I am glad that you have made this statement at this, the most historic trial that has ever been held in Scotland, when the working-class and the capitalist class meet face to face.

He had nothing to retract, nothing to be ashamed of. He had acted clean and square for his principles:

> I am a Socialist, and have been fighting and will fight for an absolute reconstruction of society for the benefit of all. I am proud of my conduct. I have squared my conscience with my intellect, and if everyone had done so this war would not have taken place . . .
>
> No matter what your accusations against me may be; no matter what reservations you keep at the back of your head, my appeal is to the working class. I appeal exclusively to them because they, and they only, can bring about the time when the whole world will be one brotherhood, on a sound economic foundation. That, and that alone, can be the means of bringing about a reorganization of society. That can only be obtained when the people of the world get the world and retain the world.

The jury felt no need to retire. They intimated through their foreman a verdict of guilty on all charges. The Lord Justice-

General asked Maclean if he had anything more to say, but no, he thought he had said enough for one day.

The Lord Justice-General pronounced sentence. He said the accused was obviously a highly-educated and intelligent man, who thoroughly realized the seriousness of the offences he had committed. The sentence of the court was that he be sent to penal servitude for a period of five years.

Maclean appeared somewhat taken aback by the severity of the sentence, but on being led to the cells he turned to his comrades in the gallery and cried: 'Keep it going, boys: keep it going!'

40/Glasgow fights

The press used every device, in addition to biased accounts of the trial, to alienate sympathy for Maclean. One Glasgow newspaper hoped to create the feeling that he had been dealt with leniently by suggesting that in any other country the penalty would have been death. The *Glasgow Herald* produced a special two-column article on the menace of Bolshevism in Scotland. 'Bolshevism, or to call it by its old familiar name, Anarchy, is not only a disease, it is a crime which, like other forms of morbid and unnatural offences, invariably brings a host of weak-minded and degenerate imitators in its train.'

The Glasgow workers, however, by this time had learned to think for themselves. Whether they understood or believed in all his ideas or not, he was their friend and their hero, and they were going to fight for him, all sections of the movement united, with the spirit that had made May Day a historic event.

Already protests from all sections were pouring in to Munro, the Secretary for Scotland. As a result of the use made of press reporters at the trial, the Glasgow Branch of the National Union of Journalists passed a resolution repudiating the action of any person who, as a press reporter, gained admission to any meeting and utilized his position to take notes for the purpose of providing police evidence.

All the Labour and Socialist organizations in the West of Scotland joined together to form the Clyde District Defence Committee, for the general purpose of providing protection for working-class propagandists, and for the particular purpose of providing economic support for Maclean's dependents and agitating for his release. The Executive of the British Socialist Party decided that the fight for Maclean was to be in the forefront of their struggle. Meetings and demonstrations must be held everywhere. The Glasgow District Council of the BSP decided to hold one big demonstration to Glasgow Green every month until the governmen was forced to give in.

The first demonstration was held at the beginning of June. Thousands of people, grim and determined, walked through the streets from George Square and listened eagerly at Glasgow Green to the speeches from three platforms. At a Peace Demonstration held by the Women's Peace Crusade the meeting was preceded by insistent demands for cheers for Maclean.

While the whole movement was thus united in the fight, there were still a few leaders who tried to disparage Maclean's actions. They would pander to his popularity among the masses by alluding to him as emphatically brave and sincere, but add with regret that he was too indiscreet and did not 'watch himself'— insinuating, of course, that they were just as good champions of the working class, and it was only their wisdom and caution which prevented them being in the same position as Maclean. Compared with their great hero, Ramsay MacDonald, he undoubtedly did lack the virtue of discretion. Ramsay MacDonald was so discreet that he had been able to gain a reputation as the great leader of the anti-war movement and at the same time gain a government pass to anywhere on the Western Front. The government had no illusions about who to send to Peterhead!

The rank and file, however, never swerved in their loyalty. The response to the 'Release Maclean!' call was so great that it soon became obvious that he was almost as dangerous in jail as at liberty. The authorities made known their opposition to the July demonstration, but in spite of that, a very large crowd assembled in George Square at the appointed hour. The police were out in full force. Instead of forming up four-deep in the usual manner, the crowd hung about till one tiny section strode off led by a band playing the *Red Flag*. Then they followed behind in mass, filling up the whole breadth of the street, so that the police could hardly interfere. Thinking they had called their bluff, the demonstration then formed in normal fashion until it reached Jail Square. There it was surrounded by a force of hundreds of policemen. Without any reason whatever, they drew their batons and a scene wilder than any witnessed in Glasgow for many years was enacted.

Hundreds of unarmed men and women were struck down violently. This brutality served only to fan the flames of anger, and thousands broke through the police barriers and crowded round the platforms on the Green. Next day the men went back to their work-shops and factories more determined than ever before to fight injustice.

The following month's demonstration passed off without a murmur. Apparently the authorities had realized the folly of repressive measures.

In October, the Election Conference of the Gorbals Labour Party was held, and, in spite of the fact that the National Executive had asked the local party to put forward Barnes once more, Maclean was adopted by an overwhelming majority. The local executive visited Party Headquarters in London in the hope of persuading them to change their minds, for by this time they had no excuse whatever for refusing to accept Maclean. Barnes was no longer a member of the party, as he had refused to accept the decision of the Party Conference that members must give up their government positions. Nevertheless the national executive would not have Maclean. '*Anyone* but Maclean!' was the appeal. But the local party was determined.

During this period the fight for his release had been going on fast and furious, but there had been no great anxiety about his suffering any serious damage to his health. The government, daunted by Maclean's defiance at his trial, had tried to soften the harshness of the sentence by allowing him unprecedented privileges. It had been agreed that his meals should be prepared by friends outside the prison, he had been allowed to see friends once a week and granted his own books to read. Thus it was felt that the strain of penal servitude would be somewhat lessened.

On 22 October my mother paid her visit to Peterhead. To her shocked dismay she found her husband thin and haggard, his hair pure white, and with the look of a man going through torture. In the presence of a warder and the prison doctor. Maclean told her that he had found the food from outside unsatisfactory and had refused to take the prison food. He had requested to be transferred to Glasgow where food prepared by his wife could be handed to him. As he had declared at his trial, he suspected that his food was drugged during his last imprisonment,* and had declared then that he would take no prison food. This request being refused, he had

---

* He maintained that not only himself, but all the prisoners were drugged.

therefore gone on a hunger-strike. He had tried to resist being forcibly fed, but two warders had held him down and had never left him day or night till he had been forced to give in.

Mother was distracted with grief and anger. She immediately wrote to E C Fairchild:

> I was up seeing John at Peterhead yesterday. I have repeatedly asked for a visit and have always been refused, so in desperation I asked for the visit due to me in November, and it was granted.
>
> Well, John has been on hunger strike since July. He resisted the forcible feeding for a good while, but submitted to the inevitable. Now he is being fed by a stomach tube twice daily. He has aged very much and has the look of a man who is going through torture. The Doctor all along has told me he is in good health, also the Prison Commissioners, and I knew nothing about the forcible feeding until John told me in the presence of the doctor and two warders. Now, Ex-Inspector Syme told me at the beginning of John's imprisonment that I need not worry about the fear of his going on hunger strike, as they dare not start forcible feeding without letting the relatives know.
>
> Seemingly anything is law in regard to John. I hope you will make the atrocity public. We must get him out of their clutches. It is nothing but slow murder. I feel very bitter at the way I have been treated. It was a terrible shock I received yesterday.
>
> I see the premises have been raided and Lenin's pamphlet taken away, so you will be having enough worry.

Her letter was published in all the socialist papers, and pressure by the Labour Party on the Cabinet was doubled. The Glasgow Trades Council begged George Barnes to perform an act of political generosity and use his undoubted influence to get his rival released. Barnes replied that he had done all he could to make things easier for him, but flatly refused to raise a finger for his release as long as the war lasted.

In parliament, the Home Secretary denied my mother's allegations. In reply to a question he said that Maclean had been artificially fed twice a day since July, but that no application of force had been required on any occasion. Maclean's condition was reported to be satisfactory.

Mr King In view of the fact that he is a probable candidate in the next General Election, and that the question of his nervous condition was evaded by the Rt Hon Gentleman, is there any intention of releasing this man, who is regarded in Glasgow as a sort of Martyr?

Mr Munro I cannot accept the last part of the question as correct, and I can see no reason at present why he should be released.

Mr King Does the Rt Hon Gentleman actually mean to say that there are not thousands of men in Scotland who regard this man as a hero and a martyr?

Mr Munro I am not aware of it.

It was not surprising that after this performance Munro decided, unlike Maclean, that discretion was the better part of valour and failed to keep an appointment to speak in St Andrew's Hall. A large audience waited for him in vain, but when a proposal was made that Maclean's supporters should leave the meeting, only a few hundred remained. The remainder formed themselves into a procession many thousand strong, marched to the Municipal Buildings, and held a rousing 'Release Maclean' meeting outside.

Letters of encouragement and sympathy poured in to our home from all over the country. 'At least our children have fathers they can be proud of', wrote Ivy Litvinov to mother. From Russia, Louis Shammes wrote:

> The whole of Russia is with you and your children and John! . . . Tell John I will fight for his liberation as he fought for Peter's and mine. Long live the Revolution!

The call 'Release John Maclean!' was never silent. Every week the socialist papers kept up the barrage and reminded their readers that in Germany Karl Liebknecht was already free, while in 'democratic' Britain John Maclean was lying in a prison cell being forcibly fed twice a day by an indiarubber tube forced down his gullet or up his nose. 'Is the Scottish Office', asked *Forward*, 'to be stained with a crime in some respects even more horrible and revolting, more callous and cruel, than that which the Governors of Ireland perpetrated on the shattered body of James Connolly?'

Meanwhile great events which must have rejoiced his heart were taking place in the outside world. The German fleet had mutinied at the end of October, and by 6 November its bases at Kiel, Cuxhaven and Bremen, were in the hands of elected Workers, Sailors and Soldiers Councils (Soviets). By 8 November revolution had triumphed all over Germany, and a German Republic was proclaimed next day. The British government was in a state of terror. John Maclean's statement at his trial, 'The working-class, when they rise for their own, are more dangerous to capitalists than even the German enemies at your gates', no longer seemed far-fetched.

Field-Marshal Sir Henry Wilson, describing in his memoirs the Cabinet Meeting of 10 November, wrote, 'Lloyd George read two wires from Tiger describing Foch's interview with the Boches, and Tiger is afraid Germany will break up and Bolshevism become rampant. Lloyd George asked me if I wanted this, or would rather have an armistice. I unhesitatingly said "armistice". All the Cabinet agreed. Our real danger now is not the Boches but Bolshevism.' The armistice was signed on 11 November.

The whole country went mad with joy—but Maclean still lay in Peterhead. Preparations for a General Election were now in full swing, and Willie Gallacher was chosen as deputy candidate for Maclean in the Gorbals. E C Fairchild and George Ebury, the national organizer of the British Socialist Party, came up from London to give their support.

The BSP was now concentrating all its forces on the agitation for Maclean's release. Demonstrations were being held all over the country. When the red banners with the slogans 'Hands off Russia!' and 'Release Maclean', were unfurled at one huge Albert Hall demonstration in London, the audience went wild with enthusiastic approval. A resolution demanding Maclean's release was passed unanimously at the special Labour Party Conference held to deal with the approaching General Election. Ten thousand people demonstrated for his release in Finsbury Park.

At last the government was forced to give in, and on 16 November mother received the joyful news that her husband was to be released soon. He wrote instructing her not to tell anyone else, as his strongest desire was to get home without one single person waiting for him at the station except herself. The very last thing he wanted was a demonstration to welcome him back, as he did not feel able to cope with it.

However, good news cannot be kept secret and by the time he was freed on 3 December, all Glasgow knew and was prepared.

41/Freedom of the city

On 3 December 1918, thousands of Glasgow men took 'French leave', and came out on the streets to welcome Maclean home in proper style. Two hours prior to the arrival of the train from Aberdeen, a huge crowd gathered in George Square and a procession thousands strong was formed. 'With light step and triumph in their voices', as was reported in *The Call*, the demon-strators made their way through the principal streets to Buchanan Street Station. The crowd swelled until traffic was almost at a standstill, and as 'Caledun' the Scottish reporter of *The Call* described:

> The whole city appeared to be on tiptoe for John's arrival. Every-body was expectant, and when the carriage with Maclean, his wife, Mrs Montefiore, and friends appeared, from thousands of fervent throats there went up the shout Hurrah! Hurrah! Hurrah! immediately followed by a vigorous rendering of the *Red Flag*.
>
> I do not believe the extraordinary and deeply moving spectacle of that evening will be easily effaced from the memory of those who witnessed it. The slowly moving carriage being dragged through the thronged streets by a score of muscular workers who had taken the place of the horses, the surging, exultant mass of people, the incessant cheering and singing, the 'icebound' traffic, and, standing upright in the carriage supported by friends, was the challenging figure of John Maclean waving a large red banner with an air of triumph and defiance. It was truly a triumphant entry. Maclean was granted the freedom of the city in a far more real sense than was Lloyd George when, behind a guard of bayonets, he received the burgess ticket at the hands of the Lord Provost.

Mrs Montefiore, the famous suffragette, recorded that on one occasion when the procession was halted for a minute in Jamaica Street, Maclean called for three hearty cheers for the German Socialist Revolution, and remarked that the shouts that rent the air were bound to haunt the capitalists of the Clyde for many days to come. She reported:

> For the best part of an hour, just when the trams were busiest taking back to their homes the daily loads of shoppers, those trams which were leaving the city had to travel, till the river was crossed, at the rate of John Maclean's triumphal, red-flag proces-sion, for his supporters, in disciplined, orderly ranks, spread across one half of the street; while from the trams going towards the city peeped timidly or with scared faces those who for the first time had seen flaunted to the four winds the emblem which now waves over the public buildings of Petrograd, Moscow, and Berlin.

The springs of the carriage collapsed, and the procession had to halt when Carlton Place was reached. Short speeches were made, but Maclean himself was unable to say a word. His throat was again badly affected, and was to give him trouble until the end of his life.

He was plunged straight into the middle of the election

campaign, but such was his state of health that he was able to do very little. He himself saw no need to make any public appearances at all. As he said, everything had been done for him. He had been selected while in prison. His election address had been written and circulated, and everything else necessary done, under the capable guidance of Willie Gallacher. But he was prevailed on to speak on the eve of the poll, just one week after his release.

Even before his release, the Gorbals campaign had stimulated intense interest. The fight between a convict and a Cabinet Minister of the government which had imprisoned him had a unique dramatic quality.

The election was very cleverly conducted by the government. The people were in the first flush of victory, the soldiers had not yet returned from the front and the sordid aftermath of the war was not yet evident. The bitterness caused by years of suffering was skilfully turned by demagogues and by the press into hatred, not of the warmakers, but against the 'Huns'. 'Hang the Kaiser!' was the slogan of the day. 'Make the Germans pay!' was the spirit expressed everywhere. 'The Kaiser has been mentioned', said George Barnes. 'I am for hanging the Kaiser.'

The Scottish press fully agreed with the socialist movement that Glasgow was to be the 'cock-pit' of the election, and most of the newspapers declared that the Gorbals contest was undoubtedly the chief centre of interest. That meant that all the big artillery of the government would be trained on that reputed stronghold of Bolshevism.

On the night before the poll, the hall was packed with people anxious to hear what the notorious Bolshevik had to say, and vast crowds waited outside, unable to get in. Maclean received a tremendous ovation, but it was obvious that he had not recovered his health. Nevertheless, all the old revolutionary fervour was there, and he advocated a straight revolutionary programme, refusing to modify his opinions to catch votes as others were doing. He told them that the election was important because great issues were at stake. On the composition of the next House of Commons the fate of the new socialist republics now struggling for freedom would to a great extent depend. A strong socialist representation could easily put an end to the capitalist endeavours to strangle socialism in Russia, Germany and elsewhere. Nevertheless, he assured them, if they failed, they must not be downhearted. The real British crisis was coming, and the struggle would not take place in parliament. They must slacken no effort after the election was over.

Still anxious to help others, as they had helped him, he took the opportunity to draw the attention of his audience to he victimization of socialists everywhere. He read out a letter he had sent to Woodrow Wilson, the American President, who was then in Europe conducting negotiations for a 'democratic' peace:

> I wish you to prove your sincerity by releasing Tom Mooney, Eugene Debs, William Haywood and all others at present in prison as a consequence of their fight for 'working-class democracy' since the United States participated in the war.

He got the audience to agree to protest against the victimization of James Leiper, an Inland Revenue Officer in South Lanarkshire, because of his active support for socialism in and around the town of Lanark. He also asked them to protest against the continued imprisonment in Peterhead of two Sinn Feiners, Joe Robinson and Barney Freel.

The result of the election was a foregone conclusion. The people had been stampeded. Out of 706 seats Labour gained only 59, and all the anti-war candidates were wiped out with the exception of Neil MacLean in Govan. There were some inspiring results, however. On a clear-cut, uncompromising, revolutionary programme, Maclean polled 7,436 votes as against 14,247 for Barnes. On the whole the results of the election showed the tremendous progress made since the last election in 1910, in spite of the unfavourable circumstances. Then the Labour vote had been 506,020. Now it was 2,482,566: but even this was no real reflection of the great change in the climate of opinion since 1910.

It was a different matter in Ireland, however. Sinn Fein, which was now a separatist, Republican Party, having declared its allegiance to the Irish Republic of the Easter Rising at the end of 1917, won 73 of the 105 Irish seats. The irony of the situation was that the majority of the new Sinn Fein MPs were in British jails!

42/Revolution in the air

The end of the war ushered in a new era in world politics, described by Maclean as 'the class war on an international basis'. The Bolshevik Revolution had made such an impact, especially in the defeated countries, that it had without doubt contributed largely to the revolution in Germany and to the Armistice.

In Britain, although the Armistice had been signed on 11 November, the government was at first reluctant to proceed with any large-scale demobilization. The occupation of the Rhine, intervention in Russia, repression in Ireland and in other parts of the vast British Empire, demanded military power far in excess of anything the regular army could provide. Moreover, the technical revolution in industry, described by Maclean in his Labour College pamphlet *The War after the War*, meant that one man could now do the work of three prior to the war. This in itself ensured increasing unemployment. In addition the dismantling of the munition works meant that many of the ex-munition workers found themselves without employment. The authorities therefore dreaded a mass influx of ex-servicemen, all expecting to be re-instated in their old jobs.

Nevertheless, widespread discontent and actual rebellion forced the government's hand. During the first week of January, 10,000 soldiers mutinied at Folkestone and refused to return to France when ordered. 4,000 soldiers at Dover demonstrated in support. Sympathetic demonstrations also took place in France. During the same week, 1,500 Royal Army Service Corps men from Osterley Park seized lorries, drove to London and demonstrated at Whitehall, and similar acts of mutiny were reported from far and wide. On 13 January sailors at Milford Haven ran up the red flag declaring that half the navy were on strike and that the other half soon would be. The government was therefore unable to delay any longer and had to proceed with demobilization on a large scale, even though it was evident that the authorities could not cope with all the re-organization necessary.

This was the situation at the beginning of 1919 and it was therefore quite impossible for a dedicated revolutionary like Maclean to retire from the struggle and take the rest he so badly needed after his ordeal at Peterhead. He saw only too clearly that if this opportunity were missed, it might not come again for a very long time, and it was obvious now that he was the dynamo, as Walter Kendall put it in *The Revolutionary Movement in Britain 1900-21*, that powered the revolutionary movement in Scotland. He could not afford to sit back at this stage.

After the General Election, he went to Rothesay for a short holiday. There he received a letter from the Under-Secretary for Scotland announcing that the king had been pleased to grant him a free pardon in respect of his convictions in 1916 and 1918. Maclean replied:

Would you be so kind as to inform the Secretary for Scotland that I do not accept your assertion that 'the King' has granted me a free pardon.

Not 'the King' (who should be in Holland with his cousin), but the fighting workers of Britain have regained me my freedom, and a healthy fear of those workers has induced you and your friends to try this bluff of a 'free pardon'. All the time, however, you are trying to pester my wife and myself through your detestable spies, popularly called detectives. I welcome their attentions, as it is a sign that you are foaming at the mouth at having to release me.

My immediate reply to this is a demand from the Government, through the Scottish Office, for the Hundred and Fifty Pounds (£150), the cost of recovery after my release last time and this, from your cold-blooded treatment in those infernos, Peterhead and Perth.

I made a claim last time for Seventy-six Pounds (£76) and was refused. The new demand includes that sum, and this new demand I intend to insist upon until it is met by the next Government or until the workers assume full control of the British Empire.

Needless to say, he received neither reply nor money.

His return to activity was signalled by a characteristic article in *The Call*, again protesting about the victimization of James Leiper and the continued imprisonment of the two Sinn Feiners in Peterhead. Along with this went the announcement that he would resume his Sunday afternoon class on 5 January, this time in the large St Mungo Hall, because he was expecting, he said, to get a class of over 1,000 students!

'Remember!' he concluded, 'The class is the centre of strength in all fights on the Clyde, and elsewhere. The hand, the heart, and the head, must all be brought into harmony in the glorious fight for the Socialist Republic!'

For the next five months, however, his educational work was overshadowed by the intense and feverish revolutionary campaign conducted by him, as a member of the British Socialist Party Executive and as the recognized spokesman for the Russian Revolution in Britain. His revolutionary strategy was outlined in an article in *The Call*, 'Now's the Day and Now's the Hour!':

We witness today what all Marxists naturally expected, the capitalist class of the world and their Governments joined together in a most vigorously active attempt to crush Bolshevism in Russia and Spartacism in Germany. Bolshevism, by the way, is Socialism triumphant, and Spartacism is Socialism in process of achieving triumph. This is the class war on an international basis, a Class

War that must and will be fought out to the logical conclusion—
the extinction of capitalism everywhere.

The question for us in Britain is how we must act in playing
our part in this world conflict. Some are suggesting a General
Strike to enforce a withdrawal of British troops from Russia, and,
I suppose, from Germany as well. That, to some of us on the
Clyde is too idealistic. Were the mass of the workers in Britain
Revolutionary socialists they would at once see that their material
well-being depended on the peaceful development of Bolshevism
in Russia and would, in consequence, strike for the withdrawal of
British forces, at the moment attempting the downfall of Russia's
Social Democracy. But the workers are not generally of our way
of thinking, and so are unable to see that their material interests
are bound up with Bolshevist stability in Russia. It necessarily
follows that we will have no success in urging a strike on this issue
especially, as the Government has the majority of Trade Union
leaders in the hollow of its hand, and can easily manipulate them
against us—with comparative safety to the leaders at that.

Some of us on the Clyde, therefore, think that we must adopt
another line, and that is to save Russia by developing a revolution
in Britain no later than this year. . . . The next question for us is
the start of the fight. How can we get the mass on the move and
pulled onward by the young, who wish to save their lives. We have
the opportunity at hand. **The demobilization has already created
a menacing unemployed problem. We can get the support of
the unemployed if we can suggest a means whereby they can get
a living. The only possible solution is a drastic reduction of
hours per week. This reduction will appeal to the employed if
they are assured of at least a pre-war standard of living. Here
we have the economic issue that can unify the workers in the
war against capitalism.** (My emphasis.)

Maclean looked to the miners to take the lead in a General
Strike for shorter hours. The war-time strength of the workshop
movement among the engineers and shipyard workers rested on the
urgent need for munitions. The situation had now changed radi-
cally. Because of the urgent need for coal, which was scarce, the
ball was now at the feet of the miners. Moreover, the miners were
in an extremely militant mood, determined not only to gain
improvements in conditions, but to prevent the return of the mines
to private ownership and control.

The Reform Movement in Lanarkshire had been flourishing
under MacDougall's lead, and a successful Fife Committee had
been formed. He had also toured the South Wales coalfield during
December, and helped to revive the Reform Movement there. A
minimum programme, in accordance with the lead given by

Maclean, was adopted—the six hour day, the five day week, and one pound a day.

Maclean began his agitational campaign during the second week of January by placing his services primarily at the disposal of the Reform Movement, and was recognized as one of their spokesmen. 'I am as proud of that honour as the one conferred by our Russian comrades', he wrote. He spent the week among the Lothian miners, and 'as a result of a week's mission, we have there now a powerful unofficial committee and movement. Shortly a Lancashire County Conference will be held at Bolton, when the movement will spread like wildfire'.

However, as he admitted later, history never happens as planned, and it was not the miners who started the ball rolling.

43/The forty hour strike

The Clyde Workers' Committee held a conference of shop stewards in the shipbuilding and engineering industries on 5 January. It was decided to go forward with the same demand as the miners—six hours a day, five days a week, and £1 a day. A committee which became known as the Ways and Means Committee was appointed, and it began the campaign by issuing a manifesto:

A 30-hour week means less unemployed.
Less unemployed means less hungry workers.
Less hungry workers means happier working-class families.
Happier working-class families means a healthier race.
A healthier race means working-class solidarity.
Working-class solidarity means you stand where the miners stand.

The enthusiasm on the Clyde was such that very quickly the trade union officials saw that, if they were not to lose their influence completely, they would have to take part in this upsurge. Their offer to co-operate was accepted, and on 18 January a conference of about three hundred delegates took place. This decided to call a strike in order to enforce a 40 hour week—a 40 hour week instead of the 30 hour week in order to bring in the less advanced English workers. A manifesto was drawn up and 16,000 copies sent to all the strategic industrial centres throughout Britain:

TO THE WORKERS—CALL TO ARMS!

The Joint Committee, representing the official and unofficial section of the Industrial Movement, having carefully considered the reports of the Shop Stewards and representatives of the various industries hereby resolve to

Demand a 40 hour Maximum Working Week

for all workers, as an experiment with the object of absorbing the unemployed. If a 40 hour week fails to give the desired result, a more drastic reduction of hours will be demanded.

A GENERAL STRIKE has been declared to take place on Monday, 27 January, and all workers are expected to respond.

Maclean tried to have the strike postponed for a month so that the miners could officially join in but the tremendous feeling would not be contained, and he was unsuccessful.

Maclean was not in Glasgow on 18 January. The Miners' Federation Conference was held at Southport on 14-15 January, so Maclean spent the whole week in Lancashire whipping up support for the Reform Movement and organizing unofficial committees throughout the county. He pointed out in *The Call*:

On the Clyde and amongst the miners the cry was 'all eyes on Southport'. . . . Thanks to the advance guard, the MFGB has at Southport agreed to the Six-hour Day. The Government is asked to enforce it by amending the Eight-Hours Act. My good old friend, Bob Smillie, at the Conference pointed out that we could produce enough in less than a six-hours day if we were not producing to make millionaires.

The Executive Committee has now to interview the Prime Minister and the Government, and failing satisfaction, must convene another conference. From our point of view this is all to the good. The onus for a strike is thus thrust on the Government, and will add to the fierceness of the fight when it comes off, as we know the Government will never concede the miners' demands. This will also give the Reform Movement time to expand their propaganda in the various coalfields and knit up more closely than ever. Let all miners who read this article buckle to and build up a powerful group in their own area.

It is now the business of all other Workers' Committees to accept the same programme and prepare the workers by leaflets circulated inside the workshops.

If no workers' committee exists in your town or urban area, seize the chance at the first socialist meeting to ask the fighters to remain behind and form the nucleus of a committee. Do it now; tomorrow may be too late. . . .

Once we get the mass on the move on the issue, we shall be able to take control of the country and the means of production at once, and hold them tight, through disciplined production under the workshop committees and the district and national councils.

Through the Co-operative Movement we shall be able to control the full distribution of the necessaries of life, and so win the masses over to Socialism.

All revolutions have started on seemingly trifling economic and political issues. Ours is to direct the workers to the goal by pushing forward the miners' programme and backing up our 'black brigade'.

The condition of the army, the navy, and even the police strengthens us in the fight. Capitalism is in the last ditch. Let us this year cover over this dripping monster and prepare the way for human solidarity on a sound world-wide workers' owned and controlled economic solidarity.

According to his diary, Maclean spoke at Leigh on 15 January, at Warrington on 16 January, at Liverpool under the auspices of the BSP on 17 January, and attended an Education Conference in Liverpool on 18 January. Next day, after taking his Sunday afternoon class in Glasgow as usual, he was back among the miners, this time in Lanarkshire, where he was given a great welcome at Bellshill, Hamilton, Motherwell and Shotts. Ten thousand of them had just finished an unofficial strike in defence of a mine manager, Willie Hughes, who had been victimized because of his connection with the Reform Movement. The strike was successful. Maclean reported in *The Call*:

I have had four splendid meetings in Lanarkshire, after a grand tour by Comrade Cook of South Wales (whose services other coalfields ought to obtain), and these meetings have come at the tail of a strike of 10,000 Lanarkshire miners to retain a comrade in a coal company's house. The Lanarkshire men assured me they would come out with the Clyde men and hinted that they should not return till they got the six-hour day for themselves.

On 27 January the response to the Joint Committee's Appeal exceeded all expectations. The shipbuilding yards and engineering shops were empty, and the strike spread rapidly over the industrial belt of Scotland. According to Maclean, 'Never was industrial appeal so widespread and never so quickly have the workers organized such a vast venture.'

A huge rally of strikers was held at St Andrew's Hall on 29 January, followed by a mass demonstration through the streets to the Municipal Buildings at George Square. There, a deputation consisting of David Kirkwood, Neil MacLean and a few discharged soldiers, managed to secure an interview with the Lord Provost, simply to ask that the Council should force the employers to grant the 40 hour week, and that, during the strike, the tramway system should be halted, as there were masses of strikers milling about in the streets all over the city and they feared accidents. Certainly there was nothing very revolutionary about these requests, but in the meantime some of the strikers had managed to fasten a huge red flag to the municipal flag pole, and that was enough! When the Provost telephoned London this was taken as a sign of 'red revolution', with the imminent danger of violent insurrection, and the government feared the worst. Acting under instructions, the Provost asked the strikers to return for his answer on 31 January, thus giving the government time to send up troops, machine-guns and tanks! The strike leaders rather naïvely fell into the trap, and agreed to return on Friday.

During that exciting week Maclean was again on his travels, this time to Cumberland to try to whip up support among the miners there, but finding his welcome not nearly so warm as it had been in Lanarkshire. Plans were made by the local Discharged Soldiers' Organization to disrupt his meetings, but he eventually managed to defeat them, with the aid of local supporters, and held successful meetings in Workington and Whitehaven, with the result that a Cumberland Miners' Unofficial Movement was started again.

On 29 January Maclean was the speaker at a huge meeting at Barrow-in-Furness. An old lady, Mrs Robertson, wrote to me recently telling me about this:

> The workers filled the Town Hall twice, and then he had to speak to an overflow crowd outside, and held them spellbound. It was the talk in the shipyards for months. He was such a wonderful speaker, and put things so simply that anyone could understand. . . . John was crucified that others might benefit, but the seed he sowed is showing results. . . . He was the kindest and most brilliant intellectual personality this country has ever seen . . . It is good to remember him while we live, as future generations (if any?) will despise us for not heeding him more while he was with us.

From Barrow, Maclean went back to London for an Executive Committee meeting of the BSP that Saturday, and a 'Hands off Russia' rally in Manchester on Sunday. He missed the excitement in Glasgow on Friday, 31 January, when thousands of strikers poured into George Square from all directions to hear the

Provost's answer, trustingly expecting no trouble. They were excited and exhilarated rather like the crowd at a Cup Final, and were shocked to find the Square lined with hundreds of policemen, many of them mounted. While their deputation went into the City Chambers to hear the Council's answer, the crowd waited peacefully outside listening to speeches from Gallacher and others. Suddenly the fall of a police horse seemed to be the signal for a vicious and unprovoked attack by the police, who began to move about swinging their batons in all directions. Men and women, surprised and unarmed, went down like ninepins, and the whole square was soon in an uproar.

The strikers, once they recovered their wits, fought back with all the bottled-up hatred of years, and used their fists against the police batons with considerable effect. The deputation inside the City Chambers, hearing the noise, rushed out to restore order. Kirkwood was felled to the ground by a baton and carried away unconscious. That was the fat in the fire, and the 'Battle of George Square' took a much more serious turn. The men tore up iron railings and used them as weapons. They commandeered a lorry filled with lemonade bottles, and used broken bottles. The police were actually forced out of the square. Then the Riot Act was read, the strike leaders arrested and the fighting died down. The shocked and angry strikers returned to their homes, having heard the government's answer—violence!

Next morning Glasgow was like an armed camp. Throughout the night trainloads of young English soldiers had been brought to the city—young lads of nineteen or so who had no idea of where they were, or why they were there. The authorities dare not use the Scottish soldiers billeted at Maryhill Barracks, in case they turned round and supported the strikers. The whole city bristled with tanks and machine-guns. Paul Johnson in a recent article in the *Sunday Times* shows that 'Winston Churchill regarded this as a merely tentative measure. He told the Cabinet: "By going gently at first we should get the support we want from the nation, and then troops can be used more effectively".'

From the beginning of the strike, the Joint Committee had been issuing a daily Strike Bulletin to combat the lies of the ordinary press.* A copy of the paper giving the account of 'Bloody Friday' was sent to every Trades Council in Britain. A manifesto was drawn up, and many thousands sent to all trade union and

---

*   Cabinet minutes reveal that £1,000 was spent on sending men to Scotland to work up a government case in local papers.

G

labour organizations in Britain. Delegates from the Joint Committee were sent everywhere to explain the situation. Support came from all over Scotland. Many thousands at Rosyth, Grangemouth, Leith, Edinburgh, Greenock, Coatbridge, Motherwell, Aberdeen, and Dundee, were involved. Messages began to come in from Barrow, London and other English centres (especially the ones which Maclean had visited) expressing solidarity and announcing that workers there were preparing to down tools.

Meanwhile Maclean was the chief speaker on Sunday 2 February, at a huge 'Hands off Russia' rally at Manchester. On Monday he went back to London, where meetings had been arranged by the London District Council of the BSP at Kentish Town, Poplar (where he spoke along with Harry Pollitt), Twickenham, and Walthamstow, ending up with a reception in his honour on Saturday. On Sunday he was again the main speaker at the huge 'Hands off Russia' demonstration at the Albert Hall, the other speakers being Cathal O'Shannon (the Irish TUC leader), George Lansbury, Israel Zangwill the novelist, Neil MacLean, and Lady Warwick. The Albert Hall was crowded to the door, and *The Call* reported the proceedings:

> the climax of this remarkable meeting was reached when E C Fairchild announced John Maclean. Round on round of applause greeted his rising, the whole vast gathering breaking into song. Holding up his hand for silence, Maclean plunged right into his speech. First, see that President Wilson releases Haywood, Eugene Debs and other political prisoners, then we may believe in his brand of democracy. Secondly, he said, give me a sign of approval that we may write and demand their release, and like lightning a forest of hands shot into the air. . . .
>
> In a fine peroration he maintained that armies and navies would never cease until production was socialized, and that the only way to help Russia was to abolish our system of industry and, by making the workshop the unit of industry, march towards socialism on the lines laid down by Russia.

He came back to Scotland to find the General Strike petering out. There had been a dramatic change in the situation when the Electrical Trades Union signified its intention of joining the strike. The government did not dare risk a 'black-out' in the present turbulent situation, and a new regulation under the Defence of the Realm Act was hurriedly introduced which made a strike by the ETU illegal. This was the turning point, because the official trade union movement, which had been terrified by 'Bloody Friday', and the arrests of Gallacher, Shinwell, Kirkwood and the others, used this as an excuse to draw out. Encouraged, the reactionary executive of the Amalgamated Society of Engineers suspended members of the Glasgow District Council from holding office for a year. Soon after, the secretary, Harry Hopkins, was arrested and charged along with the others (including George Ebury, the national organizer of the BSP, who had been in the forefront of the action from the first). So ended Scotland's first attempt at a General Strike, defeated, according to Maclean, 'more by the lack of working-class ripeness than batons, tanks and machine-guns'.

44/January aftermath

Looking back on that fateful January of 1919, it is obvious that several events occurred which influenced John Maclean's life in an unexpected way. The most important of them was, of course, the forty hour strike.

Although Maclean and the BSP had supported the strike wholeheartedly, he was not unduly upset about its outcome, except for the arrest of Gallacher and his other comrades, whose subsequent imprisonments did distress him greatly. The premature action of the strike leaders and their refusal to wait for the support of the members of the Triple Alliance, the miners, transport workers and railwaymen, meant that from the outset the strike had little hope of success. Its failure most certainly did not mean that Maclean's revolutionary strategy was nipped in the bud, because that was based on an analysis of post-war tendencies, whereas the strike was, in effect, the winding up of the war-time movement.

Certain aspects of the strike however, in my opinion, did eventually set him thinking along new lines. The conclusion he had reached after the dockers' strike in 1912 that: 'Fighting leads to new facts, thus to our new theory and hence to revolution. On with the fight!' might have been tailor-made for the January strike. The new fact that first manifested itself then was that the great swing to the left which had taken place in Scotland (although the election results belied this) had not taken place to the same extent in England. There was a slight indication that he was beginning to realize this in an article, 'Rumblings of the Revolution' which Maclean wrote for *The Call*, 30 January, as an exhortation to all to support the strike,

> With mutual confidence and self-reliance, then, into the fight, comrades, and make it a real revolutionary one. I know that socialists in the Scottish industrial belt can be relied upon. Are our brothers across the border going to funk it or fight as the Yorkshire miners have done, even though on a trifling issue? If the Midlands can be paralysed for a 20 minutes' meal hour, surely England ought to be paralysed for a drastic reduction of hours of labour. England, arise!

It is significant, also, that the final Strike Bulletin (12 February), had this to say:

> London Executives don't understand our aspirations here, and never take the trouble to find out what is wrong when a strike occurs. We have to emancipate ourselves from the dictatorship of the London juntas by building an organization which will be under our control and function when we want it to function.

Although this passage was in essence an expression of the traditional aspiration towards industrial democracy of the shop steward movement, there are also echoes of the nationalist sentiments and distrust of London administration politically which had been strongly manifested in every section of the Scottish Labour Movement, particularly during the last two years of the war. In 1918 the Scottish TUC passed the following resolution:

> That this Congress demands the establishment of a Scottish Parliament to deal with Scottish national affairs; the neglect of Scottish interests and the growing congestion of public business in the Imperial Parliament render it imperative that Scottish Home Rule should be inaugurated at the earliest possible moment; the problems of reconstruction peculiar to Scotland can best be dealt with by a Scottish Parliament; further, we demand that Scotland as a nation be directly represented at the Peace Conference.

The Scottish Council of the Labour Party had been passing similar resolutions every year since its formation in 1915.

When the Scottish Home Rule Association was re-constituted in 1918, its first president was William Gallacher of the Scottish Co-operative Wholesale Society (*not* the William Gallacher of the Clyde Workers' Committee, who was to be bitterly opposed to any kind of Scottish Nationalism for a considerable number of years). Its leading members belonged to the ILP—men like Tom

Johnston, editor of *Forward*, R E Muirhead, also of *Forward*, and the Rev James Barr.

One of the events referred to which also had an effect on Maclean's political thinking was the beginning of an association with the Hon Stuart Erskine of Mar (who preferred to be called Ruaraidh Erskine), the second son of the fifth Lord Erskine. According to *Scottish Nationalism* by H J Hanham:

> He was an opponent of the First World War. He backed the 1916 rising in Dublin (though in guarded language because of wartime censorship). He attacked Lloyd George as 'the Welsh Titus Oates' because of his attitude towards Ireland. And he welcomed the Russian Revolution with its declaration of universal brotherhood and support for national aspirations as warmly as any Arab nationalist.

Erskine could be called a revolutionary nationalist. Unlike the Home Rulers, he wanted complete Scottish separation, a Scottish republic, and, like James Connolly in Ireland, he wanted to see a Celtic renaissance. The following year he was to write a series of articles on 'Celtic Communism' in Maclean's *Vanguard*.

Like the Scottish TUC, he wanted separate Scottish representation at the Versailles Peace Conference, and had been collecting the signatures of important people to support this claim, in order to present a petition to President Wilson. When asked for his signature, Maclean had replied in characteristic fashion that he was in favour of a parliament or Soviet with headquarters in Glasgow, but that such an organization would not come into being 'through the negotiations of Scotsmen with the quack Peace Conference about to be held in Paris, but through the revolutionary efforts of the Scottish working class itself'. (*The Call* 9 January). In his letter to Erskine, he went on to show the futility of expecting President Wilson to do anything for Home Rule for Scotland, 'as he is the representative of brutally blatant capitalism in America, a capitalism that means to crush Mexico under its "heel of steel".' It was Lenin and the Bolsheviks, he claimed, who were the real benefactors of the Home Rule movement, but the only thanks they would appreciate would be the 'revolutionizing of Scotland by its wage-slave class'. He ended his letter by declaring:

> My life has been spent in making for this goal, and this year I mean to do more than ever for the ending of capitalism in Scotland —as elsewhere in the world—and the establishment of the socialist republic in which alone we can have Home Rule.

Another January event which had a profound effect on Maclean's future development was the setting up of a new Irish Parliament by the seventy-three Sinn Feiners elected in 1918. Peter Beresford Ellis gives the following account in his book *A History of the Irish Working Class*:

> Cathal Brugha presided over the Dail Eireann (the Irish Parliament) and a Declaration of Independence was read out in Irish and English which ratified the 1916 proclamation. An address to the Free Nations of the World was read in Irish, French and English, appealing for recognition for the new republic and aid to get a delegation accepted at the Paris Peace Conference. Then a Democratic Programme was adopted by the Dail.

> 'We declare in the words of the Irish Republican proclamation the right of the people of Ireland to the ownership of Ireland and to the unfettered control of Irish destinies to be indefeasible; and in the language of our first President Padraic Pearse, we declare that the nation's sovereignty extends not only to all men and women of the nation, but to all its material possessions; the nation's soil and all its resources, all the wealth and all the wealth-producing processes within the nation; and with him we re-affirm that all rights in private property must be subordinate to the public right and welfare.'

That was only the first paragraph of the Programme, but its radical nature is obvious. One of my clearest childhood recollections is a photograph of the first Dail, taken obviously a few months later as De Valera was conspicuous in the centre as President, hanging in an honoured position on the wall of our home at Auldhouse Road. I know my father was greatly excited and encouraged by this great event.

Another event took place on 21 January which was a big factor in determining his future life. On that day Govan School Board refused to consider his application for reinstatement as a teacher. He had now little choice but to continue in the role of 'professional revolutionary'. This coupled with a reckless disregard for his own well-being when he thought the revolutionary movement was at stake, led to the break-up of his family later in the year.

My mother, a gentle and retiring person, had never taken an active part in her husband's political activities. She believed that her most effective contribution was to make his home life happy and comfortable, and this she had done supremely well. Moreover, he made many demands on her to provide hospitality for socialist comrades, and I understand that our home was often like a hotel.

Her health had never been good, and it took her all her time, therefore, to cope with domestic responsibilities.

She had suffered the effects of the war-time persecution and terrorism with great fortitude, because she was one hundred per cent behind Maclean in his fight against the war. The situation after the war, however, was rather different. She did not understand the complexities of revolutionary politics. She saw only her beloved husband, a changed man, his health undermined by prison persecution on top of years of constant overwork—now continuing this overwork at an even more hectic pace and, as she saw it, slowly committing suicide. This failure to be received back into his profession was a great blow to her, not only for economic reasons, but because she felt that by resuming teaching he would be resuming a more normal life.

She did everything in her power to make him give up his political activity until he was really fit. This, however, proved the very worst course she could have taken. Maclean realized, as we have seen, that the near-revolutionary situation in Scotland would not last long, and advantage must be taken as quickly as possible. Once again, as in war-time, there was so much to do, and so few people to do it. He developed the outlook, unwisely perhaps, that those who were not with him were against him, and he became suspicious that his wife was being 'got at'. Later, when all her efforts failed, and he was immersed in the most hectic year of his hectic political life, she left him, taking Jean and me with her, with the ultimatum that she would not return until he gave up his revolutionary activity. She thought she was doing the right thing, but it was too much to ask of the dedicated revolutionary who saw what she did not—the kind of situation described by Lloyd George in a secret memorandum to Clemenceau:

> The whole of Europe is filled with the spirit of Revolution. There is a deep sense not only of discontent, but of anger and revolt amongst the workmen against pre-war conditions. The whole existing order in its political, social and economic aspects is questioned by the masses of the population from one end of Europe to another.

For the first few months of the year, there was no desperate poverty. Enough money had been collected while Maclean had been in prison to keep the family for a few months after his release. Meetings in those days were enormous, and collections, which were the main source of income for professional revolutionaries, were generous. There was still money in the pockets of the workers, after years of full-time working. In spite of the growing unemployment and the general disorganization industry was still booming. Sales of literature were tremendous. His 1918 trial speech had been published as a pamphlet, *Condemned from the Dock*, and many thousands were sold. *The War after the War*, his war-time Labour College pamphlet, also sold in great numbers.

That shortage of money was not acute just after the end of the war is shown by a story told to James Maxton in 1924 by a teaching colleague of Maclean's, Harry Ross. Ross had been caught in Austria at the beginning of the war, and interned for the duration. Shortly after he arrived home, early in 1919, Maclean, fearing that he might be destitute, visited his home when he knew he would be out and left an envelope for him containing £20. Harry Ross told Maxton that fortunately he did not need the money, but that he had the greatest difficulty in getting Maclean to take it back. 'He was always helping. There was always someone begging from him, and if John had it he gave.'

Last, but certainly not least, of the January events which had a profound effect on Maclean's career, was the meeting in Moscow which decided to inaugurate the Third International. Present were at least two of Maclean's former BSP colleagues—Chicherin, whom he had helped to free from internment in England, and Joe Fineberg, who had been elected a member of the BSP executive in 1918. On 24 January a radio message from Russia all over the world appealed for delegates to be elected to attend the founding Congress of the proposed new International.

There was never any doubt about Maclean's support. As early as 1915, both he and Peter Petroff had issued clarion calls through the columns of *Vanguard* for a new International to replace the now discredited Second. Now the proposed revival of the latter by the British Labour Party, and a meeting for that purpose arranged to take place in Berne in February, made the foundation of the new International a matter of urgency.

Litvinov had been arrested in September 1918, and deported back to Russia. From that point, during 1919, Maclean was popularly regarded as Russia's unofficial ambassador and as such was the principal speaker at all the important 'Hands off Russia' rallies held that year.

45/The Miners

If there was to be a General Strike, Maclean was convinced, as we have seen, that in Scotland it would begin with the miners, who were the largest and most militant section of the organized working class. At that time the whole industry of the country depended largely on coal, which was in short supply.

At Southport the miners had voted for a national strike if the government did not concede their demands: a thirty per cent increase in wages; complete discharge of miners upon demobilization; full wages for those who were unemployed; the six hour day; and the nationalization of the mines. They were promised support by the other two members of the Triple Alliance, the Transport Workers' Federation and the NUR, which also had wage increases, shorter hours, and nationalization of the railways on the agenda.

By the time the forty hour strike burst forth, the London executive was still negotiating with the government, but the reform movement in Scotland tried to force the issue and bring the miners out with the Clyde men. MacDougall gave a vivid account in *The Scottish Coalminer*:

In the minefields the first shots came from Fife. At the end of January a petty surface-workers' grievance was the occasion of sympathetic action, and once the men were out the Reform Committee deepened the struggle into one for the winning of the general programme.

In Lanarkshire the news from Fife was enough. The more fiery districts, Shettleston and Blantyre, were aflame at once. Then action of a fairly rough character—it could scarcely have been called peaceful picketing, the thing was really an incipient revolution—was taken to stop the laggards . . . Men might be reluctant to come out against the official mandate of the union, but once out they were swept entirely off their feet by the emotional current around them. Unpaid pickets marched by night many a rough stage in order to stop distant collieries early in the morning. The Committee was in permanent session at Blantyre.

The first day of the strike an immense mob, like a brown swirling flood, poured into the quiet streets of Hamilton to get the officials to proclaim the strike in the name of the union. The demonstrators took possession of the union offices . . . The crowd choked the street, interrupting the car traffic, and were addressed from the balcony by the Reform leaders. At a joint meeting of the union executives and representatives of the Reform Committee, it was decided that the strike be declared official.

That meant that all the 50,000 Lanarkshire miners were out. On 31 January, 'Bloody Friday', the London executive had passed a resolution opposing sectional strikes, and had notified the Scottish officials accordingly. This, together with the assurances of the local officials that the future was rosy if only the men would abide by the executive decisions, persuaded the men to return to work. This was a great disappointment to the Reform Movement, and no doubt contributed to the defeat of the forty hour strike.

The British ruling class once again showed its genius for compromise. Although there were members of the Cabinet who would have liked a 'confrontation', the miners were offered a twenty per cent increase in wages, a seven hour day (with the promise of a six hour one in the future!), and a Royal Commission on nationalization. As Maclean pointed out later in *The Call* (27 March):

> I know that huge masses of the men are against the acceptance of a compromise. . . . The chief duty of the Reform Movement amongst the miners must be immediate effort to prevent the Executive from climbing down before the Government.

However, these concessions were accepted meantime, and the miners waited impatiently for the decision of the Sankey Commission, which the government had agreed to implement.

There is no doubt that the Reform Movement played an essential part in gaining these concessions from the government— even though it was a case of aiming for the stars and reaching the tree tops! Both Maclean and MacDougall redoubled their efforts, and during February and March, Maclean concentrated his agitational work mainly among the Scottish mining areas.

February's agitational campaign ended with a large demonstration in St Andrew's Hall in Glasgow, organized by the Glasgow District Council of the BSP, at which Maclean was the main speaker. In his pamphlet *John Maclean, Martyr of the Class Struggle,* Guy Aldred gave a report of this meeting:

> John Maclean was the principal speaker . . . He protested against the exaction of indemnities, as the influx of commodities merely endangered the workers' standard of existence in Britain. The capitalist newspapers all denied this economic menace at the time. But Maclean, of course, was a thousand times right.

46/The BSP as Communist Party

The founding congress of the Third International took place during the first week of March. There was no official delegate from the BSP (which did not decide formally to affiliate until October of that year), but Joe Fineberg, now living in Russia, was present. The principles hammered out at this historic meeting were soon known all over the world.

An entry in Maclean's diary, dated 2 March, is a reminder that the slaughter going on in Russia meant sorrow to members of the Scottish revolutionary movement, in a personal as well as a political sense. Some of the men fighting in defence of the new Soviet Republic were old comrades. There had been hundreds of East European refugees working in the mines and steel works of West Scotland, especially in Lanarkshire, and some of them belonged to the BSP. The 2 March entry in Maclean's diary reads starkly—'Blantyre—Jonas Shelpuk—killed in Red Guard, joined at Omsk.'

The BSP was not entirely united on the question of affiliation to the Third International. A great controversy took place in *The Call* until the annual conference at Easter. It seems to have been initiated mainly by Theodore Rothstein, who, as Russia's official agent and the dispenser of Russian funds, soon became a great power behind-the-scenes in the BSP. The controversy took the form mainly of Soviet democracy versus parliamentary democracy, and, to some extent, industrial unionism versus craft unionism. It soon became evident that only a small minority, including E C Fairchild, who was still the editor of *The Call*, and H Alexander, the party treasurer, supported traditional 'social democracy'.

At the conference, which took place that year at Sheffield, 20-21 April, the executive's emergency resolution was carried by an overwhelming majority. This pledged the party to a 'world revolution . . . which . . . in all countries would seize the reins of power, overthrow the rule of the capitalist and landlord classes parading in the shoddy cloak of Parliamentarism and sham democracy, establish the direct rule of the workers and peasants by means of Soviets, and wind up the capitalist order of Society.' The conference decided to set up a committee of five 'to draft a scheme of unity' which would make possible the merger of the ILP, BSP and SLP into a single united Socialist Party. The conference also decided to continue affiliation to the Labour Party. This was to remain the central issue which now divided it from the small revolutionary groups like Sylvia Pankhurst's Workers' Socialist Federation and the SLP. Maclean supported this decision.

Significantly the *Glasgow Herald* made no mention of these important matters when reporting the conference. The following extract speaks for itself:

Mr John Maclean called attention to the arrest of W F Watson for a speech at the Albert Hall, London, on 8 February.

The Chairman: 'What do you suggest?'
Mr Maclean: 'Seize Lloyd George!' (Cheers and laughter).

The *Herald* also reported that during the course of a speech he complained that a leaflet written by him on the subject of 'A Soviet for Scotland' had been refused insertion in the official organ. Next day the *Herald* gave what was probably a garbled account of a speech on the second day of the conference:

Mr John Maclean, Glasgow, in the course of a vigorous speech said: 'Reference has been made to the fact that Arthur Henderson has dined with the king. I suppose I shall come in the same category, as the king gave me a free pardon. The Government can get into the unofficial movement through Scotland Yard agents, just as they can get into the official movement. It is our duty to remain in our class and face the issue. **It is entirely owing to the BSP that we have got a drift towards the revolutionary position.** (My emphasis). The Hendersons have got to go, the Thomases have got to go, and are going. The general strike will be the next stage towards getting the land and the means of production into our hands.' (Cheers).

Tom Bell recorded that Maclean moved an emergency resolution demanding hands off the revolutions in Russia, Hungary, and Bavaria. He also moved a resolution on conscription, welcoming the efforts of the Miners' Federation to end it, and insisting that it was 'being maintained in order to crush the revolutionary movement on the continent'. In the course of his speech he kept insisting that 'The capitalist class must be kept busy at home', which put in a nutshell the policy he had been advocating ever since the Russian Revolution.

The decisions taken at the conference, committing the party to a revolution in the Soviet style, meant in effect that it was now acting as a Communist Party in Britain, even though it did not formally affiliate to the Third International until October. This made no difference at all to Maclean's activities, which had been guided by communist principles, as he saw them. Now they had the official BSP blessing. During March, he spent a week in Lanarkshire, a week in Lancashire (speaking at Colne, Nelson, Burnley, etc), a week in Glasgow, and a week in Sheffield. During April, he did another week in Glasgow and surroundings, spoke at a rally in Paisley Town Hall in protest against Gallacher's imprisonment before going on to do two days in Cumberland. He spent two weeks in South Wales (sandwiching in two days at the BSP annual conference) before coming back for a week's tour of Lanarkshire.

He arrived back in time to take part in a round of May Day demonstrations. He was one of the star attractions in Glasgow, along with Constance Markiewicz, the heroine of the Easter Rising and now Minister of Labour in the Irish Republican government. That year May Day was held once again on 1 May, a Thursday, and it is recorded that about 150,000 people took part. At the crowded meeting in St Andrew's Hall that evening, he was again the chief speaker, along with the Countess and Neil MacLean. *Forward* reported that he said:

> they must not be content to have a Republic only in Ireland, but must also strike out to have a Socialist Republic all over Britain as well as Ireland, and to have in addition an international system of Soviet Republics all over the world. . . . He hoped when the Revolution came about in this country that the Celtic fringe of the population would play an important part in the struggle.

The fact that Maclean was chief speaker at another three May Day demonstrations, at Hamilton, Kilmarnock and Paisley, is witness to his great personal popularity at this period, and to the fact that the BSP was now playing a leading part in the Scottish labour movement.

47/The Scottish Labour College

During these turbulent first months of 1919, when the future of Britain seemed to be in the balance, revolutionary agitation in the industrial and mining areas naturally took precedence over all other kinds of activity. Nevertheless, Maclean's most cherished project, the setting up of a Scottish Labour College with day students like the London one, was never far from his mind. It was to him an integral part of the struggle, and the great controversies sweeping the movement at this period, especially about the 'Dictatorship of the Proletariat' and 'Soviet Democracy', made this work even more relevant. He stated later that year, 'The dictatorship of the proletariat would be a monstrous tragedy unless the proletariat has knowledge. The Scottish Labour College will play its part in supplying the requisites of working class knowledge'.

Progress towards a properly-functioning College had been interrupted by Maclean's two imprisonments. His three years' sentence had come just after the conference of February 1916, and he had again been arrested immediately after the election of the first Executive Committee in March 1918.

One of his first actions after his release had been to begin his Sunday afternoon economics class in central Glasgow, and his diary showed regular meetings on Saturday afternoons with the College Committee.

During the spring a number of district conferences took place. The centres visited were Aberdeen, Arbroath, Dundee, East and West Fife, Edinburgh, and Falkirk, and the attendances were surprisingly good. Some local branches of trade unions agreed to levy their members to support the College work in their own districts. The Labour College Committee also had meetings with the Plebs League, the English organization connected with the Central Labour College, which had been backed by the SLP, while the Scottish Labour College, of course, had been formed under the auspices of the BSP. During that spring, however, while differences between the two parties were beginning to be ironed out, the two educational organizations agreed to unite, and plans were made for a conference to take place on 24 May to prepare for the opening of day classes on 1 September.

Thus Maclean's agitational campaigns had two objectives—first, to set up unofficial committees to function as embryo soviets, and in addition to organize local Labour College classes.

During his 'Cook's Tour' of South Wales in April, he saw preparations being made to examine candidates for the eight maintenance bursaries of £75 per annum provided by the South Wales Miners' Federation for the Central Labour College. Maclean described this later as 'the greatest working-class educational effort ever made in any country', and here he gained more ideas and inspiration for the running of the Scottish Labour College.

The Conference on 24 May was again a big success, being attended by 571 delegates. A lucid and brilliant paper was read by the secretary, William Leonard, giving the subjects to be studied and the field which it was hoped the College would cover. It was hoped to form classes all over the country under the guidance of district committees working together with the College Committee and the Plebs League. After some discussion, appeals were made by Helen Crawford, who had just returned from a Women's International Conference in Switzerland, by James Maxton and by Maclean himself.

It was decided to open the College for day classes on 1 September. In August, Maclean and William McLaine, a leader of the shop steward movement in England and a prominent member of the BSP, were appointed full-time tutors.

48/Keeping capitalism at bay

In the midst of all the urgent revolutionary campaigning, Maclean never lost sight of the plight of the many political prisoners throughout the world. At a Glasgow Green demonstration on 11 May, he announced that there would be a special demonstration on 25 May to demand the release of Eugene Debs in America and other political prisoners elsewhere. That night he sat down to write a letter to Debs himself, encouraging him and telling about the fight being made for him.

Soon afterwards he received a letter from Delia, Jim Larkin's sister, asking him to come to Dublin to speak on behalf of her brother Peter, who together with twelve of his socialist comrades was still in prison in Australia. He promised to come as soon as his other commitments would allow, and meantime the agitation for Debs was carried on with increased vigour after Maclean received a reply from Debs' brother informing him about the bad treatment Debs was receiving.

At the end of May, immediately after the Debs demonstration, he made another whirlwind tour in England, this time to address many meetings in the Colne Valley and Huddersfield, the latter one under the auspices of the Trades Council. Maclean reported in *The Call* that two record meetings were held at Huddersfield and Hanley. He also informed his readers about the concrete results of his visit:

> Efforts are being made to build up a network of Workers' Committees and independent educational classes in conjunction with the Central Labour College in Yorkshire. Lancashire, South Wales, and Scotland must look to their laurels now that the dalesmen of Yorks are on the move.

After his week in Yorkshire came another week among the Ayrshire miners, taking in meetings at Catrine, Glenburn, Patna, Old Cumnock, Kilbirnie, and Drongan. Willie Gallacher once described him as sweeping like a tornado through industrial Scotland, and probably that is the best description that has ever been made. He finished this hectic week with a protest meeting on Glasgow Green, Sunday, 8 June, where he was again the chief speaker, this time to protest against the continued imprisonment of Gallacher and the other forty hour strike victims.

After a week devoted to the conference of the Glasgow District Council of the BSP, he was off again to England, this time among the Durham miners. One of the leaders, Will Lawther (later to become Sir Will!), was a special friend and much interested in the Labour College movement. Maclean was no stranger here, and received a warm welcome. Lawther's brother told me about an amusing incident at Chopwell. About four thousand people attended his open-air meeting there. A local ex-Sergeant Major tried to turn the crowd against him, but without success. The crowd, enthusiastically in support of Maclean, turned on the ex-soldier and he was glad to have police protection. At another meeting

Maclean was dealing with his favourite subject at that time, warning his audience of the danger of another world war. When question time came, one old man wanted to know just when the war would begin. As quick as a dart, Maclean replied, 'I'll need to see Old Moore about that!' The huge crowd broke into peals of laughter—the old man's name was Moore.

That month ended with another whirlwind tour of the West Lothian minefields.

By this time the Fife Reform Committee had become so influential that Willie Adamson MP made a bitter attack on the leaders at the Miners' Gala at Dunfermline on 2 June. Maclean claimed that this was indeed a tribute:

> William objects to non-miners interfering in mining affairs (he wrote in *The Worker*). As a politician, he is compelled to interfere in housing and other affairs . . . outside the coal industry. William, use your head! I interfere in mining affairs although I do not intend to cut coal. I consider it my duty. William has called us (the Reform Committee) blacklegs. The greatest betrayal of Labour was support of the capitalist war. . . . William supported the war, and betrayed his class. . . .
>
> William claimed he got me out of prison. I denied it at Dunfermline, asserting it was due to working-class pressure. He has prevented a big agitation springing up for the release of Gallacher and the others by assuring people that he could do the trick. . . . Yet William turns round on the only men who count in Fife, the only men who really struggled to get even the miserable Sankey concession.

He went on to say that this attack had publicly shown others the power of the Reform Movement in Fife and was encouraging others, like the Ayrshire miners, to fall into line. After reminding his readers that the South Wales miners were demanding full control of the mines for socialization (rather than nationalization), he went on:

> Encouragement also comes from Lancashire, where our comrade Hutcheson is busy. On Tuesday, the Nelson and District Weavers' Association held its quarterly meeting, and resolutions were passed for the thirty hour week; more money; knock-out to capitalism; a profiteering commission. . . .
>
> This means that cotton workers are adopting the same methods as the miners. Soon the woollen workers will clear the decks for action. In Bradford, Huddersfield, and the Colne Valley, the *seeds of the new revolutionary methods and ideas are germinating fast.*

In the meantime, the final report of the Sankey Commission

had been issued. The Commission consisted of six members representing the miners, and six representing the employers. Bob Smillie and Frank Hodges especially put up masterly cases for the miners.

The Commission reported in the middle of June, for nationalization, and the whole labour movement waited, with baited breath, for the government's decision. They had to wait two months.

When Maclean went to Dublin in July, he found the whole place bristling with soldiers. No declaration of war had been made, and the Dail Eireann had not yet been declared illegal, but the British Army of Occupation was there in full force. Maclean was sorry to see Scottish regiments among the troops. He arrived in time for the 'Peace' celebrations (the Versailles Treaty had been concluded):

> On Peace Saturday round the neighbourhood of College Green were thousands of policemen in plain clothes and spies galore brought in for the occasion to support the soldiers, and the police openly armed with revolvers. Apart from these and women, very few (mostly incomers like myself) witnessed the solemn farce of 15,000 soldiers with bayonets fixed, machine-guns and tanks, marching through the streets to celebrate peace.

When he found out that no demonstrations inside the city or County of Dublin were allowed, so that no organized protest could be made against the 'peace quackery', intervention in Russia, the imprisonment of Pete Larkin in Australia, or anything else, he felt like asking his fare back to Glasgow! However, Delia Larkin managed to arrange some meetings for him, and on 20 July he spoke at the Irish Workers' Hall. Describing his experiences in *The Worker* he wrote:

> There I urged that Ireland alone could never gain her freedom, that her Republic depended on the revolt and success of British Labour, and that therefore Irish Labour would not be free under a Sinn Fein Republic, but only under a Socialist Workers' Republic, and that consequently Irish Labour should support British Labour in the campaign against intervention in Russia, and should be prepared to play its part in the world-wide establishment . . . of Socialism . . .
>
> Although the meeting was attended by a large number of the men who had participated in the Easter Week rebellion, no objection was raised to my suggestion as to the attitude to be adopted towards 'Tommy'. In personal conversation, I found that these men fought not against the soldiers as enemies of Ireland, but just

as interposed tools of British capitalism, and that they had no hatred of the soldiers but of the Government that foully used them . . . although they were prepared to fight again for Ireland should occasion arise. They clearly comprehended the position I urged, and the ultimate advantage of it from the world workers' point of view.

These views, however, did not meet with approval at other meetings. He received very bitter and outspoken criticism at a meeting held for him by the Socialist Party of Ireland. Permission had been granted to use the Mansion House for this meeting, but when they approached the entrance their way was blocked by police about two hundred strong. 'An inspector obdurately refused', wrote Maclean, 'to listen to my plea that I had come on a mission to civilize Ireland. Such is humour in Ireland!' In the end they had to adjourn to the garden, and held their meeting there:

Although in the circumstances the audience was not large, it was quality undiluted, William O'Brien being in the chair.* One man desired to know why the Gordons came to Ireland after refusing to go to India. Hot stuff like that was poured into me, and through these manifestations of the Irish mind at home I began to realize the spirit that 700 years of oppression had failed to subdue. Once the workers develop a similar hatred of capitalism, things are going to move on avalanche-like. However, Cathal O'Shannon neatly but effectively supported me from a Socialist standpoint, whilst Sean McLoughlin who fought through the Rebellion urged the international position as a true supporter of Jim Connolly must. On the Wednesday evening, I was favoured with an opportunity of addressing the shop steward movement inside the Transport Union, and from the applause I received and the sentiments expressed after my address, the Irish workers clearly understand the international role of the workers. The motto of the Transport Union, as their neat little flags show, is 'One Big Union'.

The Irish workers are ever more clearly developing their class-consciousness through combats with the propertied class, through socialist literature, through the big Dublin Economics Class that soon will give birth to the Connolly Memorial Labour College.

He met most of the prominent personalities of the Irish Labour movement, and particularly liked the late George Russell, the famous poet, (better known as 'A E'): 'Never have I met one

---

*   Founder of the Socialist Party of Ireland, and a follower and friend of James Connolly.

in whom so nicely are blended the idealist and the realist. In him Ireland is seen at her best.'

While there is no recorded indication of any change in his attitude to 'the national question', it is my opinion that his personal experience of the bitter Irish hatred of British domination was at least one of the factors that led him to join later that year Erskine of Mar's 'National Committee' which had been formed to promote Scottish independence.

Next year Maclean was forced to admit that the Irish revolutionaries had been helping, far more than British socialists, to 'keep capitalism busy at home':

> The Irish Sinn Feiners, who make no profession of Socialism or Communism, and who are at best non-Socialists, are doing more to help Russia and the Revolution that all we professed Marxian Bolsheviks in Britain.

49/Capitalism resurgent

Even before he went to Dublin, John Mclean realized that the movement had missed the revolutionary boat. When he returned, the announcement that government had rejected the Sankey Commission recommendation on nationalization of the mines, was a confirmation that it had now overcome the dangerous post-war situation and could afford to take up the offensive once again.

There certainly was a tremendous feeling among the miners for a strike against the government's treacherous decision, but after consulting with the other members of the Triple Alliance, the executive agreed to wait until the TUC Congress which was to be held the following month in Glasgow.

Even though the hope of a general strike had disappeared Maclean kept up his agitational campaign among the miners; he spent some time with the Durham miners and a week with the Fife miners. Most of August, however, was spent preparing for the opening of the Labour College day classes on 1 September, and publicizing this work as far as he was able:

> I wish to remind you (he wrote in *The Worker* of 9 August), of the Scottish Labour College and its oncoming winter's work. You

have either to make the College work a tremendous success, or you are going to have imposed on you Capitalist teaching under the auspices of the WEA supported by prominent members of the landlord and capitalist class (the class that uses the police, the navy, and the army, against us), and staffed by teachers whose outlook is determined by Marshall in Economics and Cunningham in Industrial History.

He proceeded to warn that the WEA had originally been formed to counteract the Labour College movement, and was now being revived for the same purpose.

He informed readers of *The Call*:

It has been recommended that the Glasgow members of the BSP levy themselves 3d a week for the Scottish Labour College, which will open its doors on September 1st. The programme is quite a big one, covering the whole week and the fees are the lowest of the low—5/- for one subject and 2/6 for each additional one.

During August Maclean also found time to write an important theoretical article in *The Call* refuting theories put forward by an American writer, Kahn, about the imminent and automatic collapse of capitalism because of currency problems. Kahn's book, *The Collapse of Capitalism*, had been having a great vogue at economics classes and had greatly influenced class teachers. In this article and in a supporting one written in November, Maclean pointed out:

At Easter time the British press raised the alarm about financial collapse to justify the with-holding of supplies of credit to France, because France was making extravagant demands at the Peace Conference. In other words, Britain used this collapse to justify a financial blockade of France. France yielded all right. However, certain of the best Marxists in the South Wales coalfield were deceived by the press stunt, all the more readily as they had been swept away by Kahn's book. . . .

Capitalism is not based on credit or paper, but on production of commodities for surplus value in the form of interest, profits and rent. The conditions are sources of raw material, machinery and organization, skilled labour and markets. The war has opened up new sources of raw material, and coming railways will vastly extend these sources. The war waste affords vast demands for goods and the seizure and opening up of the world by the League of Thieves means markets vastly exceeding past experiences. . . .

My impression is that capitalism is more vital today in Britain, Japan, and America, than ever it was, and is preparing for expansions such as have never been made before, that if capitalism is to be 'sent west', it will only be the result of the delivery of the greatest knock-out blow ever given, and that this blow must be given by a united, revolutionary working class.

He went on to assert the real Marxist position that the only hope was the working class at its grass roots:

> Let us remember that although the Trade Union and political leaders of the working class have been afraid to be as audacious as the leaders of capitalism, have failed as ever at the critical moment and will do so again, nevertheless the mass of the people are coming more and more towards our position.
>
> Therein lies salvation. The safety of society rests not in the hands of a few leaders or heroes, but in those of masses of mankind, conscious or unconscious . . . Although the events do not seem propitious, a growing mass of workers is becoming conscious of the need for a new society. . . . The greater the drift, the more the props of capitalism will vanish and hence the pending collapse of capitalism. Quantitative changes on our side will become qualitative; in other words, newer and clearer views with higher and prouder spirits will come with numbers.

In August he took part in a huge demonstration led by the ILP against increased rents. The 1915 Rent Act, which forbade the increase of rents during the war, was now out of date, and the Housing Council was forced to take up the cudgels once again. Plans were made to hold a big demonstration in the middle of August to back up the fight against increasing rents. Both leaders and rank and file were determined to resist any kind of provocation, in spite of irritating actions by the authorities. The forty hour strike riot was still in everybody's mind. However, all passed off peacefully. Andrew McBride had challenged Maclean beforehand regarding his attitude, and this annoyed him considerably:

> I had pretty sharply to tell McBride that I was a Revolutionist, not an inciter to useless and dangerous rioting. . . . I gave him the assurance that I would do my utmost to prevent a riot, as I intended to march in the front line of the Gorbals contingent.

Over and over again Maclean had to protest against the implication that revolution necessarily means violence, rioting and bloodshed. He found that he had to keep on making quite clear that the revolution he was advocating was the fundamental re-organization of society, which he claimed could be carried out peacefully—given the adequate political education of the working class. If violence were used, it would come from the other side.

The annual congress of the TUC was held that September in Glasgow. The main issue was the resolution moved by the miners

demanding that Congress should co-operate with them in forcing
the government to adopt the scheme of national ownership and
control recommended by the Sankey Commission. Congress leaders
were quite aware of the implications of the resolution. The only
way to force the government was a general strike, but they
realized that this meant revolutionary action. The defeat of the
government at this time would be the first step towards the overthrow of the capitalist system. They temporized. They agreed that
if the government continued in its refusal, then a special Congress
would be called.

But the government now felt strong enough to take the
offensive against the railwaymen, the majority of whom wished
the industry to remain under state control. By means of the
divide-and-rule policy, by granting the locomotive-men a standard
wage similar to the war-time one and refusing the NUR the same
concession, they more or less forced the NUR to go on strike.
Maclean now ceased his campaign for a general strike:

> A General Strike should be avoided for the moment as the
> Government has shown its preparedness, amongst other things,
> by its control of food vehicles. *A General Strike should have
> behind it the impetus of a Labour attack,* whereas the impetus is
> on the side of the capitalist government. . . . A respite will enable
> . . . us to clarify the vision of our class and perfect industrial
> organization on a sound class basis, and will give us the time to
> show the Co-operative Movement that the Middle Class Union,
> largely composed of private traders, and their kith and kin in the
> professional services, has as its end the general onslaught on
> labour, the crushing of co-operation—the Commissariat depart-
> ment of Labour's Army.

What he did advocate at this point was the replacement of
the TUC Parliamentary Committee by a permanently-sitting
Labour Council, an anticipation of the General Council.
Maclean was delighted when he read in the *Scotsman* of 18
October that statements made by the secretary of the TUC, Fred
Bramley, revealed that plans were being made to enlist the help of
the co-operative movement in preparation for big strikes ahead:

> in future strikes affecting the community as a whole it is being
> arranged to introduce the machinery of the Co-operative Societies
> for the support of the striking Trade Unionists threatened with a
> shortage of supplies.

This was, of course, what Maclean had advocated in 'Now's
the Day and Now's the Hour', and he wrote approvingly to
The Call:

We cannot but be pleased at Bramley's disclosure, because it will hearten us to push the scheme everywhere. . . . The fight of the future centres around food and the armed forces. If by publicity we can win the armed forces . . . the Co-operative movement can help us to ensure that our class is regularly and properly fed during the crisis.

Although some disquieting developments had been taking place in the BSP, including the resignation of E C Fairchild and H Alexander, at this period Maclean, in public at least, declared his pleasure at the lead which the BSP had been giving:

Events of this year have proved that no organization in Britain has a greater influence than the BSP on the policy of the working-class. . . . At this stage we of the BSP can play a supremely important part. We can call into being work-shop committees with a right class basis; we can provide them with a programme identical with that of our South Wales comrades in the mining industry . . . Let us urge:

Full socialization of mines and other trustified industries.
Full industrial control by the workers involved, though modified to permit of the use of the Co-op movement.
Control of the education of the workers.
A 30 hours' week.
Fifty per cent increase in wages.
Communally produced houses.
Withdrawal of British troops from all parts of the world.
Abolition of the Army and Navy and the establishment of a Workers' Defence Force.
Transfer of the functions of Parliament to Labour's Central Committee.

That same month of October he wrote a pamphlet especially for the Glasgow municipal elections in November, called *Sack Dalrymple: Sack Stevenson: Let Labour Revenge Bloody Friday*. Here he blamed the Tramways General Manager, James Dalrymple, for acting in conjunction with Chief Constable Stevenson and providing the provocation which led to the 'Bloody Friday' riot— acting, of course, under the instructions of the capitalist town council and ultimately of Bonar Law. He accused Dalrymple of terrorizing the tramwaymen by using spies to ferret out all who were at all militant and having them dismissed.

He also made a passionate repudiation of the claim, dear to the hearts of the Fabians, that the Glasgow tramway system was an example of 'Municipal Socialism':

The tramway system of Glasgow has been boasted of all over the world as the triumph of Municipal Socialism. From the standpoint of profit-making efficiency I have no objection to raise. But Socialism implies security, comfort, and happiness for the people who actually run the cars.

Victimization is the opposite of security, and spying is degrading both to the spy and the one spied upon. Spying implies that it 'pays' to hold your tongue; it spells ruin if you speak your mind. Socialism means that you are free and entitled to speak your mind. . . .

From a Labour standpoint the 'Municipal Socialism' of the Glasgow trams is a ghastly blank. This is, of course, to be looked for from a Council composed in the main of middle-class snobs, despisers of the working class (except when a war is on), men who think the wage-earner is an inferior animal simply because he has to do as the horse has—to work for a master.

He put forward a programme for the tramwaymen similar to those being put forward for the miners by the Reform Movement and for the workers in general by the BSP:

1 A six hour working day
2 A minimum of One Pound per Day
3 Security from Victimization
4 Dismissal of James Dalrymple
5 Depot representation on the Tramway Committee

He went on to affirm that a solid vote for the Labour candidate was the first step to take. Forestalling objections from left-wingers he pointed out:

Some Socialists may object to voting Labour. In the circumstances they have to choose between the Labour men now standing and the capitalist defenders of 'property' and high rents. The Labour candidates may not be all some of us would like, but it is better to send them to power and so test them in the light of experience. They must fail to bring much relief to the workers, but at least they can be forced to avenge 'Bloody Friday'. . . .

That in itself will be a long way forward towards that complete restoration of class confidence needed for the time when a Clyde Valley Workers' Committee will control the civic affairs along the course of our river, and take the place of the various county and town councils meantime holding power in one part or other of the watershed areas; just as this Workers' Committee may guide Labour into the paths of the Scottish Communist Republic.

Ireland's great power today lies in the three election victories gained for Sinn Fein. Without these she could not have proceeded to set up a Parliament to her taste. Labour's victory in November is just that 'break-through' longed for by the older champions of the Peoples' Great Cause.

This is the kind of approach towards the municipal and parliamentary processes in Britain which was to be advocated by Lenin at the second Congress of the Third International, and which was accepted by the vast majority of the BSP.

50/A new tactic

By the autumn of 1919 it had become clear that the British labour movement had been well and truly out-manoeuvred by the government and attack had been turned to defence. At the same time, Maclean was considering what was, for the Marxist movement in Britain, a new tactic.

Just about this period, Erskine of Mar organized a 'National Committee' to press for Scottish independence and other national interests. During the period since he had first approached Maclean in January, to judge from his writings in the periodical the *Scottish Review*, he had been steadily moving to the left and wrote in one issue:

> Praise to the Bolsheviks! Honour to the Revolutionaries! It is the Russian Revolution that has set the Chancelleries of Europe by the ears, and now bids fair to inscribe in large and indelible letters on the pages of the great Book of Universal National Rights certain priceless principles . . . Self-determination for *all* Nations; no annexations; and no Treaty-made premiums on after-war enmity and greed. . . .
>
> Until the people reign—until the Proletariat is everywhere in undisputed power—it were folly to expect enduring Peace, drastic retrenchment, or honest and searching reform. . . . It is possible, of course, that the Proletarian rule may disappoint in practice the glowing expectations formed of it by its friends, and may show itself to be as little dependable as . . . Monarchy, Aristocracy, and government by the capitalist class have proved themselves to be . . . but the Dictatorship of the Proletariat, how dismally soever it might fail, could not possibly sin against humanity more deeply and unforgivably than the other systems of government have done.

The most prominent members of the new body were William Graham MP, Bob Smillie, James Maxton, David Kirkwood, Tom

Johnston of *Forward*, Angus MacDonald of the Highland Land League, R E Muirhead and Joseph Duncan of the Farm Servants' Union. According to H J Hanham's *Scottish Nationalism*, Maclean 'joined Erskine's "National Committee" late in 1919, and like Erskine became identified with the view that the Scots should follow the example of the Irish, though in Maclean's case this was by following the example of the Irish labour movement rather than that of Sinn Fein'.

It should also be noted that the *Scottish Review* was the first journal to carry a serious article (by H C MacNeacail) advocating the policy of Lockhart of Carnwarth in the eighteenth century, that the Scottish MPs should withdraw in a body and reconstitute the Scottish parliament which 'was not dissolved, still less abolished; it was merely adjourned'.

While emulation of the Irish movement was undoubtedly one of the factors which led to Maclean's new tactic of support for Scottish independence, in my opinion the main factor was his realization, brought acutely home to him by his campaigns in England throughout 1919, that the tremendous swing to the left which had taken place in industrial Scotland and led to a near-revolutionary situation, had just not taken place in England.

Allegations that this tactic meant that Maclean was no longer an orthodox Marxist are quite unfounded. The principle of self-determination for small nations was taken for granted in the revolutionary movement. Marx stated, in a letter dated 9 April 1870, that the special task of the Central Council in London of the First International was ' to awaken the consciousness in the English workers that for them the National Emancipation of Ireland is no question of abstract justice or human sympathy but the first condition of their own emancipation'.

Polish independence was the subject of a fierce controversy between Lenin and Rosa Luxemburg. Rosa maintained that under capitalism there was no possibility of real national independence, while Lenin insisted that Russian socialists should fight for the right of the Poles to have a separate state if they so wished. In answer to the argument that separation would undermine the solidarity of the Polish and Russian workers, he instanced the case of the secession of Norway from Sweden in 1905: 'The close alliance of the Norwegian and Swedish workers, their complete fraternal class solidarity gained from the fact that the Swedish workers recognized the right of the Norwegians to secede'.

Unlike the majority of the Bolsheviks, Lenin wholeheartedly supported the Easter rising.

Bukharin claimed that the call for the liberation of nations *within* capitalism diverted the workers from the real Socialist solution. Lenin disagreed:

> the dialectics of history is such that small nations, powerless as an *independent* factor in the struggle against imperialism, play a part as one of the ferments of the bacilli which help the real power against imperialism to come on the scene, namely the socialist proletariat. To imagine that social revolution is conceivable without revolts by small nations in the colonies and in Europe . . . means repudiating social revolution.

Another factor contributing to Maclean's new tactic was the change going on behind the scenes in the BSP itself. According to Walter Kendall:

> After Litvinov's deportation in September (1918), Theodore Rothstein became chief Bolshevik representative in Britain. Instead of experiencing a direct political struggle for power between Fairchild and Maclean the BSP, through Rothstein, now became increasingly dependent on Soviet financial aid, and came ever more under Russian influence. What began as a native British move towards revolutionizing the BSP became distorted after the foundation of the Communist International into a successful endeavour to link the BSP with the Comintern and then to remodel its thought and action on the Bolshevik pattern.

So far, as we have seen, the policy advocated by the BSP, under Maclean's leadership, was more or less the policy already evolved by the revolutionary movement on the Clyde—a combination of workers' committees and Marxist classes, and the advocacy of democratic centralism, not only with regard to the party itself, but with regard to both the co-operative movement and the trade union movement. This policy of large-scale centralism in all the working-class organizations was determined by the nature of capitalism itself. Large, amalgamated organizations, with a centralized professional administration were becoming more and more of a necessity, to combat the growing trustification of capitalism, not to mention the inevitable growth of monopoly capitalism. Centralism was regarded, not as a virtue, but as a grim necessity, with a tendency to undermine democracy—hence the importance of the unofficial workers' committees. These tendencies in the revolutionary movement had been reinforced by the Bolshevik victory, and John Maclean did not in the least object to the BSP being remodelled on Bolshevik lines—as understood prior to 1920. What he ultimately objected to was the dictatorship of the

Communist Party (the totalitarian party, if you like), a policy forced on the Bolsheviks by the exigencies of the Civil War and foreign intervention.

In the meantime, it appears that he disagreed with Rothstein over the functions of the 'Hands off Russia Committee', of which he had been the chief spokesman. According to Harry McShane, Rothstein wanted Maclean to become the paid organizer of the Committee, to give up his industrial agitation, and to devote his whole time to its activities. Maclean considered that the only way to defend Russia was 'to keep capitalism busy at home', not to hold large rallies all over the country with all sorts of people, as Rothstein wanted. In addition, he did not want to make himself dependent on Russian money—and did not like the situation developing in the BSP, which was becoming more and more dependent on Russian subsidies. He remembered the situation where Hyndman maintained his domination of the party by financial means and felt that 'The man who pays the piper calls the tune'. Most of all, he did not like Lieutenant-Colonel Malone, whom Rothstein had introduced to the 'Hands off Russia' Committee and who a few months later became a member of the BSP's executive committee.

Later, in the *Vanguard* which he resurrected in 1920, Maclean spelled out his objections to Malone:

> The less Russians interfere in the internal affairs of other countries at this juncture, the better for the cause of Revolution in those countries. Rothstein's activities drove Fairchild out of the BSP, and his approaches to me created a situation that compelled the BSP to gently slip me out. The leadership of the BSP then fell to Lieut-Col Malone MP, who in 1918 was on the executive of the Reconstruction Society, the body that flooded the country with leaflets poisoning the minds of the people against Russia and the Russian Revolution.
>
> To ask me to work with Malone for Revolution is a joke. A man like that ought not to be allowed in a Revolutionary Marxian Party. Whatever may be contended against Turati, Kautsky, Hilferding, Hilquit, Longuet and Macdonald, ought surely to apply with greater force to men such as Malone. To allow a Malone to lead a Revolutionary Party after a record such as his is high treason to Communism. You might as well appoint Churchill 'honorary' President of the Russian Republic!
>
> If England is to be led by Malone, then let us Marxians in Scotland forge ahead on entirely independent lines. Scotland is firmer for Marxism than any other part of the British Empire.

In the meantime, this introduction of Malone into the leadership of the party reinforced Maclean's distrust of Rothstein. Although he had played an outstanding part in the fight against Hyndman's jingoism before the war, Rothstein had resigned from the BSP in disgust at the beginning of the war. He played no part in the struggle against the war, although he wrote under the pseudonym of John Bryan in *The Call*. During the war he worked as an interpreter in the War Office, and it was only natural that those who had borne the brunt of persecution in the anti-war struggle should look askance at his growing power.

All this was in the future, however, and in November 1919, Maclean was still regarded as the spokesman for the Russian Revolution. He was the main speaker at a large anniversary demonstration in the Kingsway Hall, London. His theme was:

> We in this country are moving in the rapids of revolution. The Shop Stewards' Committees are driving forward the 'labour leaders', especially in the mining districts. The Spartacists of Germany are preparing a revolution and soon our chance will come.
>
> The Triple Alliance of Labour must come to take the place of Parliament. On with the class war.

Later in the month he was again the chief speaker at a Hands off Russia demonstration in St Andrew's Hall, Glasgow. This was reported in *The Call* under the headline 'John Maclean's Great Speech':

> Glasgow is a truly wonderful place. For an hour before Maclean was booked to appear, trams from all over Glasgow were unloading crowds at the Olympia doors. It is a remarkable tribute to John's personality and power. Those who got inside had a treat. The machinations of the Government were ruthlessly exposed, and he explained in detail the relationship of Bradburys to prices in a manner which . . . no other public speaker is capable of. A pin would have been heard to drop in his concluding oration.

51/Educational work

In November, Maclean was asked by the Executive Committee (of which, of course, he was a member, having been re-elected at the annual conference), to write a series of articles for *The Call* on high prices. The country had been flooded with paper currency, called John Bradbury's, to pay for the war and prices had risen in proportion. The cost of living had more than doubled since July 1914 and had trebled since the beginning of the century. Yet since the beginning of the century on average wages had only doubled and no more:

It follows then that the living of Labour has fallen in the last 24 years despite two wars for 'freedom'—the Boer War and the Great War.

The only course open to Labour is the absolute destruction of capitalism . . . The way to victory must be through prosecution of the class struggle . . . and Labour must see that the living of the workers is raised either by raising wages or lowering prices, or both. The fight for higher wages is a sectional one even inside the ranks of the five million organized wage-earners. The unorganized get little or no benefit, and therefore can be pitted against the organized.

On the other hand, a fight for lower prices involves all organized workers at the same time, and favourably affects the unorganized, with the consequent possibility of bringing them within the ranks of the organized. From a class point of view, then, the fight for lower prices is a better course, especially as many workers have had wages stabilized till September, 1920. . . .

Before the war the gold and the bank notes needed to circulate wealth amounted perhaps to no more than £150 millions. This increase in paper money above the £150 millions is the principal cause of the high prices.

When gold payment was resumed in 1919, prices began to fall. Labour's cry, then ought to be 'Burn Bradbury!'—not the man, but the effigy. . . .

If these notes were burned and gold payments resumed, supported as before by the usual bank notes, prices would at once fall to half their present level. If prices go down, wages cannot be broken except at the risk of revolution. Lord Milner expressed this fear in the Lords the other day, and hence favoured keeping up prices. 'Burn Bradbury and down with prices!' must be our reply to Milner.

He wrote several long and complex articles, giving a multitude of economic facts to support his contentions. Tom Bell says in his book on Maclean, that this campaign to reduce prices inside a capitalist economy was quite unrealistic, as Maclean himself had pointed out in 1912, but Bell misses the whole point of the exercise. The government did not dare to reduce prices, because this would increase real wages, which would make Britain less competitive in the big commercial struggle with America which was taking place. On the other hand, the government did not dare to reduce money wages in the climate of opinion at the time, for that would have been to risk revolution. The formulating of transitional demands, obviously reasonable like the reduction of prices, but which capitalism cannot grant, was part of the classic Marxist tactic of which Bell, who had received his training in the unorthodox SLP, did not approve.

Before the end of the year the work of the Scottish Labour College had become so successful that the movement began to attract unprecedented attention. William Diack, a well-known trade unionist, wrote a long article on the 'Scottish and Irish Labour Colleges' in Erskine of Mar's *Scottish Review*:

At present there are thirteen evening classes at the College in Glasgow, with an attendance of 565 students. The district classes throughout Scotland number 43, and when the full returns come in at the end of December it is expected that for the whole of Scotland there will be a roll of over 2,000 students. That is a wonderfully good record for two years' work.

Diack made the usual ILP criticism about too much emphasis on 'the crude materialism of Karl Marx'. But another, more relevant point, perhaps made John Maclean think twice.

Diack pointed out, after giving a list of the books recommended for pupils, that there was not a single one bearing directly on Scottish history, Scottish land and labour problems, or on any phase whatever of Celtic literature. 'Scottish authors are conspicuous by their absence. And that, too, in a Labour College for Scottish working-men and women!' He criticized the choice of *Working men Co-operators*: 'no one would ever suspect from reading it that the pioneers of Co-operation in the United Kingdom were a little group of Scottish miners who discovered the merits of associated trading, thirty or forty years before the Rochdale pioneers founded their historic store. . . . Scotland may be relegated to the background in our ordinary schools and colleges, but there is no reason why Scottish history—and particularly Scottish political history, of the past 120 years, should be omitted from the Labour College curriculum.'

He concluded:

> The cause of Scottish national independence has been placed in the forefront of its programme by the Scottish Labour Party, and the union of Scottish Labour and Scottish Nationalism ought to find a fitting reflex in the curriculum of the Labour College. I think I may confidently predict that when the James Connolly College is opened in Dublin the promoters will not be open to the reproach that they are interested in the social and industrial history of every country but their own.

It seems likely that Maclean did take account of this indignant reproach, but what excited him at this period was the realization that the *employers* were now very much aware of Marx's economic theories, and were using them for their own benefit. In *The Worker* of 1 December, he pointed out that,

> The Yankees, having no fear of Marxism in America, long ago adopted the Marxian point of view, and hence it is by no accident that Taylorism and Scientific Management sprang up across the Atlantic. The war compelled Britain to accept and adapt the first fruits of Taylorism. The new view was typically expressed by that up-to-date capitalist, Lord Weir, who, in an address to the business men of Glasgow, insisted that the main factor in production is man-time . . . so therefore labour-time is the main factor in production—the mighty fact refuted for generations by University dons, but now preached by Scotland's engineering capitalist top-notcher!

Maclean advised every Shop Stewards' Committee to buy *The Weir Bulletin,* a magazine which had been issued for the first time in September to the employees to explain the function of the new Planning department. He explained that the importance of the Labour Hour as a unit of measuring value was brought out here 'more sharply than ever I have heard or read before'.

Maclean returned to the theme of the capitalists picking the brains of the socialist movement in an article 'Away with the Idle Rich', in *The Call*, 22 January 1920:

> The Government is . . . trying to get workshop committees established. It accepts the Guild Socialist notion, and foists on Labour the spurious Whitleyism. Recently *The Call* quoted Dorman of the Dorman Long Group on the Teesside as urging virtually 'One Big Union'.

H

Why all this? Obviously to stave off real Bolshevism. The Marxian Theory of Value applied under capitalism increases production and increases exploitation. Workshop committees, Whitley Councils and Industrial Unionism, under the guidance of the capitalists and the Capitalist Coalition mean greater harmony, greater peace, inside the workshop and inside the whole sphere of production.

Because the capitalists accept our theory and the type of structure we as Marxians may suggest, that is clearly no reason why we should scrap our theory and mechanism for the control of production after we displace our enemy from power. They played the same game in the old days when they stole our socialist thunder and our socialist programme for election purposes.

52/American imperialism

Well before the end of the war the rise of American imperialism began to haunt Maclean. America had derived great benefit from its initial lack of involvement in the war, and, as he pointed out in his Labour College pamphlet *The War after the War,* had now 'definitely passed from being a borrowing to a lending country'. By the time Britain managed to manoeuvre America into the war in the spring of 1918, it had already become the 'supreme economic power in the world'.

All during 1919, Maclean kept hammering away at the danger involved in the growing bitter commercial rivalry between America and Britain, and wrote a pamphlet called *The Coming War with America* in which he began by laughing to scorn the prevalent euphoria about the new League of Nations being able to prevent future wars. He showed that America's foreign trade had trebled during the war and was still increasing:

The New York bankers have united forces to finance exhausted Europe. The loans, of course, will take the form of foodstuffs, raw materials and machinery to re-establish economic life. This will give America a grip on European markets and on European peoples in the event of war with Britain. America is naturally seizing the opportunity, too, to get a grip on other world markets, especially on those of South America and China. . . .

America is exploiting Ireland's distress and this explains the mighty reception given to De Valera, backed up by loans in due course. In case of war Ireland would be a fine naval and air base against Britain. Britain could be kept out of the Atlantic, and if cut off from the continent by a ring of opposing powers her course as the Mistress of the Sea would be run. This explains Britain's madness in suppressing the Dail Eireann (the Sinn Fein Parliament) and Irish papers, and the imprisonment of Irish patriots. America is exploiting this all right. She is showing herself as the 'righteous democracy' whilst at the same time she is absorbing her own little Ireland—Mexico, to wit.

He gave many examples of the commercial rivalry ever growing more acute between the two powers:

Both combatants know that the country that can sell cheapest and yet make immense profits, is the one that is able to create its wealth in the least time. The less the time to do a job, the less the cost. To produce in less time the worker is now being urged to work harder and harder, to increase his production. The gospel is work hard! harder! hardest!

He continued by detailing the various methods by which the workers were induced to work harder: profit-sharing, scientific management, improved machinery, trustification, scientific research and education—and now welfare work:

Shorter hours, better conditions, football and cricket fields, baths, clubs, mid-day meals, and other expressions of welfare work all make for health, and health makes for the vitality and energy essential to production at the highest pressure. Everyone now knows that it is possible to do more work in 48 hours than in 56 hours a week, even on the land.

In conclusion he asked his readers to choose: 'world Bolshevism now or a few years hence another world war':

However Labour may attain power, it must do as the Bolsheviks are doing; it must get full possession of land and all means of production in order to use these co-operatively by the whole community in the creation of wealth for the advantage of all. That this would have been done peacefully and fairly in Russia but for the venomous intervention of British capitalism, aided more or less by world capitalism, must now be admitted by every fair-minded man. It can be done everywhere without bloodshed unless the propertied class in devilish glee prefer the course of social destruction to that of reconstruction along the lines of socialism.

It is the duty of workers to get into One Big Union along the lines of industry right away and not wait for the snail-like movements of the Parliamentary Committee of the TUC; and to fall into line with the miners, who have conducted a great and growing campaign, not only to benefit miners, but the rest of the workers as well. The programme must be widened so as to make the objective not mere nationalization of trustified industries, but the complete socialization of production and distribution. Nationalization implies the payment of rent and interest; socialization means the payment of neither rent nor interest.

Maclean's attitude in this matter was fairly widely held at this period. It was by no means unique. William McLaine, one of Maclean's SLC colleagues, reviewed the pamphlet in *The Call* (26 February 1920), making it clear that the BSP shared his opinions:

> The new work by Comrade Maclean marks another stage in the campaign initiated by the BSP—the campaign of warning and enlightenment as to the real relationship between Britain and America . . .
> Of course, everybody says that Britain and America are friends, and could not possibly go to war. Everybody from Lord Haldane and the Kaiser downwards (or upwards) said the same about Germany, and the war came. . . .
> This pamphlet by a Marxian shows why a lending country must dominate. It shows the imperialism of America to be no less insistent and insidious than the imperialism of Britain and Germany.

At this period, Maclean could see no possibility of one or the other side winning without a war, but Maclean's first biographer, Tom Anderson, twelve years later, saw the situation in a different light. Commenting on Maclean's statement, 'The Marxian contention is that war cannot be avoided if capitalism lasts, and many Marxists are of the opinion that the principal antagonists in the next war will be Britain and America', Tom Anderson said:

> In the light of events of today that statement made by Comrade John was prophetic. Britain must find a way out, but America bars the way; she holds the trump card, the economic power, and she will not let go her hold, and Britain in her death struggle will be compelled to go to War with America or surrender and become a vassal of the Almighty Dollar. There is no middle course for our bourgeois.

The Vassal of the Almighty Dollar! Surrender without a struggle! It took another world war to complete that process.

53/Break with the BSP

The only myterious part of John Maclean's life was his break with the BSP at Easter 1920. The impression has been given by Tom Bell and Willie Gallacher in their respective books, and also by Harry McShane in his pamphlet, *Remembering John Maclean*, that he resigned, but he himself declared otherwise.

I have already quoted a passage in which he stated categorically:

> Rothstein's activities drove Fairchild out of the BSP, and his approaches to me created a situation that compelled the BSP to gently slip me out.

Next year in his 'Open Letter to Lenin' (*The Socialist*, 30 January 1921), he repeated his allegation:

> After his visit to Russia, Malone addressed meetings about the conditions of Russia, and last year joined the BSP, after Rothstein's attempt to buy Fairchild and myself brought on Fairchild's retiral from the party and my secret expulsion.

It seems to me that this process began at the St Andrew's Hall Russian Revolution Commemoration meeting in November, when Malone was one of the speakers along with Maclean. It seems clear from frequent subsequent references to him that Maclean strongly suspected Malone of being a government agent, worming his way into the confidence of the BSP leadership. Later, in June 1920, Maclean wrote in *Vanguard*:

> Since I spoke with him in St Andrew's Hall, Glasgow, I have denounced him as an agent of the Government soothing the Socialists whilst the Government was preparing for a Spring offensive against Russia.

It was by now common knowledge that Malinovsky, who for years had been a trusted member of the Bolshevik Central Committee, was indeed a police spy. Scottish history, including the ill-fated 1820 Insurrection, has been riddled with the activities of government agents. It therefore did not seem far-fetched to Maclean to suspect that there should be 'informers' and 'agents provocateurs' in the ranks of the socialist movement any more than it had seemed to him far-fetched that convicts in Peterhead Prison should be drugged and their spirits broken. With regard to the prison persecution, he always maintained that the class struggle did not cease behind prison doors. While he may have been unduly suspicious, probably sometimes of the wrong people, that did not mean that he was suffering from persecution mania, as Gallacher later maintained. Gallacher was by no means the 'dangerous man' of the Clyde, and himself suffered nothing like the severe punishment meted out to Maclean.

On 26 February, *The Call* advertised a 'Hands off Russia' demonstration to be held at the Albert Hall, London, with both Maclean and Malone on the list of speakers. Subsequently the paper reported this meeting, but there was no mention at all of Maclean. I have been informed that he refused on this occasion to speak on the same platform as Malone. That appears to have been the beginning of the end of his long membership of the SDF/BSP. He duly attended the Easter conference and was reported as having moved an addendum to another resolution 'to the effect that, should the Allies cross the Rhine, we should use our best endeavours to bring about a General Strike in this country.'

There were no further references to Maclean in *The Call*, so I can only deduce what happened from several references to the conference by Maclean himself. Commenting on the Unity Convention in August, at which the new Communist Party of Great Britain was formed, he wrote:

> I myself was automatically excluded from this London show, through the trickery of the Cockney, Cant, who refused to recognize the Tradeston Branch of the old BSP, of which I became a member on the death of the Pollokshaws Branch. My objections to Inkpin & Co were stated publicly and privately at the 1920 Easter Conference of the BSP. I have no objection to the programme of the London gang, but to their honesty and to Col Malone, who was on the EC of the Reconstruction Society. (*Vanguard*, November).

So one of the bones of contention was Malone, who was actually elected to the Executive Committee of the BSP at the conference which expelled Maclean. The other bone of contention was obviously the money and jewels which had been coming from Russia to finance the revolutionary movement. This was of necessity a completely 'hush-hush' business, and could not be openly discussed. This is the factor, of course, which makes his expulsion so mysterious. Later (*Vanguard*, September) he was to refer to the

BSP as 'a party that has been corrupted by money, no one clearly cares to say whence its origins'. This seems to suggest that he thought some of the money might be coming, not from Russia, but from the British government. This ties up with his suspicion of Malone, and possibly of Rothstein as well. When Gallacher talked later about Maclean's 'hallucinations', but never said exactly what they were, I imagine he meant his suspicion of Malone and his antagonism to Rothstein and himself.

After his expulsion, he struck out on his own, and re-issued the *Vanguard*, this time published by himself. In the first issue he referred to the paralysis of both BSP and SLP and it seems likely that he meant not so much that these organizations had been daunted by the success of the government's anti-working-class strategy, but that they had been corrupted by 'easy money'. In addition, there is no doubt that he regarded as sterile a great deal of the in-fighting going on as a result of Lenin's directive that the new party must affiliate to the Labour Party and take part in parliamentary activity. In the event, the heated and endless arguments going on about Labour Party affiliation turned out to be quite academic, as the CPGB's application for affiliation later in the year was turned down in a most decided manner.

The interminable arguments about the respective merits of political and industrial action he regarded as fiddling while Rome burned:

During the first four months of this year nearly £200 million have been invested as new capital. That surely shows how the bosses are piling up capital on which more and more profit must be paid by the workers, the Henry Dubb class. All the time the Socialists are discussing **whether Lenin can wink as well with the right eye as the left eye.** (My emphasis, to show that Lenin was now the new 'Pope' of Marxism.)

By the time he was expelled, therefore, Maclean had apparently reached the conclusion that the BSP was finished as far as revolutionary activity was concerned, and he did not fight against his expulsion, as far as I know.

In his first copy of *Vanguard* (May), his leading article gave a resumé of the recent events leading to his present action:

MacDougall went to work in the mines in Lanarkshire, and started among the miners there the finest piece of Socialist propaganda ever conducted in Scotland. *Forward* carefully suppressed references to MacDougall's work as his policy of revolutionary direct action was antagonistic to that of the editor and the fossil-types inside the ILP. None the less, the work was done, and that explains the fervent support Lanarkshire gave to the premature Forty-Hours Strike, and to the policy of aggression last year that lifted the British miners into the forefront of the workers' movement throughout the world.

The skill and cuteness of the Government prevented a strike of the miners, who might have received the support of the rest of the workers to the detriment of the British proposals at the Peace Conference, to the defeat of Britain's Anti-Russian policy, and to the endangerment of British capitalism itself. Whilst giving free scope to Smillie and his colleagues at the Coal Commission —now seen to be a farce to stave off revolt—the Government set itself to the task of breaking up the miners' reform movement and driving MacDougall out of public life. This accomplished, it then faced up to the Miners' Federation itself, and has now succeeded in driving Smillie out of the fighting ranks, has defeated direct action for nationalization of the mines, and has isolated the miners from the other trade unions.

The reference to the defeat of the miners concerned the special TUC congresses, of which the movement had had such high hopes. The congress of December 1919 had fended off the miners' claims by promising to conduct an intensive educational campaign on nationalization. The congress of March 1920 came right out against any kind of direct action and re-affirmed the traditional view that the only way to obtain nationalization was through parliament. Regarding Smillie, according to a short biography in *The Book of the Labour Party*:

A period of bad health and failing eyesight followed the strenuous months of the Commission, and resulted in the resignation of Mr Smillie from the Presidency of the MFGB, although he still retained his chairmanship of the Scottish Miners.

Maclean went on to warn:

At the same time it (the Government) has paralysed the BSP and the SLP, and may do so to the ILP as well, so as to clear the ground for a safe and sane Labourism, safe and sane because it is dominated by ideas of the reform of capitalism rather than by a determination to destroy capitalism and inaugurate the Workers' Republic.

And he concluded:

Dissatisfaction with the plight of the BSP maimed by this year's onslaught of capitalism has compelled us to resurrect the *Vanguard* in the hope that we may concentrate the minds of the workers on the revolution to be gone through in this country as well as on the one gone through in Russia. The main use of the Russian workers' success is the inspiration we ought to derive from it for the accomplishment of a similar feat within the bounds of Britain.

Do what it may, the British Government cannot prevent the revolution. Bribe and destroy whom it may within the ranks of Labour, it cannot prevent the mental evolution of the masses who are being kicked into line by the disillusionments of the war's aftermath and the transformation of joint stock companies into One Big Trust.

If this modest little paper can play its tiny part in breaking the spell the dominant propertied class hold over the minds of the workers then it will justify its existence.

54/The 'Vanguard' campaign

When John Maclean turned up at the Glasgow May Day demonstration (still being held on 1 May) selling the new *Vanguard*, it caused quite a sensation. He had so long been faithful to the BSP, through thick and thin, that it would have seemed quite inexplicable had conditions been normal. But, of course, conditions were not normal in the revolutionary movement. It was in a state of flux; the different parties were in the melting pot, and old party loyalties were rapidly disappearing.

Maclean was not long alone. He was quickly joined by young Harry McShane, also a foundation member of the BSP, and a member of the 'suspect' Tradeston Branch. McShane, an engineer, had been a shop steward at Weir's Works, the cradle of the Clyde Workers' Committee, and had played a prominent part in all the 'Red Clyde' activities. He helped to sell the paper and offered to chair the meetings which Maclean was advertising in the *Vanguard*: every Sunday night at the corner of Renfield Street and West George Street; the subjects during May to be: The Economic Need for Communism, the Historical Evolution of Communism, Methods of Attaining Communism, and Reconstruction under Communism. I imagine that Maclean was planning these meetings as a rallying ground just as the Bath Street meetings had done in 1915, and that the *Vanguard* would play a similar role.

Although the first number of the *Vanguard* was of necessity a one-man band, half was devoted to 'May Greetings to Russia', with long articles by Zinoviev and other Bolsheviks (taken from other periodicals, of course) giving vivid pictures of the situation inside Russia.

The central feature of the new paper, however, was the 'Fighting Programme' around which he planned to conduct a big revolutionary industrial campaign, as he had done in the spring and summer of 1919. In his introduction he began with a dig at the socialists who were, in his opinion, keeping back the revolutionary movement:

> In the ranks of the Socialist movement are still to be found those who parrot today as they argued in 1914, that no Social Revolution is possible until the vast majority of the wage-earners are conscious, revolutionary Socialists. They remind us of the Socialists at the other extreme who argued that society would slowly evolve into Socialism with an accompanying improvement in the lot of the labouring class and an increase in their happiness.
>
> The latter failed to see that since at least 1900 the real wages of the workers were diminishing and that after trying political action through the Labour Party the more intelligent urged the others on to direct action, creating a general unrest directly traceable almost in every instance to the reduced purchasing power of frequently shrinking wages.
>
> The former appear likewise to be blind to the possibility, nay probability, of a revolutionary impulse of the masses as a consequence of an economic break-down on the Continent leading to a similar phenomenon here. Should that impulse come and the masses get on the move, this human avalanche will sweep the political power of the present ruling class into the historic past and assume power itself.

He went on to urge that the socialist vanguard in this country should lead the way by pushing concrete immediate demands, just as the Bolsheviks had done with their slogan of 'Peace, Bread, and Land!':

> Very well, then ours is the duty to formulate an immediate programme that will appeal to all workers and so prepare them for united action. We must have such a programme that no capitalist will concede, one that necessarily must bring about a clash with the dominant class; a programme that may not immediately inspire the workers to action, but one that in a crisis might so rouse them that by effective spontaneous effort they will sweep the capitalists out of power.

A SUGGESTED PROGRAMME

1 A six-hour maximum working day.

2   A minimum wage of £1 a day.
3   Reduction of prices to half the present level.
4   Rationing of work to absorb the unemployed.
5   Payment of full wages to the unemployed.

This was obviously an elaboration of the Minimum Demand Programme of the Miners' Reform Movement, and Maclean explained that the first two items had already been accepted by the Workers' Committees' Movement, and should now be universally acceptable. He pointed out, also, that the third demand, the reduction of prices, was now being pushed by Bob Smillie and the Scottish miners. Regarding the last two items, he explained that Tom Mann, the engineers' leader, had been 'going strong' on economic security, the rationing of work, and full pay for the unemployed, so these items should also be acceptable.

He called on all left-wing socialists to push these demands through their unions, as had been done in South Wales, and continue to demand another special TUC congress. 'The prosecution of the industrial class war will break the capitalist shell sooner or later'.

During the month of May he set forth on another of his tornado-like campaigns, helped by Harry McShane, who had lost his job and whom he persuaded to become a professional revolutionary like himself. James Clunie (a close friend, and later Labour MP for Dunfermline), recorded in his *Portrait of John Maclean*:

> During the early stages of the Russian Revolution and the formation of the Communist Party, when financial aid was being freely given but often to the wrong people, John Maclean always advised me that he could get all the funds he wanted from the workers on the Clyde.

This was certainly true of this period, before the great depression clamped down with terrible strength towards the end of the year. Collections at the mammoth meetings and the enormous sales of literature brought in ample money to finance more literature, more activity, and provide a living for the two men. Later there was enough money to provide for another three propagandists, and also to produce literally millions of leaflets which were to be distributed all over industrial Scotland.

Later Maclean was able to report in the June *Vanguard*:

> Although doing this work largely on my own to begin with and arriving everywhere practically unadvertised, I have had most encouraging welcomes (especially from 'drunks'!) and have had the able assistance of the Left-Wing Socialists. Through the

sale of some copies of *Condemned from the Dock,* I expect soon to have £20 on hand. With this I intend to issue a leaflet on the programme for free distribution at the works. I trust shop stewards will help with this work.

During May he wrote to Tom Mann asking for his help with the Fighting Programme, which was freely given, and demonstrated by articles which he wrote for practically every edition of *Vanguard.* He also wrote to the Foreign Secretary, Lord Curzon, requesting permission to visit Russia during the months of July and August, when the Second Congress of the Third International was to take place.

Towards the end of May he visited Dundee to promote the Fighting Programme, and recruited another member for his propaganda team. This was Alexander Ross (usually called 'big Sandy'), an ex-policeman who had lost his job when he went to prison as a conscientious objector during the war. He had been a member of the ILP, and he brought in another ex-conscientious objector and ILPer, Peter Marshall of Glasgow. Peter had been a Post Office clerk before the war, but he also had forfeited his career, and was now unemployed. MacDougall, whose health had improved again, was also brought in. These men, with the exception of Sandy Ross, were of the best type of 'worker intellectuals'—able to speak, lecture, and write well. Ross was a complete extrovert and no intellectual. Peter Marshall told me that probably he had not even read through a pamphlet. However, he had a flamboyant personality and a ready wit. He could draw a crowd and make it laugh and this was valuable to Maclean, who was always deadly serious on the platform. Marshall was also jocular and witty, and later proved to have a special talent for lecturing on economics. I had my first lessons from him many years after; and if John Maclean was better, then he must have been brilliant indeed. Harry McShane was called the 'boy', and did a lot of the donkey work. Later he proved to have a special talent for political writing. One day later on Maclean referred to his team as 'The Tramp Trust Unlimited', and the joke stuck.

While in Dundee Maclean took the chance to push the Labour College work as well as the Fighting Programme. A Dundee and District Committee was formed and the secretary, E G Carr, reported in *Forward* (5 June):

Last week we had a course of 19 lectures on 'Economics and the Social Revolution'—tutor, John Maclean. After an attempt to get the University Lecture Hall for our course, we had to fall back on the ILP Hall . . . The hall holds only 200, so we had to

confine the number of the class to the size of the hall. Easily
double that number of tickets could have been sold, so many were
disappointed. . . . Maclean worked like a Trojan, and well deserved
the thanks given at the closing lecture. Every day at a work-gate
Maclean held aloft the flag of socialism, and the message was
straight and clear, and did a lot of good.

On the Saturday following this marathon educational course,
Maclean and Carr organized a Labour College Conference at
Arbroath and formed a District Committee there. At this conference
it was reported that the Dundee Committee had already gathered
£50 towards the appointment of a full-time tutor for the coming
winter session.

The annual meeting of the Scottish Labour College was held
on 29 May and was attended by 530 delegates. It was reported that
district conferences had been held at Aberdeen, Dundee, East and
West Fife, Edinburgh, Falkirk, and Arbroath. In Aberdeen and
Edinburgh, local branches of unions had agreed to levy their
members twopence, and sometimes threepence, per head per
annum, to help the College work in their own districts.

It was also reported that the College had received about
£2,000 during the previous year, that the Fife miners had put aside
£450 for bursaries to send three day students for a year during the
1920/21 session, and that the Lanarkshire miners had allocated
£300 for the same purpose. So it appeared that Maclean's most
cherished dream, a Day College, might be fulfilled in the near
future.

During the previous year the work of the College had been
so successful that the general public was greatly surprised, according to an article in the *Glasgow Herald* of 5 June. This article
criticized the College severely for its narrow curriculum and 'ill-
balanced teaching, based almost entirely upon Marx'; it recommended that the College should co-operate with the WEA 'which
has a connection with the Universities', and that it should amalga-
mate with the Central Labour College in London (where the tutors,
reflecting the general political outlook in the south, were not so
extreme in their views!) Maclean, as we have seen, was uncom-
promisingly against any co-operation with the WEA, but some
members of the College were apparently not so determined. It
appeared that John McClure, formerly of the SLP, had during the
war moved the dismissal of Maclean during the latter's imprisonment. He had joined the ILP at the end of 1919, and was now
being boosted by the element inside the ILP which supported
MacDonald and Snowden and which Maclean called 'the official

wire-pulling gang'. The latter backed the WEA. Maclean once again warned that any attempt to fuse the Scottish Labour College with the WEA would be disastrous, and gave, as an example, Ruskin College.

In the June *Vanguard*, Maclean called on all shop stewards and believers in industrial solidarity and action who were willing to promote the Fighting Programme to attend a conference on 5 June. This was a great success and it was decided, among other things, to issue a hundred thousand leaflets explaining the Fighting Programme. Soon the Tramp Trust was busy all over industrial Scotland.

55/Hands off Ireland!

Maclean was able to blazon on the front page of the June *Vanguard* 'THE FIGHTING PROGRAMME WELCOMED', and the rest of the paper also showed that it was no longer a one-man band. It included a splendid article by Dora Montefiore, which was a review of Upton Sinclair's latest book *The Brass Check*. Maclean's never-ceasing concern for Russia was reflected in the publication of an article by M Katz, 'Lenin the Seer', together with an appeal from the Kiev Soviet of Workers' and Red Army's Delegates 'To the Workers of Europe and America', graphically describing the savage Polish onslaught. In another article, 'Russia's Triumph', Maclean kept his readers up-to-date with news about Russia, and ruefully declared that his attack on Colonel Malone for soothing the Socialists 'whilst the government was preparing for a spring offensive' had been justified.

But he ended triumphantly:

> We are glad to hear that the London dockers have struck against sending supplies to Poland. Let it become a General Strike.

However, it was an article by Maclean on 'The Irish Fight for Freedom' which demonstrated the direction which the *Vanguard* campaign was to take more and more in the coming months. During May, appalled by events in Ireland and the almost complete ignorance in this country of what was actually going on, he wrote a powerful and moving pamphlet *The Irish Tragedy: Scotland's*

Disgrace, giving the brutal facts about the campaign of terrorism.

He pointed out that the recent war was supposed to have been fought to defend the rights of small nations, yet Ireland at the General Election of 1918 and at the municipal elections and county elections of 1920, had voted with a vast majority of four to one for an independent republic. What did Ireland actually get, however? An army of occupation with 'aeroplanes, tanks and other blessings of civilization'!

He also showed that the excuse that Russia was at the mercy of a 'dictatorship of terrorists' had been used to justify the spending, by Winston Churchill, of almost two hundred million pounds in the direct and indirect attempt to overthrow the Russian Republic during the past year. But, he maintained:

> To any right-thinking person Britain's retention of Ireland is the world's most startling instance of a 'dictatorship by terrorists', as Britain rules Ireland against Irish wishes with policemen armed with bombs and a huge army equipped with over 40 tanks and as many aeroplanes, machine guns galore, and all the other beautiful manifestations of Christian brotherhood, love and charity.

He also laughed to scorn Britain's contention that it was holding Ireland in order to defend the Orange Protestants who, it was maintained, would have a rough time of it if the Irish Catholics were in power:

> Just remember Britain's excuse for entry into the war. Was it not to defend poor little Belgium against Germany? Even Lloyd George tried on that 'wheeze' on Xmas 1915, in St Andrew's Hall, Glasgow, when he came to persuade the Clyde workers to accept dilution of labour. But everyone ought to know that the Belgians are Catholics and the Prussians Protestants.

> Does anyone really believe that Britain fought the greatest world war to protect Catholics against Protestants on the Continent, and now is preparing to turn the Emerald Isle red with Catholic blood to protect Protestants?

Maclean then asked the question: what was Britain's *real* reason for desperately hanging on to Ireland? He maintained:

> Ireland stands between Britain and the Atlantic Ocean, on which British ships must freely sail, in case of war, to preserve the people's food supplies. If Ireland were an independent republic and formed an alliance with America, which Bottomley in *John Bull* now calls 'Britain's Next Enemy', then in the event of war . . . Irish ports would be the base of operations of the American fleet

and Irish soil would be the base of operations of the American Army.

He went on to describe some of the repressive measures which had been taken against the Irish people and declared that it was impossible to expect the Irish to suffer this kind of terrorism without some kind of retaliation.

He proceeded to describe how Irish dockers and railwaymen had followed the example of the London dockers who refused to load the *Jolly George* with ammunition for Poland and were now refusing to supply the Army of Occupation with the 'ammunition that may be used to kill themselves when off industrial duty'. Irish railwaymen were now asking the Executive Committee of the NUR to take action to prevent ammunition being sent to Ireland, but that body was at the moment trying to pass the buck to the Triple Alliance and to the TUC, so Maclean demanded:

> Are the rank and file going to submit to the usual dilatoriness, or are they going to force the pace themselves by taking direct action themselves?
>
> Britain is pouring more and more troops into Ireland . . . A terrible tragedy may be perpetrated by Britain before Labour has realized the full gravity of the situation . . .
>
> The real centre of the Irish fight is Liberty Hall and the Transport Workers' Union.
>
> A General Strike, then, for the withdrawal of British troops from Ireland, and the demand of the release of Jim Larkin (America) and his brother Pete Larkin (Australia).

Harry McShane has recorded that twenty thousand copies of *The Irish Tragedy* were sold throughout Scotland in the following months.

Meantime, the reactionary NUR leader, J H Thomas, had persuaded his executive to demand that Irish railwaymen should return to work, and that all should agree to the handling of ammunition not only for Ireland but also for Poland and Roumania. The result of this traitorous move was, as Maclean explained:

> The Government has seized hold of the NUR advice to its members to assume that the British workers will condone any bloody deeds in Ireland. . . .
>
> This is the greatest question confronting Scotland today, for if speedy action is not taken a horrible tragedy will be enacted, and Scotland will be disgraced for ever. This is more important than protesting against higher rents or the high cost of living. **It is acquiescing and participating in the murder of a race rightly protesting its own right to rule itself.** (My emphasis.)

In accordance with these sentiments, the Fighting Programme in the July *Vanguard* ceded pride of place to Ireland. The article 'Scotsmen Stand by Ireland!' filled the front page, and the 'Hands off Ireland!' campaign was carried on concurrently. This took a great deal of courage, because of the large Orange population among the Scottish working-class. However, it wasn't until the end of June that the Tramp Trust ran into trouble in what Maclean described as 'the Battle of Motherwell'.

On 29 June all five members descended on the Wishaw and Motherwell area armed with thousands of leaflets called 'Proposed Irish Massacre' (a hundred thousand were distributed in central Scotland), and held mid-day and evening meetings to advertise the big meeting in Motherwell the following evening. Maclean described what happened:

> Prompt to time the meeting started, Marshall setting off. Immediately interruptions arose from a crowd of Orange hooligans directly in front of the speaker, but Peter kept on in an unperturbed manner till the natural close of his witty and eloquent address. By this time the street was absolutely packed. . . .
>
> Then came the real fun of the evening. As soon as I started the howling started in earnest. Shouts of 'traitor!', 'Peterhead', 'square head', and even obscene language were hurled at me whilst policemen and plainclothes men were in the audience. Had Socialists acted thus and used such language at a Carson demonstration (and I am a better man than lawyer Carson any day), the police would at once have arrested fifty (probably innocent) persons and had them fined heavily or imprisoned up to six months. Had Irishmen treated Carson thus, fifty would have been sentenced to a year each, and the mocking boss press of Britain would have rung with paid indignation against the 'brutal intolerance' of the Irish, and would have drawn the necessary moral as to the fate of the saintly Orangemen living inside an Irish Republic.

He described how he warned his 'vast, quiet, attentive and patient audience' to expect no reasoned and consecutive address from him because, from his past experience of Orangemen, he knew what would happen. He himself, however, must have become unusually irritated by the interruptions, because he proceeded to taunt the Orangemen:

> when I told the crowd that the Sinn Feiners and nationalists by vote in January had captured 'Derry and that therefore 'Derry walls had surrendered, this galling statement was too much for the hooligans who had come to enrage me. Like mad bulls amidst shouts of 'Up 'Derry!' they rushed down on me. My friends dived

forward, too, to save the bag and the literature in front of the ILP platform. In the scramble the platform collapsed.

Just at this moment, to my surprise, up rose the determined shout, 'Up Dublin!', and with that a company of young Irish Volunteers, who had kept as quiet as Pussyfoot all through the Orange rowdinesss, rushed from behind in frontal attack on the hooligans.

After the Orangemen were routed and order resumed, he went on with his lecture in peace. Even during the first years of the war in the days of war madness, he had never been subjected to an attack like this.

He ended his article with a passionate plea for the Scots to line up with the Irish:

My lecture on Ireland is meant particularly for Scotsmen in view of the fact that the Government intends particularly to use Scottish regiments to do their dirty work in Ireland. My desire is to prevent Scotsmen being used to smash our sister race, the Celts of Ireland, for English capitalists who are descended from the Germans. Scotsmen have been taught to hate the Irish as a different race. They are not. The Welsh, the Scots and the Irish are all of Celtic origin, so that from a racial point of view the Welsh and the Scots ought to line up with the Irish.

He ended the article in his usual optimistic style:

The Irish workers are now organized in the Irish Transport Workers' Union. . . . These workers are revolutionary in outlook and are bound, on the establishment of a Republic, to convert it into a Socialist Republic with Celtic Communist tradition as a mighty driving force.

Until the Orangemen fall into line with their class we ask the wage-earners to combat them mercilessly. Up, Ireland! Up, Scotland! Up, the Social Revolution!

On the front page of the August *Vanguard* was a full-page cartoon showing the Connaught Rangers refusing to fire on the Indians, and Maclean entitled it 'The Greatest Deed in British History!' In an article, 'Up India!', he enlarged on the significance of this event:

It was a gloriously stupid piece of folly for the War Office to send Irish soldiers to India as it is now learning to its cost. . . . *Manchester Guardian*, stimulated by the 'down guns' of the Connaught Rangers wrote a 'leader' pointing out the coming disaster in Ireland. It warns the Government to be cautious, since Irishmen in large numbers are to be found in every regiment and battleship. If a Civil War starts, the MG sees the possibility of every regiment being rent in twain and a mutiny in every vessel of the navy, as well as an Irish outburst all over the Empire.

We see, further, that other soldiers will learn the CR lesson and refuse to shoot their class when called upon—and even take Labour's side. That happened in Russia and elsewhere on the Continent . . . The Irishmen in the bosses' army and navy will be the centre of such revolt. The Irish situation, obviously, is the most revolutionary that has ever arisen in British history, but unfortunately lads who fancy themselves the only revolutionaries are too stupid or too obsessed by some little crochet to see with sufficient clarity the tight corner the Irish are placing the British in.

56/Fighting for a Scottish Communist Party

Maclean's increasing interest in the question of Scottish independence naturally meant an increasing determination to have a separate Scottish Communist Party.

In the meantime he had received the following reply to his request for permission to visit Russia:

Lord Curzon is unable to give a reply to your request at this moment, but if you will apply to him again towards the end of June he will consider whether the necessary facilities can be granted to you or not.

Maclean accordingly re-applied on 17 June, adding that he trusted that 'Lord Curzon will this time reply favourably in view of the new situation arising out of the government's negotiations with M Krassin.' This referred to the trade negotiations going on between the two countries.

Having nevertheless been refused permission, Maclean applied through Cook's Touring Agency for a passport for Denmark and Sweden. Eventually this was also refused, to his great chagrin. Among those who had been allowed to go to Russia were two members of the ILP: the chairman, Dick Wallhead and Clifford Allen, a member of the Executive Committee. Their visit was the result of pressure from the large number of members who were sympathetic to affiliation to the Third International. Thus the delegates to the annual meeting of the Scottish Division had, in January 1920, voted by a large majority in favour of leaving the Second and affiliating to the Third.

There is no doubt in my own mind that this swing towards revolutionary socialism in the Scottish ILP was due to Maclean's marathon campaigns in 1919, when many of his meetings had been held under ILP auspices. Another factor was, of course, complete disillusionment with the old International. The formation of a Communist fraction took place at the Easter conference in 1920. This became known as the 'ILP Left Wing'. Wallhead and Allen met the Executive Committee of the Comintern. After a series of informal discussions with Lenin and other Bolshevik leaders, they drew up twelve questions which were submitted to the Committee on 25 May. On their return the replies were published by Harry Glass on behalf of the ILP Left Wing and boosted by Maclean in *Vanguard:*

> This pamphlet must play a greater part in the moulding of British thought than even Marx and Engel's *Communist Manifesto* did in the past. Out of it we who claim to be Communists must get the basis of Communist Unity in Britain. . . . Before the winter Scottish Communists ought to come together in conference and discuss unity on the basis of this momentous document.

This is the first record which shows that Maclean was himself proposing to form a Scottish Communist Party. This may seem odd to those who do not understand the extent of Maclean's support among the Scottish masses, or that he was still regarded by the Bolsheviks as the standard-bearer of Communism in Britain. When the invitation had come to the BSP to affiliate, it had come, not to the BSP as a whole, but to John Maclean and his friends. Even now, after Maclean was out of the BSP, the Executive Committee of the Comintern, according to the ILP pamphlet, still equated him with the Bolsheviks and held him up to the ILP as an example to follow.

This pamphlet, of which Maclean so enthusiastically approved, was an elaboration of the Twenty-one Points, strict adherence to which was imposed on all organizations affiliated to the Comintern, but it is interesting to note in passing that the Comintern rather differed from Lenin regarding Labour Party affiliation. A big change in the Labour Party constitution had taken place during 1918-19. Individual membership was introduced and a definite political programme, including the famous Clause IV was adopted. The Comintern noted this change:

At the present moment there is a tendency of the opportunist leaders to make the Labour Party a real party with local organizations and a programme. They aim to create a large opportunist party which is to retard the revolutionary development of the masses. Were this tendency to succeed, the Labour Party would never afford the socialist organizations which form part of it the right to an individual communist policy, nor to the propagation of the revolutionary struggle. It would bind their freedom hand and foot. It is thus evident that no kind of organization seeking to carry out a communist policy could possibly belong to the Labour Party.

Maclean, of course, agreed with this. He had voted at the 1919 BSP conference for continued affiliation to the Labour Party, but once the new party began to take shape he never again supported affiliation.

Before Rothstein left Britain to attend the Second Congress, according to Gallacher in his *Last Memoirs*, he met Maclean and tried to bury the hatchet:

> Theodore . . . told him that he was the representative of the Bolshevik Party in Britain and that the comrades in Moscow were very anxious for John to take a leading role in the foundation of the new British Party.

Most of the people with whom I have discussed the matter think that Maclean made the biggest mistake of his life in not going illegally to Moscow, as Gallacher and others did. It may be that Lenin, who did not understand the national situation in Britain and always referred to Maclean as 'Maclean of England' (as did also the Comintern in 'Moscow's Reply to the ILP'), would have agreed to a separate Scottish Communist Party, as indeed he apparently agreed to a separate Irish Party. In the end, though, it was not only a *Scottish* revolutionary party that Maclean wanted, but also one that was independent of 'outside dictation and finance', as he said in a letter to James Clunie. At the moment, however, he saw the corruption as being centred in London and wanted no truck with it.

At the beginning of August a Communist Unity Convention was held in London, when the majority of the BSP branches and a section of the SLP (called the Communist Unity Group), united to form the new Communist Party of Great Britain. Scotland, however, was not well represented. Only seven Scottish BSP branches, one Communist Unity Group from Glasgow, and one ILP branch sent delegates, together with one delegate from the Greenock Workers' Social Committee. The Social Committees were the brainchild of the *Worker* group, who wanted to form Committees not only at the place of work but also at the dwelling places of the workers. This had been evolved, according to Maclean, 'to dish the BSP', to which most of the *Worker* group had become hostile, because of its support for Labour Party affiliation.

The decision of the new party to apply for affiliation to the Labour Party, according to Walter Kendall,

> provoked hostility among the Scots communist groups. On 14 August, the *Worker* called the decision an 'unpardonable mistake' adding that the Communists in Scotland are nine-tenths anti-Labour Party, and that there was 'not the slightest prospect of the Communist Party in its present form making any headway north of the Border'. In the next issue, Alex Geddes, who attended the Unity Convention as a delegate from the Greenock Workers' Committee called for a 'Scottish Communist Party'. Discussions amongst the groups centred round the *Worker* began almost immediately, and were held in the paper's office.

Later, when he came back from Russia, Gallacher was to sneer at the idea of a Scottish Communist Party, but in the meantime Maclean had the backing of most of the Scottish communists. His next step was to call for a Communist Council of Action. In August there was a scare that Britain, pressurised by France, was going to declare war on Russia. The Labour Party formed a joint Council of Action along with the TUC, with the possibility of a general strike in the background. For various reasons, Maclean believed this was a put-up job, engineered by Lloyd George who was not ready for war with Russia (being fully engaged in Ireland!), but who also did not want to disagree with France, and used the Labour leaders to frighten the latter.

Maclean's reaction was to issue a reprint of the pamphlet *Russia's Appeal to the British Workers* which had been scattered amongst British soldiers when they occupied Russian territory in 1918-19. He added a preface calling for a *Communist* Council of Action, explaining:

> The Labour Councils of Action will not fill the bill. There are plenty of honest men acting as leaders of Labour, but proved traitors are at the helm—the Hendersons, the Thomases, and the Clynes.
>
> We Communists are the only ones that can lead society to Communism. Therefore we must form a Communist Council of Action to assume the real power when the proper moment arrives.
>
> In the process I favour a Scottish Communist Republic as a first step towards World Communism with Glasgow as its headquarters. We must have a rank and file dictatorship through

delegates directly representative of the various workshops and industries.

We must start Scottish Communism round the organization of the Scottish Co-operative Society and the distributive branches, as food supplies are the first requisite.

With this pamphlet Maclean issued a leaflet, 'All Hail! The Scottish Communist Republic!', which Harry McShane recalls created a sensation when it was distributed at a large housing demonstration at Glasgow Green. In it he gave expression to the Connolly tactic—the combination of communism and nationalism:

Scotland must again have Independence, but not to be ruled by traitor kings and chiefs, lawyers and politicians. The Communism of the clans must be re-established on a modern basis. (Bolshevism to put it roughly is but the modern expression of the communism of the Mir). Scotland must therefore work itself into a Communism embracing the whole country as a unit. The country must have one clan, as it were—a united people working in co-operation and co-operatively using the wealth that is created.

We can safely say, then: Back to Communism and Forward to Communism.

The control must be in the hands of the workers only, male and female alike, each workshop and industry sending delegates to District Councils and the National Council.

The National Council must be established in or near Glasgow, as half the population live within a radius of twenty miles from Glasgow.

In the period of transition a Wage-earners' Dictatorship must guide production, and the adoption of the machinery and methods of production, to Communist methods.

Many Irishmen live in Scotland, and, as they are Celts like the Scots, and are out for Irish Independence, and as wage-earners have been champion fighters for working-class rights, we expect them to ally themselves with us, and help us to attain our Scottish Communist Republic as long as they live in Scotland. Irishmen must remember that Communism prevailed amongst the Irish clans as amongst the Scottish clans, so that, in lining up with Scotsmen, they are but carrying forward the tradition and instincts of the Celtic Race.

The September *Vanguard* contained the first of a series of articles by Erskine of Mar on 'Celtic Communism'. Maclean also poked fun in that issue at the *Glasgow Herald*'s horror at Erskine's

---

*   Erskine and Maclean that year founded the Scots National league, the object of which was the 'The resumption of Scottish national independence.'

declaration at a Sinn Fein demonstration at Trafalgar Square, London, that the Scottish Gael was 'preparing to overthrow the English Government and proclaim Scotland's independence.' The *Herald*'s comment has a rather topical ring about it:

> We are discussing serious schemes for removing the local administration of Scotland from Westminster to Edinburgh, and we do not want to have their consideration interrupted by absurd caricatures of their meaning.

Maclean commented:

> By the time this appears we expect to have . . . in circulation 100,000 leaflets urging on towards a Scottish Communist Republic. Our vast audiences are catching up the idea already all right; and ideas win in the long run against ridicule and force.

In the same article, Maclean paid tribute to the Tramp Trust Unlimited, declaring that it was the greatest institution Scotland had ever produced:

> In three months it has published, paid for, and distributed almost half a million leaflets. In the same period it has collected and realized off literature sales over £500. That is a record for four or five men that stands unchallenged. **If there were fifty of us working thus in unison** we would put the *Glasgow Herald* and the robbers of Scotland out of action in six months. **Let Lenin realize that we are the real leaders of Communism, and not the men who have got through to Russia,** and that we are creating that Communist outlook that must make for Revolutionary Mass Action. Come together, comrades, into the Scottish Communist Council of Action as a first step to a clear and clean Scottish Communist Party. (My emphasis.)

When it is realized that the *Vanguard* and most of the pamphlets being sold were only twopence the real magnitude of this achievement can be measured. About sixty thousand items of literature had been sold in three months, literature which was packed with solid Marxist propaganda and educational material.

It should be realized that Maclean fully intended to bring the Highlands into his plans for a Scottish Communist Republic. In August he attended the Highland Land League annual conference, and was asked to second the resolution on Scottish independence. Resolutions were also passed in favour of public ownership of the land, economic rent to be paid to the government. Maclean reported that 'there was general approval of Communism under the control of the industrial workers, the fishermen, and the crofters and other land workers. . . . A real Gaelic revival as well as a Lowland revival must result.'

In pursuit of his concern about the Highlands, Maclean made his way to the island of Lewis in the Hebrides during August. Lord Leverhulme, the Sunlight Soap magnate, had floated a company called *The Lewis and Harris Welfare and Development Ltd*, apparently for the purpose of developing industry in these Hebridean islands. It was decided to clear the islands of its crofters, but many of them were recently demobilized ex-servicemen who had been promised land by the government after the war. Some of them refused to be evicted, and the farms of Coll and Gress were 'seized'. Maclean visited Coll to see for himself what was going on. He met four of the 'raiders', and later published a long article in the September *Vanguard* called 'The Highland Land Seizures'.

Maclean saw in this government-backed development something more sinister than the usual capitalist industrial enterprise:

> Leverhulme has insisted that he requires Coll and Gress Farms as part of his scheme for dairy farming purposes to supply milk to Stornoway. This excuse is a joke, as I saw on MacBrayne's boats milk cans that had brought milk from Aberdeenshire. If milk is now being brought in, it can surely be brought in afterwards when the population of Lewis has been shepherded into Stornoway as his 'Lordship's' wage-slaves.
>
> I am convinced that my first impression is correct, that Leverhulme is preparing Lewis and Harris for the navy in case of war with America. The 'Mac Line' of trawlers (now transferred to Fleetwood) were to sail from Stornoway right north to Iceland and perhaps Greenland, and most of the catches were to be canned at Stornoway. A breed of fishermen would thus be fostered who would know the waters and be handy in case of war. . . . Remember that Britain has forced Denmark to give Iceland independence, and by the use of methods now well known to Leverhulme the inhabitants of Iceland will be induced to take the side of Britain against America. Britain controls Greenland; so that by this chain she would have a continuous sweep right across the north of the Atlantic to Canada.

He advised the Lewis men to hold fast, and not to play the game of either English or American imperialism. The workers on the Clyde were prepared to help the families of the raiders if they were put in prison. However, the raiders were ultimately persuaded to give up their farms, and Maclean commented on the Highland situation in *Vanguard*:

In the autumn we intend to make 'a big push' on the Highland question . . .

Lord Leverhulme must not be allowed by bribery and corruption to use Highlanders to oust Highlanders out of their native land. We must encourage the Highlanders to co-operate communally, to cultivate the land with the latest machinery and with the latest discoveries of science, and to communally catch fish as well. . . . If the Bolshevik notion of world Communism through national Communism is scientifically correct, then we are justified in utilizing our latent Highland and Scottish sentiments and traditions in the mighty task confronting us of transforming Capitalism into Communism.

Every edition of *Vanguard*, apart from the first May issue, had a leading article dealing with the world situation, and included in the September one there was a significant paragraph dealing with the situation of the British Empire:

The British Empire will soon burst under the various national pressures. Egypt is being granted a nominal independence, and this sham concession will inspire India, S Africa, and other parts of Africa, and Ireland to greater activity. . . .

Even in Scotland the demand is being made, not for an anaemic local Government, but for complete Independence. An Independent Scotland would refuse to let her lads fight the battles of the maniac English who hold the obsession that the world was made by God for them to rule and rob. An Independent Scotland would fight with Ireland and not against Ireland.

Since the British Empire is the greatest obstacle to Communism it is the business of every Communist to break it up at the earliest moment. That is our justification for urging a Communist Republic in Scotland.

57/One big union

Like Connolly, Maclean coupled this aggressive anti-imperialist policy with the advocacy, industrially, of the speeding up of union amalgamation. The formation of the Amalgamated Engineering Union, in place of the old Amalgamated Society of Engineers, prompted him to publish in July, Tom Mann's article, 'The Passing of the ASE', taken from the *ASE Journal*. Along with this, Maclean included an article by himself called 'One Big Union', setting down for the first time as far as I am aware, his ideas on union organization, just as he had done for co-operative movement organization nine years previously:

> Tom Mann's admirable little article on the death of the ASE suggests a discussion on the whole question of organization, industrial and social.
>
> We Communists believe that the working class is a unit, and in organization ought to be a unity; in other words, that in industrial affairs there should be One Union, inclusive of all workers, subdivided according to industry for economic purposes, and re-subdivided again for technical or craft purposes since craft crosses industries.
>
> All know, for instance, that engineers are found in all industries requiring machinery. These ought to be aggregated inside the industry they are engaged in, and also brought together with comrade engineers as well on a craft basis for purely technical purposes.
>
> This double shuffle is only possible inside One Union for All Workers. Two factors are making for solidarity . . . First of all, labourers constantly migrate right across a host of industries, and hence their unions are being forced together with at least a million and a quarter members.
>
> One can easily imagine that once this amalgamation takes place every labourer in every industry will have to show his or her union card and badge. The numbers must soon rise to at least five millions. This General Labourers' Union, or whatever may be its baptismal name, will consequently overshadow all the old skilled and semi-skilled craft and industrial unions, and wrest organized power from them.
>
> It is, surely, clear to all that the struggle to retain power will force the skilled unions to carry the amalgamation process a stage or two further on towards the One Big Union for All. Engineers will have to amalgamate with iron and steel workers, and then with shipbuilders. One textile union must come into being, and so on . . .
>
> Another factor—the main one—making for the One Union is the process of trustification at present evolving very rapidly towards One Big Trust of all British industries . . . Trustification means specialization of the various works in an industry. This, with standardization of parts, means mass production of uniform work. In these circumstances a man is confined to one machine and one job for life perhaps. He loses his craft skill or never needs to learn it. He thus becomes only a 'handy man'. The machine thus becomes a leveller, a breaker of craft and skill barriers. . . .
>
> This is the main factor in driving 14 unions into the AEU,

of which Tom Mann will be the secretary. Still the AEU is inadequate against Beardmore and Vickers, as these Capitalists control several industries. Not organization, but profit, determine the line of activities . . .

The One Union implies workshop committees representative of everyone inside particular works—a scientific re-organization from the bottom up through the district to the national committee. The national committee must be a permanent one, linking up all industries and organizing the production and distribution of wealth, and in conjunction with political representatives will do the work that ought at present to be done by the Capitalists' Parliament. Parliament must fade away when Labour unites scientifically, and commands control of the land and workshops of the country.

58/Pioneering again

As the summer of 1920 wore into the autumn, the campaign for the Fighting Programme was shoved into the background, first by Ireland and then by unemployment. Later, at the beginning of January, Maclean wrote 'An open letter to Lenin', (*The Socialist*, 30 January 1921), in which he accused Gallacher of giving Lenin an exceedingly over-optimistic view of the situation here:

He has led you to believe that there is a workshop movement in Scotland. That is a black lie. I have been at work gates all summer and autumn up and down the Clyde valley, and I am positive when I say that victimization after the premature forty hours' strike crushed the workshop movement. Unemployment today has struck terror into the hearts of those at work, as starvation is meant to tame the workless. No industrial movement of a radical character is possible at present outside the ranks of the miners.

It should be explained here that Maclean and his associates never at any time led their supporters or their audiences to believe that a revolution was inevitably just round the corner! Mother told me that prior to the war, Maclean believed that it would be about fifty or possibly a hundred years before Britain would be ready, but that the war and the Russian Revolution transformed the situation.

By this time it had become obvious to Maclean that the massive revulsion against the Liberal Party amongst the workers as a whole was being expressed, not in a revolutionary upsurge as had been hoped, but in 'a safe and sane Labourism'. Maclean had to admit this in an article 'Still the Fighting Programme':

> Such vast masses of workers and their wives live lives of unremitting toil relieved only by pictures, 'boose', betting, and sports that in matters of social and political affairs they do little more than drift along in the current. As the strongest current is now the Labour one, they sympathize with everything attached to Labour true or false, and are prepared to vote Labour now on till death.
>
> Yet hosts of these people, when reading the above programme, have shaken their heads and declared that we could not get it. If our sympathizers are so lacking in knowledge about the mass of wealth produced by Labour and stolen by the boss class . . . then it is evident that we revolutionists must buckle to more strenuously than ever in the work of widening the concepts and outlook of our class.

He went on to acknowledge, also, that perhaps the *Vanguard* had been too dull and too heavy, with too much theory—'untrained and particularly exhausted workers cannot be bothered about theory', but at the same time he pointed out that many of them, instead of backing up the Fighting Programme and demanding shorter hours to absorb the unemployed, were clamouring for overtime to augment their diminishing wage packets. This Maclean saw, as he later saw gambling, as a kind of counter-revolution and protested:

> Stop everywhere all overtime. Striking is of no use if you work overtime after to make bigger profits for the boss . . . Instead of allowing overtime, a real fight for the shorter day ought to be commenced. If the working day is shortened without proportionate increase in output more men will have to be employed.
>
> Everyone knows that the greater the number employed the fewer there must be unemployed. The fewer 'signing the books' the less the competition for jobs. In these circumstances Labour gets bold and demands more money. If by the reduction of hours one can increase one's rate of wages per hour, so that in the end as much can be earned in six hours as formerly in eight, one's obvious duty is to fight for the shorter working-day. It is short-sightedness more than greed that makes Henry gasp for 'overtime'.

As the number of unemployed grew astronomically, Maclean saw that they must be organized, and in October began holding regular unemployed demonstrations in Glasgow. At the first one a deputation was appointed to meet both the Trades Council and the Town Council. In the November *Vanguard* he described the Town Council's reaction:

The Town Council had to receive our deputation since it was the last meeting prior to the Elections. A refusal meant a sure win for Labour.

We demanded food at municipal restaurants as the most urgent question of all. Then work on farm colonies at trade union rates of pay, with representation on all committees employing the unemployed. We requested houses to shelter full families on the colonies. We urged the Corporation to proceed with all available work of a new and repair character . . . Finally, we requested use of a city hall in which the unemployed might meet and comfortably discuss the situation.

. . . Under powers from the meeting, the committee right away interviewed Bailie John Stewart, convener of the Municipal Restaurants Committee, and Bailie John Wheatley, convener of a special committee to find work under Corporation auspices for the unemployed.

The Committee has also urged the Distress Committee to meet it, as well as the Parish Council and the Education Authority.

We have found up-to-date every committee willing to convene a special meeting to discuss matters with us.

Bailie Wheatley's Committee met our delegates and agreed to *grant the City Hall three times a week* and agreed to convene the heads of departments to get work under way. The next day this was done. . . . The Restaurant Committee meets on 28 October and the Distress Committee on 29 October. Never before in the history of Glasgow was such alacrity shown. Why? Because our committee appears every day lobbying Labour Councillors and others on every issue.

We wish the Education Authority to proceed with boots, clothes and food for the children. We wish Barnhill Poorhouse to be placed at the disposal of the homeless.

In fact, we mean to exhaust every constitutional method of safeguarding the unemployed of our class. Whatever happens after that we certainly will not be to blame.

At this point he deprecated the action of the *Worker* group (mainly Gallacher, J R Campbell and John S Clarke) in encouraging men discharged from the Albion Motor Works and Beardmore's to seize works as some of the unemployed did at Coventry:

To rush a works just now would mean split heads and a defeat for the Labour candidates . . . A Labour Town Council will respond to our pressure more readily than a bourgeois one. If Labour fails then a forceful revolutionary fight is the logical next stage. Unemployment has not really begun yet, neither has the winter. There is ample time for desperate deeds before the winter is over if other and more 'constitutional' means fail.

Only provocateurs would rush the situation at this juncture. Had the Clyde Workers' Committee pursued the fight for the shorter working week after Bloody Friday we might see reason for their anxiety about the unemployed at the present time. . . . They have done sufficient this last eighteen months to earn the contempt of every real Revolutionist.

J R Campbell retaliated by trying to 'capture' or break up the Unemployed Committee founded by Maclean. Meanwhile the Trades Council also reacted, and a Trades Council Unemployed Committee was formed, consisting of one representative from each trade union, two from the Trades Council, two from the ILP, two from the Town Council Labour group, and four from Maclean's Unemployed Committee. A preliminary demonstration was organized to meet in the City Hall on 9 December, and Maclean warned:

Remember that the bosses are now beginning to use the Unemployed Army as a weapon to break wages. A slump in wages may take place after the New Year, when the trade slump comes, unless Labour is organized, united, alert and combative.

At the November municipal elections, forty-four Labour councillors were elected, but the Tories held power. It is interesting to note how the Unemployed Committee was received after the elections, as told by Maclean in his Trial Speech in October 1921:

When December came I saw that in January unemployment was going to be very severe and thought the Corporation was not doing enough. I urged our Committee to again try to see the Corporation Committee or the whole Corporation, but the Town Clerk said it was against the Standing Orders of the Corporation to hear the Unemployed Committee a second time because a special Committee of the Corporation was carrying out that work and he referred us to that Committee. I urged that it was not working hard enough. We led the Unemployed in front of the Municipal Buildings, but we were kept out by the policemen; every entrance was barred. I asked to see some of the Labour Councillors, but the Lord Provost would not grant us permission to enter as a deputation. We saw a big number of policemen in the Courtyard of the City Chambers, and although we tried again and again to get in, we were refused.

59/No Scottish Communist Party

Meanwhile the fight for a separate Scottish Communist Party had been going on vigorously. A meeting between Maclean's supporters and the *Worker* group held on 11 September had been successful and another meeting called for 2 October 'with the object of the definite forming of a Communist Party composed of all the Left Wing element in Scotland.' (*The Worker* 25 September.) When Gallacher returned from Russia on 27 September, the situation changed completely. Later, in the December *Vanguard*, Maclean described him as 'going the rounds ridiculing the idea of a "Scottish" Communist Party because he has been to Russia and poses as the gramophone of Lenin'. Gallacher now began to assume the mantle of Lenin and the Russian Revolution, and brought his influence to bear heavily against a separate party in Scotland. Lenin had decreed that there was to be one party in Britain (Ireland was not now regarded as part of Britain, however, as a separate Communist Party *was* formed there).

This must have had its effect on the *Worker* group, because Maclean and his supporters apparently did not attend the meeting on 2 October, at which a Communist Labour Party was formed, with John MacLean (of Bridgeton) as secretary. Most of the left wing in Scotland believed that the appointment of this other John MacLean was deliberate, in order to confuse the public. Maclean certainly thought so, and in an article called 'The Irish Tragedy', he for the first time gave vent to his angry feelings. The Irish situation took pride of place in this article, and it must be pointed out again that at this time his determination to fight for an independent party was linked with his support for the Irish struggle.

He began with a passionate denunciation of Lloyd George's speech at Caernarvon on 9 October, when Lloyd George had admitted that the real reason for holding on to Ireland was to hold on to her ports: 'Hand our ports over to Ireland, the gateway of Great Britain! They might starve us. No!'

It was in this context that Maclean denounced the formation of the Communist Labour Party:

Why did I visit Arbroath on Saturday, 11 September, but to protest the hollow mockery of the sex-centenary celebration of the Scottish Parliament's declaration of independence to Pope John XXII, whilst Scottish boys dressed in the garb of the English Government were then and now daring the Irish to set up a free and independent Irish Parliament elected by the overwhelming vote of the Irish people? . . .

Have I not urged the establishment of a Scottish Communist Republic as a means of arousing the wage-slaves of Scotland to the immediate and urgent need of withdrawing Scottish lads from Ireland, and Scotland itself from English-paid Edinburgh KCs and the English boss class? Did I not try to have formed a Communist Council of Action as a preliminary to one substantial Revolutionary Wage-Slave movement with headquarters in Glasgow and with Scottish inspiration behind it? Was not this sidetracked by Messer and that shadow now mis-named 'The Scottish Workers' Committee', who neatly used the name of John MacLean of Bridgeton to have established a Communist Labour Party, this time to dish the SLP as the same clique's 'Social Committees' served to dish the BSP branches?

Gallacher and *The Worker* have sneered openly at the idea of a 'Scottish' Communist Party, although all connected with *The Worker* have been compelled to trade under the name of the 'Scottish' Workers' Committee. There is no reason for the existence of a Communist Labour Party, as its object is the very same as that of the Communist Party of Britain. . . .

The formation of the CLP is a shameful bewilderment of honest Socialists disgusted with the babyish tactics of the wire-pullers of the ILP . . .

Such brutally wanton shattering of the hopes and spirit of the best fighting elements in Scotland becomes a base betrayal of the wage-slaves of the world and the subject peoples of the world at such a critical juncture as this. . . .

The tragic situation that Lloyd George is now openly admitting justifies the existence of an honest Scottish Communist Party. The geographical cleavage makes the situation quite clear.

We refuse to be bluffed by Gallacher that Lenin says we must have only one Communist Party in Britain. Why does Gallacher help to start another Communist Party if he is so anxious about Lenin? *I for one will not follow a policy dictated by Lenin until Lenin knows the situation more clearly than he possibly can know it from an enemy to Marxian Economic Classes* as Gallacher privately declared himself to me to be.

I

On 13 November, Gallacher in *The Worker* insisted that the Comintern was now the authoritative voice of world communism, and had decided that there could be only one Communist Party in Britain. In the December *Vanguard*, Maclean announced that he was summoning all in Scotland who favoured the Comintern's 'Twenty-one Points' to join together with the SLP, now the only group of any size outside the CPGB, and form a Scottish Communist Party, which was to be founded on 25 December, at a special conference.

In an article, 'A Scottish Communist Party' in the same issue (which was also to be the last) he stated:

> We are of opinion that the SLP will raise no vital objections to the preliminary conditions laid down by the Bolshevik International at Moscow. Until 'real delegates' can get a chance to meet our Russian comrades in open and mature conference, the 'points' enumerated are but provisional, and need cause no heat or undue excitement. The main thing is to get the clear-headed and honest Marxian Revolutionaries into one camp. We in Scotland must not let ourselves play second fiddle to any organization with headquarters in London, no more than we would ask Dublin to bend to the will of London.
>
> Whatever co-operation may be established between the Revolutionary forces in the countries at present composing the 'United Kingdom', that co-operation must be based on the wills of the free national units. . . . Let attention be paid to Point 17: 'Each party must change its old name to that of Communist Party of such and such country, section of the Third International'. . . . Nothing in Point 17 precludes the formation of a Scottish Party as Scotland is a definite country. . . .
>
> Scottish Marxists are surely not going to accept as an authority on Marxism a man such as Gallacher, who never was a Marxian, but an openly avowed Anarchist. Lenin, Trotsky, and the Bolsheviks were and are very rigid Marxians. Because of their faithful adherence to principles they have won through and are holding out with amazing success.
>
> A real Revolutionary Party can only be established here on Marx, not on Bakunin, by fully avowed Marxians of long years of standing. If Lenin tells us to unite with elements who are Anarchists, we must reply by asking the Bolsheviks to unite with the Mensheviks or Social Revolutionaries. **We stand for the Marxian method applied to British conditions. The less Russians interfere in the internal affairs of other countries at this juncture, the better for the cause of Revolution in those countries.** (My emphasis.)

Prior to the Christmas conference, Gallacher saw fit to write

a letter to the Executive of the SLP warning of Maclean's 'hallucinations' etc. A copy of this letter was sent to Maclean who, naturally, was extremely angry. It was no surprise, therefore, that when Gallacher and his supporters turned up at the conference, uninvited, there was some trouble.

MacDougall was elected to the chair, and Maclean's opening speech analysed the developing crisis of capitalism, emphasizing the revolutionary potential of both the Irish in Britain and of the unemployed. Before the business of the evening could proceed, however, the question of Gallacher's letter cropped up, and the fat was in the fire. During the bitter recriminations, Maclean accused Gallacher of being 'no better than a government agent' and that he had come to 'burst up this organization'. Some of those present almost came to blows, and the whole affair was blown-up in the capitalist press, presumably reported by an informer in their midst. The meeting ended in a defeat for Maclean's ideas when an SLP spokesman informed the audience that the SLP was not prepared to fuse into a Scottish Communist Party. Maclean and his supporters were fully prepared for this eventuality, however, and the conference ended when Maclean moved a resolution calling on unattached socialists to join the SLP.

He later explained this move in *The Socialist*, when he called the SLP the 'only clear Marxist organization in Britain', and said that he now 'thought it opportune to fuse with the SLP rather than form a new Party for Communism inside Scotland, especially as Glasgow is the area where most of its best work has been done. . . . The SLP has at least to its great credit the printing of the finest Marxian literature in the world. To allow the SLP Printing Department to be crushed would be a crime to Marxism, upon which alone a successful revolution can be based. It is the duty of all determined Marxists to rally to the SLP'.

In this article he also pointed out that his support in Glasgow was stronger than ever before:

On the Monday after the conference, 27 December, at the unemployed meeting in the City Hall, J R Campbell, Gallacher's comrade, came for the third time to capture the meeting. He was voted down, and would have been struck down as well but for my intervention. If that is not proof of confidence in me by the unemployed . . . what is?

He also pointed out that although Gallacher and his men had sneered at him for emphasizing the need for a Scottish Communist Party, yet they had been advertised to speak at the International

Hall on 6 January, under the auspices of the 'Scottish Communist Labour Party'!

On the day of the Unity Conference of the CPGB held at Leeds on 30 January, Maclean published in *The Socialist* his 'Open Letter to Lenin', in which he warned him to be very chary of anybody coming from Britain:

> You will recognize that it is the business of the British Government to deceive you and get you to make false calculations, as it made the Kaiser form wrong estimates.

He pointed out that if the capitalist class found it necessary to use a Labour government as it had used Lloyd George and the Liberal government, then:

> A sham Labour Government, with our beloved friends MacDonald and Snowden (and ethereal Ethel too) will be formed although the real work will be done by the 'Old Gang' under the guise of the Privy Council.

He knew, of course, that Lenin had the real measure of the Labour leaders, but he warned him also about the 'leaders' of the Communist Party being formed that day!

> Now *The Communist*, the successor to *The Call* when the BSP was transformed into the CPGB, has passed into the control and editorship of Mr Meynell, who retired from the directorship of the *Daily Herald* when Lloyd George charged him with bringing jewels to England from Russia to subsidize the *Daily Herald*.
>
> If Lansbury and he thought it good tactics to dissociate the *Daily Herald* from Meynell, why is it that Meynell now assumes editorship of what is recognized as the official organ of the CPGB? Who is Meynell and what is Meynell? is a very appropriate question. To my knowledge he never was in the SDF or the BSP. He has as much standing in revolutionary circles in Britain as Malone.
>
> It is only in a country such as Britain, ruled by the most unscrupulous and cunning capitalist class that has ever disgraced this earth, that totally unknown, untried, and inexperienced men could be thrust to the front.

Maclean then went on to relate some of the events already described and emphasized,

> Do not place reliance, then, on the United Communist Party that will be formed today, and do not rely on the workshop movement either.

He also warned Lenin that the only Russian who really

understood the situation in Britain was Peter Petroff:

> Petroff is the only Russian who knows the working-class movement intimately in London and Glasgow. Until his imprisonment in 1916 Petroff stayed with me, and worked with MacDougall and me to build up the mass movement that is now beginning to manifest itself in Scotland. . . .
>
> It is by no accident that Dr Shadwell, after a recent tour over Britain, wrote in a series of articles to the London *Times* that the Clyde was the most revolutionary centre in Britain. Dr Shadwell is perfectly correct. Ask Petroff the reason why.
>
> The unemployed are better organized in Glasgow than elsewhere in Britain . . . Three thousand five hundred unemployed meet twice a week in the City Hall, so that we may discuss principles and tactics applied to the present situation from a Marxian point of view.

He went on to say that this mass movement was bound to be augmented as more and more men were thrown idle, and because many of the wage-slaves in Scotland were Irishmen, 'whose country is being more and more cunningly and cruelly tortured.'

He concluded this agonized appeal:

> This I let you know, so that you may not despair altogether of Britain, although you had better examine more critically than ever the fairy tales that are likely to be poured into your ears by conscious and unconscious tools of Lloyd George and the propertied class of Britain.

60/Organising the unemployed

The seven months' episode of the Tramp Trust Unlimited, the only period of his twenty years' political activity during which Maclean was not a member of a political party, has been used by his enemies, particularly during the Stalinist period, to prove that he did not believe in 'the party', or that he was of such a quarrelsome temperament that he could not submit to the discipline of a well-organized party, and more nonsense of this description. In actual fact, it was Gallacher and his supporters who did not believe in the political party, until Gallacher was converted by Lenin in the summer of 1920!

Already Maclean, with a prescience engendered by his profound knowledge of Marxism, had put his finger on the fatal flaw of the Comintern, which was to become, because of the failure of the world revolution, a supra-national rather than an international organization. The tendency displayed during the Second Congress to emphasize the role of the Communist Party, organized on an authoritarian basis, rather than that of the Soviets, was expressed by Zinoviev:

> The Communist Party must be strictly centralized, with an iron discipline, with a military organization. Yes, with a military organization. In **England** (my emphasis) we have four or five separate Communist groups . . . This must be put an end to.

Events had forced a system of military discipline on the Bolsheviks, who still saw the Comintern as the body that was to lead the world revolution, and were quite certain that it must have the same system of military discipline. This meant, in effect, Russian domination, with the national units having little say even in the formulation of tactics. Eventually this was to play right into the hands of Stalin and his friends.

After his seven months' uninhibited freedom of expression in the *Vanguard*, Maclean was now, voluntarily, a member of a party whose views he had never supported one hundred per cent. But because it was mainly a Scottish party and its organ, *The Socialist*, was centred in Glasgow, he thought that he might be able to build it into the Scottish revolutionary party he thought necessary.

In the meantime he had to submit to party discipline, just as he had done during the years in the BSP, and he was not able to express his own ideas on Scottish independence or support for the Irish struggle. Through the columns of *The Socialist*, therefore, we can trace only his activities in the developing Unemployed Movement, which had the total support of the SLP leaders, of whom Tom Mitchell, editor of *The Socialist*, and James Clunie, Maclean's SLC colleague, were two.

The Labour Group in the Glasgow Corporation and the Trades Council Unemployed Committee, were proving quite ineffective, and Maclean realized that the unemployed would have to help themselves, organized in the Unemployed Movement. In addition to constant deputations to the City Chambers, and the bi-weekly meetings in the City Hall where 3,500 men were taught the elements of Marxism, demonstrations outside in the streets were regularly held.

The dole was only fifteen shillings a week for a short period, after which, if men could still not find work, they had to apply for parish relief, administered under the old Poor Law system. Able-bodied men could be refused 'outdoor relief'—that is, they had to live in the poorhouse at Barnhill, separated from their wives and families. Even when relief was granted, the amount was at the discretion of the local Parish Council, and was generally lower than the amounts granted in England.

The Unemployed Movement, therefore, began a campaign to force the Parish Councils to grant the larger amount. Huge demonstrations were organized at the different Parish Council Offices all over industrial Scotland but especially in Glasgow, and Maclean and his 'ragged army' became the terror of all the parish officials. Charles Doran, now a member of the John Maclean Society, but then a young immigrant from Dublin, and a member of Guy Aldred's Anti-Parliamentary Communist Federation in Glasgow, described one incident which was typical of the kind of work Maclean did at that time:

> Matthew Foy, one of Bridgeton's down-and-outs during the tragic slump days, speaking to me one day after John's death, could hardly control his emotion as he told me of the morning he went to John's house in Newlands to seek his help against the Parish Authorities who offered the Poor House to Matthew and outdoor assistance to his wife and family. John took Matthew by tramcar up to the City Chambers at George Square. As John entered the Council Offices, several clerks hailed him with 'Good morning, Mr Maclean!' John brushed all that aside and demanded 'Send Reynard to me!' Mr Reynard was the Chief Officer. He came along, and John told him 'Here is this man. You know about him as you consigned him to the Poor House when you refused him outdoor relief.' Reynard tried to argue in terms of law. John was quite brusque, and threatened a demonstration. That was enough for Reynard, as he was well aware that John Maclean could organize a gigantic demonstration, as he had done on previous occasions. So Matthew Foy was sent at once to the Cashier with an authorization from Reynard for a cash payment.

Direct action with a vengeance!

MacDougall and Marshall were concentrating mainly on the Labour College work, which Maclean was inclined to neglect occasionally in favour of his work with the unemployed. Nevertheless, he was very happy with his day students, and spent a great deal of time with them.

In an article called 'The Unemployed: Will there be a General Strike?' in *The Socialist*, 27 January, Maclean gave a report of the special Joint Congress on Unemployment organized by the Trade Unions and the Labour Party. He did not expect any real action, he wrote, only bluff, but he did welcome the proposed formation by the TUC of a General Council, instead of the parliamentary committee, which was a part-time, voluntary body. Maclean had advocated the organization of such a body over a year ago, as we have seen, and now he had great hopes that its formation might lead to a situation of 'Dual Power' in the country:

> Thus may be built up outside Parliament the instrument that will take the place of Parliament, that will as well take over production and exchange of wealth from the Federation of British Industries, the Chambers of Commerce and the Institute of Bankers.

He also saw this new organization taking over the educational work now being done by the Labour Colleges:

> That the science of society in its evolution and its functioning may guide the workers in the mighty transformation that is preparing, it is necessary that we hammer the fundamentals of Marxism into the brains of our class. This can be most systematically done by the new Trades Union Congress Committee taking over the Labour College, London, and the Scottish Labour College, and making these the basis of a series of colleges and a network of evening classes all over the country.

Here he was much too optimistic, just as he had been about the Labour Party when it was formed. Actually, forty-three years later the TUC did take over the National Council of Labour Colleges, but by that time the latter had become a completely emasculated organization.

On 10 February McShane was able to report that the efforts to organize the unemployed were meeting with unprecedented success. Committees were now being formed in other districts, 'with the object of creating local interest and bringing pressure to bear on the local representatives.'

A Scottish Conference, bringing together representatives of all the Unemployed Committees throughout Scotland was held on 19 February at the International Hall. There the following proposals were agreed to:

1 That we urge Joint Conference to recommend a General Strike
2 That we ask London Unemployed Committee to represent us at the Joint Conference
3 Exemption from payment of rent for unemployed
4 Opening up of trade with Russia. Independence to and peace with Ireland, India and Egypt
5 Cancelling of war indemnities
6 Granting of one year's credit to continental nations
7 Reduction of retail prices
8 Maintenance of present rate of wages
9 Release of all political prisoners
10 All resolutions to be sent to the House of Commons, Labour Party, and TUC

A Scottish Provisional Committee was formed; Sandy Ross being appointed chairman and John Maclean, secretary.

McShane reported that the Glasgow Committee held a 'monster procession' soon after the Conference. In front was carried a banner with the inscription: '1914, Fight: 1921, Starve!' This banner became famous, as big demonstrations were held more and more frequently. Charlie Doran described them to me:

When John held meetings on weekdays in Glasgow Green at the base of Nelson's Monument, he would often feel inspired to suggest a march round the West End to 'frighten the bourgeoisie'! This was usually at night. The crowd, always a large one when John was the speaker, would agree. It might be 9 pm. John would then say: 'Form up in sections of four. I shall march at the head. At certain points I'll give the signal with a white handkerchief, and you will all shout *in unison* the slogan agreed upon'. . . .

On one occasion John, anxious to show solidarity with a comrade 'Big Sandy Ross', who was then in Duke St Prison, suggested two slogans—'We want grub!' and 'Release Sandy Ross!' Sandy Ross was a large, beefy fellow, and one could imagine him quaking in his cell, if he heard, which he probably did, 5,000 voices in unison chanting that unfortunate double slogan.

This is anticipating our story by a few months, of course, for in February Sandy was still at large, and 'larger than life'.

61/The mailed fist again

While much of Maclean's energy that winter had been spent in trying to organize a Scottish Communist Party, in agitating for support for Ireland, and in pioneering the Unemployed Movement, the routine work of agitation, education, and organization went on all the time. Since the beginning of 1919, his industrial campaigns had centred round the miners, and this continued in 1920. On 16 October the Datum Line strike began. Negotiations had been going on between the executive and the government since the spring, about rises in wages to keep up with rising prices. In addition, the miners were determined to keep the national minimum wages which had prevailed since the government took control in 1917. The executive got nowhere, however, and on 16 October a national strike was declared.

On 21 October, the NUR's special delegate meeting courageously over-ruled their reactionary leader J H Thomas, and announced that the NUR would come out on strike in support of the miners unless their demand was met in full. Next day, the government introduced its already-prepared Emergency Powers Bill, and rushed it through parliament within a week. The miners got their rise very quickly, however, but in the form of a bonus to be paid on output beyond a national level which became known as the 'Datum Line'. Maclean was disappointed about this outcome, and especially in Bob Smillie for accepting it; but pleased that the rank and file had voted against:

> Our reliance on the miners as the champion shock battalion of Labour is absolutely justified. . . . Whatever compromise the leaders patch up with Horne and Lloyd George, let the rank and file of the miners refuse to toil harder. Let the workers in other industries follow suit . . . All hail the miners!

By March, the depression had reached an unprecedented depth, with the number of unemployed amounting to a million. Maclean had already predicted that the government would begin a great offensive against Labour in March, and this indeed began with their abandonment of control of the mines, which were handed over once again to the tender mercies of the private employers, who immediately began to cut wages. The miners were threatening to come out, and many of them, especially where the Reform Movement had been strong, did strike to preserve the national minimum wage. The mine owners, now in a very strong position because of the vast number of unemployed, shut down the mines on 1 April, and the big lock-out began.

The government had been preparing for this eventuality by arresting, on trumped-up charges under the Emergency Powers Act, most of the militant leaders throughout the country, and sentencing them to the statutory three months. According to Maclean, they were trying to create the impression that an attempt was being prepared to start a revolution. At the same time the government began to make allegations about a Sinn Fein/Communist plot, and before 1 April, sixteen alleged Sinn Feiners were brought to trial at the High Court, Edinburgh, and some of them sent for long periods to Peterhead. Then English marines were brought up to Glasgow, under the impression that they were being sent north to fight not the workers, but a Sinn Fein army.

Meanwhile attempts were being made to trap Maclean into using strong language, so that he too could be sent to prison. He was very well aware of this, and made the following report in *The Socialist:*

> Even the *Daily Record* on 14 April, in a leading article entitled 'Why?' had to write thus:
> There is a new note in the public utterances these days of Mr John Maclean and fellow Communist leaders. Impassioned exhortations to heroic deeds have given place to the cautious counsels of pacific measures. It is all very strange . . . it may be there is more to fear from such men cooing like turtle doves than breathing fire and slaughter.

In Fife, the *Dunfermline Press* reported that, on 13 April, 'Cowdenbeath rate-payers woke up to find that the burgh had, overnight, been converted into what was virtually an armed camp'. Through the night, buses packed with soldiers had poured into the town, and also into another mining town, Lochgelly. Both were Maclean strongholds. Eight miners were arrested. In Glasgow, Bellahouston Military Hospital was cleared, except for a few beds. According to Maclean, the government was preparing to spill plenty of blood in Glasgow and 'give us a taste of Paris at the end of the Commune in 1871'.

On May Day, Maclean could keep up his 'cooing' no longer and threw down the gauntlet, declaring that no matter what powers the police might have under the Emergency Powers Act, he now intended to speak his mind in public.

On 4 May, an armed attempt was made to rescue an Irish prisoner from a 'black maria' conveying him from the Central Police Court to the prison. In the attack a police inspector was killed. The press at once blamed Sinn Feiners and thus gave the police the excuse to raid all suspected premises and arrest anyone in Scotland. That night a raid was made on the premises of the Scottish Labour College, but nothing was found. The secretary, Peter Lavin, told me years later, when I was trying to find old records of the College, that in a panic he had burned all the old documents, even the minute books, and that nothing had been left. Next day Tom Mitchell, editor of *The Socialist*, and manager of the Socialist Labour Press, was arrested. In Maclean's opinion this was not for publishing any seditious material in *The Socialist*, but because he had published the Sinn Fein paper, 'Dark Rosaleen' as a business proposition.

That day, Maclean addressed a huge meeting at Barrhead and advised Irishmen to stand steady and calm. When that night explosives were used to blow up telegraph and telephone poles near Barrhead, everybody blamed the Sinn Feiners. Maclean, however, suspected that it might have been done by police provocateurs to stir up trouble:

> The whole situation is wonderfully suspicious when thus knit together, and justifies us asking Irishmen and the workers generally to calmly watch developments. This is no plea for passive starvation, but for refusal to resort to childish displays of petty force when the Government is ready to give us a deluge of blood. Keep Bellahouston Hospital empty.

As it transpired later, the government had been determined to get him even before he threw caution to the winds on May Day. Rallying the miners and the unemployed had taken him all over the Scottish mining areas. (It was at this time that, as McShane recorded, he had saved up £5 for a badly-needed new suit, but gave it to the miners instead). He was especially involved in Lanarkshire, where he was trying to win enough support for a full-time tutor for the Scottish Labour College. One of his regular stances was at the corner of Hallcraig and Hill Streets, Airdrie, and there, on 26 April, the Chief Constable of Airdrie was detailed to take notes of his speech. He spoke that day as advertised, along with Sandy Ross; Harry McShane taking the chair. Soon afterwards both he and Ross were arrested and released on bail. Their trial was fixed for 17 May at Airdrie Sheriff Court, the charge being for 'addressing an audience of the civilian population and using language calculated and likely to cause sedition and disaffection among His Majesty's Forces and among the Civil Population'. They were indicted on eleven counts.

In the meantime, Maclean took time to sit down and write to his two absent daughters, Jean and myself. Mother had left him in the autumn of 1919, putting myself into the care of Maclean's younger sister, Aunt Lizzie, while Jean went to live with Mother's brother and his wife in Maryhill. Mother herself had gone out maternity nursing, living in with each case. However, that winter I had succumbed to a bad dose of pneumonia which no doubt would have killed me but for Mother's devoted nursing. For a long time afterwards I was in poor health, and she made up her mind that Glasgow, with its fogs and polluted air, was not for me. She took us both to live with her older sister, Aunt Rose, who was the infant mistress in a small country school situated in the beautiful Border countryside near Hawick. We lived at Blacklee, near Bonchester Bridge, and were having the time of our lives.

Maclean's letters to us, which from 1921 onwards were preserved, reveal the human personality beneath the fiery revolutionary, and for this reason I propose to quote extensively from them. All his letters were a mixture of light-hearted, rather whimsical fun and nonsense, and didactic teachery advice. His first letter began in typical whimsical style:

> What a great life you must be having at Good-camp Bridge! Fancy finding nests with eggs and young ones in them! I wonder what kind of language the young birds speak. Is it the Bonchester language or the Langside one? . . .
>
> You should both have been in Glasgow on May Day with the whole host of boys and girls who drove in lorries to the Glasgow Green singing the Red Flag and other songs. Sing the Red Flag every day and don't forget it. Remember every day that the masters rob the workers and that Socialism is the only thing to stop the robbery.

This paragraph and the next one show that he was concerned that our young minds should not be corrupted by the very different environment in which we now lived. We had never been allowed to take religious instruction at school, remaining outside the classroom along with the Jewish children, and he warned us:

> Don't worry about the ghost stories in the bible and the silly stories about a good god who lets soldiers kill other men to please the rich robbers.

The next week, on 14 May, he wrote, knowing that he would be sentenced to the statutory three months on the 17 May:

> I am so busy going up and down the Clyde to meetings that I have no time to kill the weeds in the garden let alone gather flowers. I think you had better both come back and keep the garden in tidy condition. . . . A lot of nice people everywhere are always asking for both of you.
>
> Now I expect to be going on holiday for three months as your mother will explain, so you will not require, perhaps, to write to me again for a long time. So be good girls, and learn hard to be clever.

On 17 May, as McShane reported in *The Socialist*, 'all roads led to Airdrie'. A large contingent of supporters, accompanied part of the way by Ross and Maclean, marched to the Court from Glasgow, and large crowds waited outside hoping to get in. The Court, however, held only a few hundred, so many were disappointed.

The eleven counts of the indictment were read out, most of them consisting of garbled extracts from the speeches of Ross and Maclean. The first prosecution witness was the Chief Constable, whom Maclean cross-examined for over two hours. Then he began to reel, and Sandy Ross explained that he had taken no food that day, and was preparing to go on hunger-strike if sent to prison Sandy continued with the cross-examination until Maclean recovered.

During his evidence, Maclean gave an outline of the speech in question, which, he pointed out, was just the same as he had given at many other places, with different illustrations perhaps, and which McShane reported in *The Socialist* as follows:

> He said that he had given the arguments in other mining districts although the illustrations sometimes varied. He said that the revolution he advocated was the coming to power of the working class. He was not in favour of fighting with Navymen, as they were not to blame. He did not believe in exhorting men to violence when they had not the accoutrements of war. He had consistently warned the workers not to run their heads below batons, nor their stomachs against bayonets. The object of the meeting was to encourage the miners, and this was clearly stated by the Chairman. . . .
>
> The Fiscal, cross-examining, questioned Maclean about what he meant by revolution. Maclean held out both hands, one above the other; he said they represented the two classes in society, the top

one being the capitalist class. He then swung his hands round to the reverse position, and said that was revolution.

Both men were found guilty, Maclean being sentenced to the expected three months and Sandy to three months plus a £20 fine (failing payment of which, another three months). On this occasion, it was thought advisable that Sandy's fine should be paid.

Maclean's threat of hunger-striking won for him the privileges of a political prisoner, unprecedented in Scottish prisons, and he was granted his own clothes, books and newspapers, bed and furniture, food, and private toilet necessities. He was also allowed two visitors a week and to write a letter once a week. Harry McShane was in charge of all these arrangements, and he told me that this was an exacting job, entailing for him a lot of work and worry.

On 21 June Peter Lavin, the Scottish Labour College Secretary, wrote to Mother, telling her that he had visited Maclean in Barlinnie and found him in good health and looking extremely well. He informed her that Harry McShane was visiting him every week, taking one of the college students with him, and also gave her news that was not so good:

> Before John was sentenced, he arranged that in the event of his being imprisoned half of his salary should be sent to you, and half given to the teacher who would come in his place. However, money is coming in but slowly, and our Treasurer, whom I saw on Saturday, informed me that nothing has yet been sent you. My delay in writing you was due to waiting for money.

It was MacDougall who took over most of Maclean's college work, but whether he was ever paid for it or not, I do not know.

There was a large attendance at the Scottish Labour College annual meeting in June. Peter Lavin reported that there were only two full-time tutors in Glasgow, John Maclean and A M Robertson, and one full-time tutor in each of six other districts— Aberdeen, Dundee, Fife, Edinburgh, Stirling and Renfrew. This full-time staff was supplemented by a number of voluntary tutors. 1,800 students had enrolled during the session, 800 of them in Glasgow.

MacDougall, in opening the discussion, pointed out the many difficulties which had faced them, including the scarcity of money in the mining districts. The Lanarkshire miners, 50,000 strong, had been able to send only three full-time students, but he hoped they would be able to send twelve next session.

J McClure noted the fifty per cent fall in the College income, a sure reflection of the desperate position of the miners at that time.

Maclean was duly released on 17 August and within hours was appearing at the Central Police Court, along with Sandy Ross, when he appeared as a defence witness for McShane who had been charged with contravening the bye-laws by selling socialist literature on Glasgow Green! Maclean, defending, said that he had been selling socialist literature at Glasgow Green for almost twenty-three years, and although on some occasions he had seen as many as ten detectives at his meetings, the sales had never before been stopped. McShane was actually fined five shillings! Such were the times.

62/I for one am out for a Scottish Workers' Republic!

Maclean immediately plunged once more into his manifold activities, especially his work among the unemployed. Because of the failure of the Corporation Labour Group to make a hard enough fight for them, the Glasgow Unemployed Committee decided to adopt new tactics, and to run Maclean and McShane as candidates in the forthcoming municipal elections, the former in Kinning Park and the latter in Kingston. They began holding unemployed meetings through the day and election meetings in the evening. Harry McShane has recorded in his pamphlet *Remembering John Maclean:*

> While the preparations were being made John was arrested once again for a speech he had made in Gorbals to the unemployed . . . John Maclean was charged with telling the unemployed to take food rather than starve. The Chief Detective, Lachlan MacDonald, who had tried for years to catch John Maclean out was in his glory.

Sandy Ross was also arrested for telling the unemployed to take food. Maclean was refused bail and his trial fixed for 25 October before Sheriff and jury. Meanwhile MacDougall had been arrested, tried and sentenced to sixty days' imprisonment for a similar offence, which so enraged Maclean that he went on hunger strike in protest, he was sent to the observation ward, and for a short period an attendant was kept with him day and night!

Meantime he issued his Kinning Park election address, which is worth recording. It consisted of immediate demands and his ultimate aim. Some of his immediate demands are only now being considered, whereas his ultimate aim of 'Socialism or Communism' seems as far away as ever:

Unemployment Our first consideration is to secure work or maintenance for the unemployed, the cost to the Corporation to be met by the Government unless where Corporation work is done.

Shelters for the Homeless No rent to be paid by the unemployed.

Municipal Restaurants To provide free meals for the unemployed and cheap meals for other citizens, and to feed striking and locked-out workers.

Municipal Management Of loading, unloading, and storage of foods at the docks in conjunction with the Dockers' Union. When dock work is slack, the dockers to be given other suitable work so as to ensure steady employment.

Housing Every family should have a house with at least a scullery, bathroom, kitchen, parlour and three bedrooms. Such houses the Corporation should build with Government loans, interest free, so as to keep down rents. We favour pre-war rents for pre-war houses.

Municipalization Generally We favour the city supplying all needs and amusements. We urge a milk, bread, beef, fruit and other food supply in association with the co-operative movement, as a step to final control by the Corporation.

We favour municipal theatres, music halls, picture houses, and other forms of amusement for the people. A huge Social Centre should be erected with a suitable public hall . . . We believe that all employees ought to have better wages and conditions than private employers provide, as an incentive to employers. Employees ought to be represented on every Corporation Committee, and workshop committees ought to be consulted by managers.

A Provincial Council Glasgow ought to embrace the Clyde Valley and so include Lanarkshire, Renfrewshire, Dunbartonshire, and perhaps a bit of Stirlingshire and Ayrshire. A Council representing this area is now necessary for large undertakings.

OUR SOCIALIST OR COMMUNIST AIM. Even supposing we had this programme carried out, we are far from the Goal of Labour—the social or common ownership of everything managed by the chosen representatives of the workers. Only when the world is run by the workers of the world for their own benefit, and not for the benefit of a landlord-capitalist-class will security of livelihood and peace between nations be obtained. That is Communism. That is why we are Communists. To convert Capitalism into Communism is a Revolution. In that sense we call ourselves Revolutionists. The Revolution can be helped by Labour voting itself into power.

The result of the election was: Moderate, 5,749; Maclean, 2,421; Labour, 1,885.

So, even though he was in jail, he was able to beat the Labour candidate.

On 25 October, Maclean conducted his own defence as usual. I have already quoted in a previous chapter his introductory remarks, giving a short account of the formation of the unemployed movement. Further excerpts help to give a picture of the desperate straits of the unemployed and the efforts to help them:

The only time Ross and myself made any public utterance to these people was in the City Hall . . . Ross's message to them was that if there were any who could not hold out it was their business to go and take food rather than die of starvation. We held to this principle, and it is one I shall hold to as long as I live. . . .
I deliberately did not use the words 'Take food if you are hungry'. I said 'There is plenty of food in the country and round about—don't starve!'

He proceeded to object to the jumbled statements mentioned in the fourth charge:

I said something on every point as mentioned there, but I said it in my own way and not as mentioned there. . . .
I for one am out for a Scottish Workers' Republic. I have even issued 100,000 leaflets for a Scottish Communist Republic. I said we must first vote ourselves into political power. I said that if we in Scotland made an effort to get a Scottish Communist Republic the British Government might then take the initiative against us . . . I then referred to the position of Ireland and said I hoped the workers of Scotland would not allow themselves to be frightened by force. I said we would not use violence; violence would be used against us.

He was then cross-examined by Sheriff Boyd for some considerable time. On being questioned about his means of subsistence, Maclean replied:

My means of subsistence come from the Scottish Labour College at which I am a tutor, and you know that.
Sheriff How did you come to organize the unemployed?
Maclean Because nobody else would.

Sheriff How many follow your banner?
Maclean I do not know.
Sheriff Does it not seem absurd to hold yourself up as the self-appointed leader of the Unemployed?
Maclean No. The Unemployed at a meeting held last October appointed me.
Sheriff What is your explanation in leading those people to the churches; do you suggest these methods were altogether peaceful?
Maclean The motive was to let the church people really see those who are starving.
Sheriff What about the Cathedral and the Infirmary?
Maclean I led the unemployed up to the Cathedral to get shelter there for those who were lying out in George Square and elsewhere.

After more interrogation of this nature, Maclean addressed the jury:

All I am out for is food for my class, and I am not afraid to say it . . . I am glad of this prosecution today because it has brought out that John Maclean is not prepared to see human beings die of starvation.

63/In prison again

The jury found him guilty and he was sentenced to twelve months' imprisonment, which he served in Barlinnie Prison. He was again granted 'political prisoner' privileges and took the opportunity to do the kind of study which his constant political activity had hitherto prevented. This must have relieved what, to a man of Maclean's restless and highly-strung temperament, was the torture of inactivity.

He had already arranged that William Montgomery, a member of the SLP who lived in Pollokshaws, should live, along with his wife and daughter, at our home at Auldhouse Road, and look after it for him. Now he wrote to his friend telling him what books he wanted:

You might bring Cohen's *Organic Chemistry* . . . Otto's *German Grammar* ought to be among the loose books. Also fish out Marshall's *Principles of Economics*, and another of similar size Cunningham's *Industrial History* . . . Gibson's *Introduction to the*

Calculus . . . Also Thomson's *Zoology* and Haliburton's *Physiology*.

He wrote many letters. Most of those preserved were to his good friend, James Clunie, but others to Peter Marshall, Hugh Hinshelwood, Roy Butchard (a member of Dundee SLP), and one to Will Lawther of the Durham miners, also bear witness to a lively, well-informed and well-balanced mind. They also show that he was greatly interested in the personal lives of his friends, that he was reading books and periodicals dealing with a wide variety of subjects and that he was following outside political events with the keenest interest. They were written in a light-hearted, humorous style, with not a trace of depression or undue resentment about his plight—and certainly not a trace of persecution mania!

Tom Mitchell, the editor of *The Socialist* was, during Maclean's first months of imprisonment, also in prison, and Clunie had come to Glasgow to edit the paper and take over the Socialist Labour Press in his absence. Harry McShane, who again was in charge of all arrangements, arranged for Clunie to visit the prison. Later in *Portrait of John Maclean* he gave a moving account of this visit:

> On the one occasion I visited him in Barlinnie Prison, he was so considerate for others, so noble in his grotesque surroundings, silenced by his persecutors, a torrent of strength in his captivity, beloved and hailed by his people, that I left with a gnawing feeling inside me to leave such a friend.

More than forty years later the Rev William Fulton, who was then Assistant Chaplain at Barlinnie Prison, told John L Broom (author of an unpublished biography of Maclean written ten years ago), about his friendship with Maclean. He had already heard of Maclean from his teacher sisters, who admired him:

> As a political prisoner he had certain privileges. He wore his civilian clothing, had his food brought in, was allowed to receive newspapers and books, and had his hour's exercise alone between nine and ten o'clock each forenoon. This was the chaplain's quiet hour so, relieving a warder, on my days on duty I was allowed to walk round the exercise ground in company with John. He proved the best of company, could talk freely on any subject or about the books he was then reading. I should say that he had around fifty books in his cell, but at that time he was intent on psychology. This had, he said, been neglected in his earlier education. I remember telling him he had nothing to learn about 'mass' psychology, which greatly amused him.

He told him how he had persuaded Maclean to attend church services to break the monotony of the life:

John was classified as a Quaker for prison purposes and received visits from a worthy friend of mine who professed this religion. There were no Quaker services but I persuaded him to come to our weekly Prison Service—as otherwise he was confined to his cell from Saturday until Monday exercise periods. I told him that to come to the Church services would at least give him a change for an hour on Sunday forenoons. He said he liked the way I put it— there was no catch in it. So it was arranged for John to attend the Church Services. It was known that he was a prisoner but apart from the staff few had seen him. Now here he was in person and I could sense the tension from the pulpit as he was brought in and seated at the back of the chapel . . .

Summing up I do not hesitate to pronounce John Maclean as one of the finest men I have ever met. Stockily built—quiet and reserved in bearing—straightforward in speech—of strong convictions with a ready flow of good sound commonsense—never particularly robust in health—even while in prison the fire within burned fiercely and very fiercely at that. It burned him up and burned him out in the end, for if any man ever deserved the name of martyr to the causes he espoused passionately it was John Maclean.

He had been accustomed from time to time to give James Clunie advice on his writing. Clunie was a house painter by trade, entirely self-educated, and readily accepted the older man's criticisms. In a letter of March 1922, Maclean advised him:

It's the weakness of *The Socialist*, I think, that it confines itself too much to abstractions. Marx is only of use in so far as his theories enable us to use the data and criticize the theories of our opponent, and enable us to put forward our suggestions at every moment of society.

In July he was enthusing about the theory of relativity:

I'm reading Einstein's popular little book on 'the Relativity Theory', as well as Prof Eddington's on the same subject. This relativity theory is a natural philosophical application of the Hegelian concept, and that's why it has been pushed by Haldane. It seems to me to have emerged fundamentally as a result of Hegel's philosophy, and particularly as a result of problems raised by the electron theory and astronomical theories as to limits to the universe and the position of the solar system in it, together with advances and applications of mathematical theories and formulae. Einstein, in his elementary treatise, refers very briefly to the work of others in the spheres of natural science and maths drawn upon by him for his resultant theory of relativity. If you have studied mensuration, algebra, and geometry to any extent you would be able to appreciate to some extent the step forward made by him, and its connection with Marxism.

Apparently, although I myself have no recollection of the event at all, Jean and I were taken during the summer holidays to see him in prison, but were not allowed inside. He had deliberately not written to us while 'inside', but was to comment on this in his first letter after his release:

> I was so very, very sorry that the wicked men who kept me a prisoner wouldn't let you in to see me, although you had come so far expecting to get in.

For months before his release, he was making plans for his future activities, and Tom Bell records that he wrote Hugh Hinshelwood on 13 February 1922, suggesting that he should organize a class again in Greenock, mentioning that his last class there had been a huge success.

Just before he was released he wrote again to Hinshelwood:

> I'll accept all arrangements made by you cheerfully, since you know the situation and I don't. But just one point, since I saw you the Unemployed Committee in Kinning Park write me asking if I'd again stand for the Town Council. I've consented. The election is on Tuesday, 7 November . . . So, therefore, if you could defer the opening till Wednesday, 8 November . . .

So, he already had his work cut out for him.

64/A new initiative

When the prison gates clanged behind him for the fifth and last time, on 25 October 1922, John Maclean faced a very different world to that of 1918. The tremendous upsurge of support for direct action had died away, and the revolutionary energy generated in Scotland had been skilfully directed by the Labour leaders into constitutional channels.

There were no waiting crowds to welcome him. He had lost his wife, his family, his career, his party, his reputation (in 'communist' circles at any rate), and his livelihood. For although one of his first actions as usual was to begin his Sunday afternoon economics class, his work in the Scottish Labour College was now on a voluntary basis. The College had suffered again by his absence, and during the 1922 session was not able to afford any full-time tutors. In addition, he was penniless, and indeed found himself in debt. He was faced with accounts for election expenses, literature and so on, which he thought had been paid. 'Never in my life', he wrote to Clunie, 'have I had an experience, in money matters, such as this.'

He had also lost his lieutenants of the Tramp Trust, with the exception of Peter Marshall. MacDougall, after his imprisonment, was out of action for some years. Sandy Ross, on his release from his second imprisonment, decided that he had had enough of revolutionary politics, and eventually emigrated to India, where he found a job in Calcutta in a jute mill. Harry McShane had joined the CPGB, of which he was a loyal member for many years.

The mass movement which Maclean had built up around the unemployed movement and the miners, had been 'captured' by the CPGB. One of the ablest leaders, Allan Hannah, a member of the International Ex-Servicemen's Association, had been offered £4 a week by the CPGB for his services, but he had refused. Others, however, had not been able to withstand the powerful pressures which the Communist Party was able to bring to bear. As well as ample funds, the enormous prestige conferred by its association with Russia had succeeded in bringing into the fold practically all the 'lost sheep'.

Why then did Maclean not follow the majority of the revolutionaries, join the CPGB, and make the best of it? I think the answer is contained in a certain passage of his future Gorbals election address of November!

> In spite of my keen desire to go to Russia, in spite of my equally keen desire to help Lenin and the other comrades I am not prepared to let Moscow dictate to Glasgow. The Communist Party has sold itself to Moscow, with disastrous results both to Russia and the British Revolutionary Movement.

The situation which he had previously denounced, of Russia paying the piper and calling the tune, had intensified, and he was sure the CPGB had embarked on a disastrous course. He had now broken with the SLP, although keeping on friendly terms, because it could not go along with his policy of Scottish independence. I am sure he had already made up his mind to form a new revolutionary party based in Scotland, but it was several months before he was able to get on his feet financially.

In the meantime there was the municipal election to contest, and he was also determined to oppose Barnes at Gorbals again in the parliamentary election at the end of November. His first action, however, was to sit down and write to Jean and myself, telling us he was free again and how sorry he was that we had not been allowed to see him.

> I was amused to read Jean's letter, where she said she was going back *only* to Julius Caesar in history. That's right, Jean. You tell your teacher about Wells's great *History of the World* and how your father took you back two hundred thousand years before Julius Caesar was born at all. Your Uncle Bob (*a Latin teacher*) will show you books written by Julius Caesar describing France, which the Romans called Gaul, and Great Britain, which he called Britannia, and Scotland which he called Caledonia.

He had been sending us the fortnightly parts of Wells's book, and now told us that he was going to send us regularly Harmsworth's *Children's Encyclopaedia,* which was also coming out in parts at that time. I can remember yet how thrilled I was with the glamorous, colourful pictures in both.

In his next letter he was able to tell us the result of the municipal election:

> Last Tuesday in KP I got over 4,300 votes against 5,800 for a Mr McFarlane; so, altho' I lost I got a great vote.
>
> I'm now busy in the Gorbals and expect by Wednesday, the election day, to have about lost my voice. If you come thro' at the New Year you'll have to use the dumb language of finger-signs to speak to me. What a joke that'll be, to be sure.

That same letter contained a very revealing paragraph, because it showed his unselfish attitude to life:

> You, Nan, did quite right in giving the first prize to the girl who came second, but perhaps you might get your teacher to keep your name and result out of the list so as to give other girls a better chance. That will keep them your chums without you being any stupider. *Your ambition must be to get knowledge and use it for the benefit of others and not to beat others.*

I remember, even at that early age of nine, I was well aware of the unfair advantage my academic background gave me in competition with other girls whose fathers were shepherds, joiners, blacksmiths, gardeners, ploughmen etc—skilled men with great natural intelligence but with little academic education. I felt guilty about always being 'first' in class, and understood quite well how empty it was.

Soon after he issued his Gorbals parliamentary election address. Ever since 1918 he had been determined to oppose 'traitor' Barnes. Now, however, it was to be ILPer, George Buchanan, he was to oppose. Barnes had intimated that he would not stand in Gorbals again, but would leave the field open for the official Labour candidate, *provided it was not John Maclean*. There was, of course, no fear of that, as Maclean had not been a member of the Labour Party since his break with the BSP. Harry McShane has recorded that the Labour Party did not find it easy to find anybody to oppose him, but eventually George Buchanan agreed. His mother begged Maclean not to oppose him, and he good-naturedly attacked neither Buchanan nor his party.

His was certainly no vote-catching campaign, but he used the occasion of heightened political interest to conduct a campaign of intense political education. His 'Electioneer' consisted of a review of his own political career, a statement of his Marxist principles accompanied by a survey of the political and economic state of both Britain and the world, ending with his own policy. After an explanation of the international circumstances which had led to the downfall of Lloyd George and his replacement as Prime Minister by the Tory, Bonar Law, he gave his interpretation of the state of the British Empire, ending with the sad words:

> The cruel torture of Ireland has largely ruined Ireland already. Clearly, then John Bull's empire is breaking up politically and economically, . . . By no accident has Bonar Law, a Canadian of Scottish parentage, of Glasgow business training, and representative of the business Central Division of Glasgow, been appointed Tory Premier; and by no accident did he outline his policy in the St Andrew's Hall, Glasgow. He must retain Canada's loyalty to London as a Canadian and as a Scot, he must keep the colonies also loyal—colonies largely run by men of Scottish birth or descent.

> Against him I stand out as the Scottish Workers' Supreme Champion. I wish a Scottish Workers' Republic, but Scottish workers to be joined in ONE BIG INDUSTRIAL UNION with their British comrades against INDUSTRIAL CAPITALISM. I wish Scottish comrades in Canada to establish a Canadian Workers' Republic independent of John Bull or Uncle Sam politically, but linked with all other American workers in ONE BIG INDUS-

TRIAL UNION. I wish Scottish comrades in other colonies to do the same.

If we can break up John's blood-soaked Empire by separation we shall probably avert a war with America. If not, John must do his own bloody work himself. We must refuse to murder our fellows of this planet at his autocratic bidding.

When all empires are broken up and the workers by political control start to make land and wealth-producing property common property, when of the wealth produced all get sufficient to give them life abundantly with leisure and pleasure and education added thereunto, then all the independent republics will come together into one Great League or Parliament of Communist Peoples, as a stage towards the time in the future when inter-marriage will wipe out all national differences and the world will become one.

To get a Scottish Workers' Republic I shall not go to the London House of Commons, but stay in Scotland helping the unemployed, standing by those at work, educating in the Scottish Labour College, and carrying the Revolutionary Propaganda all over Scotland (and into England too).

I'll support any fight for palliatives honestly started by the workers until OUR DAY ARRIVES.

If you understand the above fully you'll see that no detailed programme is necessary in this address.

If you cannot agree with me then vote for George Buchanan, the representative of the Labour Party. On no account vote for anyone else.

Yours for the World Revolution,
JOHN MACLEAN.

In another section he enlarged on the policy already given, and explained that to carry out the work necessary in the fight for Scottish Workers' Republic he could not go to Westminster:

To carry out such work effectively, I have resolved to stay in Scotland even if the winner in the Gorbals, and so will adopt the Sinn Fein tactics. My battle with Bonar Law will become all the more striking and important.

He also made an attack on Willie Gallacher which, even though warranted, seems a bit out of place and uncharacteristic in this passionate attack on capitalism, unless to highlight his firm belief that he, and not Gallacher, was the standard-bearer of real communism in Scotland:

Whilst I was carrying on the exhausting work with the unemployed, William Gallacher, Communist Candidate for Dundee, did his utmost to break up my work and the unemployed movement, as he had tried to break up the Scottish Labour College.

With this election address he issued two leaflets. One was his 1920 'All Hail! . . .' one, but with 'Communist' altered to 'Workers'—'All Hail! The Scottish Workers' Republic!'—probably to dissociate himself from the Communist Party. The latter was now advocating a diametrically opposite policy—the One Big Union *Politically* (the Comintern), and division on the industrial front—the Red International of Labour Unions (RILU), which organized left-wing breakaway unions—one of the worst mistakes in working-class history, later called the 'Minority Movement'.

The other leaflet was an article, later to be published in the November *Socialist*, on 'The First Great "Pacific" Conference of Powers'. This dealt with the conference held on the other side of the world which had opened on 25 October at Honolulu. It had been convened by the Pan-Pacific Union, consisting of all the countries bordering the Pacific Ocean, and was allied with the Pan-American Union. Maclean saw it as part of the tremendous struggle for world supremacy between the two Empires, the British and the American. He saw the USA winning hands down, giving as an example the extent of American foreign investment compared to the aggregate investment of all the other countries in the world. In 1919 it had been thirty times larger, and in 1922 was still seven times as much! He gave the exact figures. Soon afterwards Britain reacted by convening an Imperial Trade Conference, which received great publicity in the press, whereas the USA's Pacific Conference went unreported.

Thus all the literature issued by Maclean at the 1922 General Election was a political education in itself for Gorbals electors, and it was no wonder that when he founded the Scottish Workers' Republican Party some months later, a hundred should immediately join the Gorbals Branch.

Summing it all up in a letter to James Clunie he wrote:

> In my Gorbals campaign . . . I refused to talk on rents, taxes, or capital levy. I kept to the question of trade and the world political and economic complications. I urged a 'Scottish Workers' Republic'. My business now is to create a keen desire for it, and so lay the basis for a Scottish Communist Party or a Scottish Workers' Party . . . In due course a monthly or weekly paper could be issued and branches opened up all over the country. The CP is going 'rocky', and as it fades the ground will be cleared for a real fighting party **independent of outside dictation and finance.** (My emphasis.)

And he added:

Last Sunday in St Mungo Hall, despite the great MP send-off, I had two 'packed' houses.

It is no part of this biography to recount the dramatic happenings of that election. Of the twelve Labour candidates put forward, ten had been elected, all members of the ILP, and the atmosphere in these constituencies was indescribable. In Gorbals, Buchanan received 16,479 votes as opposed to Maclean's 4,027, but the latter had defeated the Liberal, who got only 1,456. On the night the ten ILPers departed for Westminster, their supporters packed two of the largest halls in Glasgow—the City Hall and St Andrew's Hall—and later a huge contingent in a state of almost religious fervour accompanied them to the station to see them off to London to bring in the millennium and Maclean led his St Mungo Hall audience there in a torchlight procession. Michael Donnelly records that at the St Andrew's Hall meeting James Maxton declared:

> people talk about the atmosphere of the House of Commons getting the better of the Labour men. They will see the atmosphere of the Clyde getting the better of the House of Commons. All the Labour members are personal friends. We are not leaving Glasgow as so many individuals but as a team working towards a goal— and that is the abolition of poverty.

Michael Donnelly further records in a style I cannot better:

> Eighteen months later in the same Hall, Maxton had a very different tale to tell. In unambiguous terms he illustrates the inevitable loss of vitality and growing frustration of the group when separated from their popular roots, and confronted by the arrogance and contempt of English MPs who regarded them as parochial bumpkins. Maxton clearly anticipated the danger to political integrity . . . such surroundings would breed, and his solution was a short and unequivocal one. The Clydesiders must return to the Clyde and take up the challenge of creating a Socialist Commonwealth in Scotland.

Donnelly then went on to quote from Maxton's speech in May 1924, when he referred in hopeful terms to the Home Rule Bill which George Buchanan was to bring before the House in a few months:

> They hoped he (Ramsay MacDonald) would give such facilities to Buchanan's Home Rule Bill that on a particular day . . . they should be able to go to Euston, St Pancras or King's Cross, and book a single ticket for Glasgow. He for one would never go back again. He might go to the international or to hear the Orpheus

Choir, or something worth while, but never for the sake of legislating for the British Empire.

He would ask no greater job in life than to make English-ridden, capitalist-ridden, landowner-ridden Scotland into the Scottish Socialist Commonwealth, and in doing that he thought he would be rendering a very great service to the people of England, Wales and Europe, and to the cause of internationalism generally.

This was indeed a vindication of John Maclean's stand in 1922.

One of Maclean's last actions that year was to take up the case of Bernard Murdoch, an ex-soldier and unemployed worker, who had died in the Southern Police Station on 28 November 1921. Maclean had read about it while he was in Barlinnie, and, in the light of his own experiences with the police, suspected foul play. As soon as he was released, he collected the newspaper reports, interviewed the widow and her solicitor, and sent copies of the special post-mortem examination to the Prime Minister and the Glasgow Group of Labour MPs, demanding compensation for the widow. He published a pamphlet called *The Glasgow Police Murder Hush-up,* which certainly did not endear him any more than previously to Glasgow's police force.

His Christmas letter to Jean and I, however, revealed that he was having some fun out of life, in spite of all his difficulties:

Fancy your father at a dance on Thursday night, going to another this Thursday, and one on 2 January! As Shakespeare should have said— 'All the world's a whirl, and all the men and women merely dancers'. Aunt Rose may read you what S really did say in *As you like it.*

I've been so busy going to unemployed meetings and classes at night that I've no time to read, let alone write, and dancing has left me so tired that I think I'll go off to Robinson Crusoe's Island and sleep for twenty years like poor Rip Van Winkle whose story is told by a wonderful Yankee writer called Washington Irving . . .

I'm going to Mr Ross's for my Xmas dinner and then to the football match as we did long years before you chicks (beg pardon, big young ladies!) were born at all—when you were fairies flying through space with Gulliver on his wonderful travels, or sailing with Jason in his quest for the Golden Fleece.

On New Year's Day I'm going out for dinner, to . . . then booked seats at the pantomime . . . so I'm sure you'd both like to be here . . . I suppose Jean is getting bigger and bigger, and heavier and heavier. If she goes on that way the County Council will be buying her up as a steam road roller, or perhaps Jules Verne will take her on his submarine journey of Twenty Thousand Leagues under the Sea.

65/The Scottish Workers' Republican Party

John Maclean was soon immersed again in his usual round of activities. But he had to admit to James Clunie in a letter on 29 January that he had been forced to give up his regular Sunday night propaganda meetings at St Mungo Hall before the end of 1922:

> I had the hall packed, but the money was not forthcoming, so had to go to Kinning Park. That halved the crowd till after the New Year; then came the revival, so we 'ettled' on opening up Oatlands (Picture House). We're getting it cheaper than St Mungo, so if the crowd keeps up, even to last Sunday's, we can pull thro' till the summer. . . . Perhaps we'll get it packed this Sunday . . . 2,000.

As usual he devoted a good deal of time and energy to the Scottish Labour College. He had started his Sunday afternoon class as soon as he was released, and one in Greenock organized by Hugh Hinshelwood for him. But the SLC had suffered severely because of his imprisonment, although organizational changes had been taking place. It had in October 1921 joined up with the other Labour Colleges in Britain to form the National Council of Labour Colleges. This should have been a decided financial advantage. Amalgamation of English and Scottish Unions had been proceeding at great speed throughout the first years of the century, and now most of the bigger unions were centred in London.

Organizational control had been passing into the hands of J P M Millar, the secretary of Edinburgh District Council of the SLC, now a member of the ILP. During January, Maclean was asked by the Executive Committee to prepare a draft for a new constitution to be submitted to a meeting of the National Committee at Edinburgh on 27 January. He duly did so but apparently he clashed with Millar, who had also prepared a constitution. He told Clunie:

> Peter and I were at Edinburgh on Saturday. Millar's chance

whilst I was in Barlinnie came, and he seemingly took it. His bent seemingly is to kill our day college ideal and make Scotland an adjunct to the London College. . . . Now, Millar must be fought.

On the 29 January he wrote to us as well as Clunie, this time a very long letter, in which he showed anxiety over Jean's future education. She was now almost twelve years old and almost ready for secondary education:

> In preparation for a secondary school, a little of the beginnings of algebra will prove useful, as well as some general notion of geometry.
>
> A good geography book and an atlas should always be at your side to enable you to know as much about the earth as possible. A general history of the world in all times should prove useful. Perhaps your aunt may be able to tell you about the great civilization of ancient Egypt, the mummies, and the tombs of the Pharoahs or emperors, and of the recent discoveries at Luxor on the Nile where the tomb of King Tutankhamen has just been found and is causing excitement all over the world.

At the same time he wanted Jean to widen her horizons a little:

> You have reached an age, too, when you should try to read and understand the papers. You'll know that the French have entered the Ruhr Valley in Germany, and that may lead to another war. The only way to end war and prevent all wars is for the wage workers of the whole world to unite and tell the wealthy that the workers themselves will rule the world. For advocating that, your father was sent to gaol and may be sent again. But sooner or later the workers will do as your father wishes them to do. So your father is helping to make modern history, because he has read past history to understand all that is described in the papers and books of today, and all that goes on around us today.

From February onwards, until the last days of his life, most of his political activity was concentrated on building up the new revolutionary party, the Scottish Workers' Republican Party. He started to build it up round the remnants of the unemployed movement which had not become attached to the Communist Party, and gained publicity by fighting every municipal by-election that eventualized, thus carrying out Lenin's policy of using the traditional political machinery as a revolutionary platform. The first one was in February, and his election address and future ones are the only records I have been able to obtain of the policy of the SWRP:

I come before you at this election at the request of many members of your ward as a COMMUNIST or RED LABOUR candidate. Pink Labourism is of no use to the workers, never will be. Your poverty and misery are more intense today than ever before. Thirteen out of every hundred in Glasgow are getting Parish Council Relief, and the number is growing. World developments are bound to make things still worse, even if Britain is lucky enough to avoid another world war . . .

As unemployment is a weapon to cow the workers into accepting lower wages and a longer week, it must be clear that the main problem before the workers of Glasgow is unemployment. That was my attitude in October 1920, when I started the present unemployed movement in Glasgow; that is my attitude today. I propose, if returned, to place before the Corporation a scheme that would absorb all the unemployed of Glasgow. The gist of my proposal is to reclaim all the moorland lying round Glasgow, and establish a system of co-operative or collective farming on scientific lines. Out of this vast experiment would arise experience enough to modernize Scottish agriculture. . . .

I am in favour of municipalizing every industry suitable for local control, as a briefly intermediate system leading on to social ownership, ie, ownership free from interest payment.

I wish to see the city extended so as to control the whole of the Clyde Valley; in other words, its conversion into a Provincial Council so as to enable the workers more adequately to control all the industries in this very clearly defined area.

The limits imposed by Parliament on the Corporation necessitate a Scottish Parliament. I wish and am striving for one independent of England altogether, for reasons beyond those of Glasgow's immediate interests. I wish a Scottish Workers' Republic, within which the workers in control can evolve present-day capitalist property into working-class property as a stage on the road to communal use of all the wealth produced.

Meanwhile efforts were also being made to give organizational form to One Big Union idea. A 'Unity Committee' was formed, which was intended to consist of delegates from all left-wing organizations, but in fact only those who had not yet joined the Communist Party supported it. Tom Anderson, in his pamphlet, gives the names of the delegates. Some were members of the SLP, others were old comrades of the BSP like Tom Anderson himself (who had stuck to him through thick and thin), and others were from the Unemployed movement. The only member of the Tramp Trust who remained was Peter Marshall.

For some time, large meetings of the unemployed had been held regularly in Helen Street Cinema, Govan. The Manager of the picture House, James Hamilton, was dismissed because he continued to permit these meetings, so Maclean and his comrades conducted a boycott of the cinema, holding meetings outside every night to advise patrons not to attend the shows. This boycott was so successful that at one performance only five people were present. Hamilton was reinstated as manager of the Ardgowan Picture House, but Maclean and one of the SWRP members, Tom McGregor, were charged with breach of the peace. Both were found guilty and fined, being allowed some months to pay. Both refused to pay.

By this time he was again gathering around him a real mass movement, consisting mainly of the most under-privileged sections of the community. By the end of March advertisements like the following were appearing in the press:

> Roll-up, Glasgow Reds, and join the new Revolutionary Party for a Scottish Workers' Parliament, allied to Russia, one big industrial union, Marxian education under the Scottish Labour College.

Open-air meetings at Glasgow Green, Paisley Road Toll, and West Regent Street were regularly advertised, Also Sunday evening meetings now at the Ardgowan Picture House.

Already Gorbals had a branch of a hundred or so, and other branches were being formed in different districts. By May Day (still on 1 May, but this was the last year—and the end, in reality, of the 'Red Clyde'), he was heading a large contingent with the new banner 'All Hail! The Scottish Workers' Republic!', out in front.

Thereafter advantage was taken of every by-election to gain publicity and members. One was fought in May, the election address being very similar to the February one, and he commented to Clunie:

> My address is every time bringing out sharper and sharper the difference between the pinks and the reds—the dialectical process in the political process, or rather, the political part of the process.

He triumphantly described the outcome of another one in June:

> The by-election in Kingston last Tuesday ending in my defeat of the Pink, Peter Campbell . . . has created a profound impression in working-class circles in Glasgow, as all realize now that a deadly fight has started between the 'Pinks' and the 'Reds'.
>
> Against us were the Trades Council, the Labour Party, the ILP, and the CPGB—the last-named playing it very dirty. One of them, Malcolm McFarlane, got the Unemployed Committee in Kingston

K

to support P Campbell. We used this in public, with the result that the unemployed movement is smashed. The CP have thus smashed the Unemployed Movement all over Glasgow, and are in consequence of the 'United Front' with the Pinks smashing their now discredited party.

He also informed Clunie that Countess Markiewicz, who was at that time in Glasgow to edit one of the Irish Republican papers, had spoken thrice for him. After this, the SWRP received nothing but the most bitter hostility from the members of the 'United Front'.

Soon events were moving fast and furious. On the day after the Kingston poll, Harry McShane was evicted from his home in Gorbals and a vast protest demonstration was organized by the SWRP. A collection was taken for another member of the CPGB, Tom Hitman, who was lying in Duke Street Prison charged with sedition. Then the demonstration marched to Hitman's home and handed the money to his wife. Maclean later told Clunie about these events, mentioning that they had created a profound impression in view of the hostility of the CPGB.

On 19 June he attended a meeting of the Glasgow District Council of the Scottish Labour College called for the purpose of considering the formation of classes during the coming winter session. The annual meeting had been held in April, and there it had been made clear that the College had been in a bad way financially during Maclean's imprisonment. Not only had all the tutors been forced to work on a voluntary basis, but because of the 'uncertain financial position at that time' no delegates had been sent to the annual meeting of the National Council of Labour Colleges at the end of 1922, although affiliation had been renewed for another year. Maclean was now determined to get the College on its feet again, and to see that it would be run in Glasgow on a scale 'never known before', in spite of the opposition of Millar and others, who disapproved bitterly of the SWRP.

At the end of June, Maclean arranged to spend a few days to visit James Larkin, who was now free and home in Dublin. He was accompanied by Peter Marshall and James Hamilton, the latter paying all expenses as a token of his gratitude in connection with the Helen Street Cinema affair. Maclean was all ready to depart that Monday morning, when a policeman arrived to arrest him and take him to Govan Police Station for his term of imprisonment. Maclean just pooh-poohed, brushed the whole thing off, and airily told the bobby that he was too busy to come then, but would look in when he came back from Dublin!

When he did arrive home, he gave himself up as promised, was treated with the utmost politeness, given a cell for the night, and treated to a ham-and-eggs breakfast in the morning. Then he was told he could go. He never found out what had happened, but presumed somebody had paid the fine. He and Peter Marshall, who told me about this incident, were highly amused about the healthy respect (if not fear) with which he was treated by the police force.

He wrote to Jean and I on 3 July telling us about his visit, and as his account brings us up-to-date with affairs in Ireland, I shall quote the major part of it:

When we landed on the river Liffey at the North Wall we made tracks for the headquarters of the Irish Transport Workers' Union called Liberty Hall, a hall that was blown down by cannon shot at Easter, 1916, when a friend of mine, James Connolly, started a Revolution to keep Ireland out of the war. He took up his position inside the large post office in O'Connell Street (called after the great Irish orator, Daniel O'Connell) along with other brave men and held it till the British blew it into a mass of ruins.

After Connolly was wounded he surrendered, and the dirty English Government had him shot, along with other brave Irishmen. This aroused Irishmen all over the world against England, called by us John Bull. After the war Irishmen, calling themselves Sinn Feiners, made an effort to start a Republic in Ireland, independent of John Bull; but John sent soldiers, called because of their dress 'Black and Tans', and killed many Irishmen. The Irish killed many in return and destroyed buildings owned by the English. One such building, called the Custom House, along the North Wall near to Liberty Hall, we saw in absolute ruins as we walked along the quay.

We asked for Jim Larkin at Liberty Hall, but found he was not there. We were told to go to Parnell Square, off O'Connell St. As we walked up O'Connell we saw other vast ruins of huge hotels, blown down by the Free State soldiers fighting the Republicans inside. . . .

In 1921 Lloyd George, premier of Britain, offered the 26 southern counties of Ireland what he called a 'Free State'—if the Free State members of Parliament swore allegiance to King George ('Wee Geordie'). Some Irishmen agreed and formed the 'Free State' alongside the Orange Government of six counties round Belfast. Other Irishmen refused to accept Lloyd George's offer, and started civil war against the Free State for an Irish Republic independent of England. Here were Irishmen, who had stood shoulder to shoulder against England, now killing one another whilst England looked on and laughed. Just a year ago this fighting started, on 29 June, when the Free Staters blew down a building as large as Glasgow's Municipal Buildings, called the Four Courts. From then till May Day bridges and buildings have been destroyed all over Ireland.

On May Day Jim Larkin returned to Ireland from the United States, where he went in 1914, and on that day De Valera, leader of the Republicans, called for a truce. There were plenty of soldiers about Dublin, and we were searched as we came off the Burns-Laird steamer, the 'Maple', but in Dublin all was as quiet as in Glasgow.

Besides the hotel ruins I've mentioned is the statue erected to the memory of Chas Stewart Parnell, the leader of the Irish MPs in the London House of Commons many years ago. Near this statue we found the Square, but Larkin was not there. On the way to his house, strange to say, we met his brother, Pete, Jack Carney, and another man married to Larkin's sister, Delia Larkin. We soon got to the house and there were welcomed by Jim and Delia. I hadn't seen Jim for ten years, as he was in USA, and whilst there he had been kept in prison over two years. They all invited us to stay, so there we stayed.

Jack Carney had been in USA, also, and he also was in prison there. Pete Larkin was in Australia during the war, and there because of his fight against conscription was sent to prison, and was kept there four years. So we were all a fine company of pirates, weren't we?

Jim Larkin is the greatest man in Ireland and is out for an Irish Workers' Republic as I'm out for a Scottish Workers' Republic. Remember his name, and remember what I say. . . .

On Sunday at 1 pm who steps into 42 Auldhouse Rd but Pete Larkin, and he's staying here for a week, speaking and selling Jim's paper, *The Irish Worker*.

On 10 July he reported to Clunie that Pete Larkin had just finished an eight day visit to Glasgow, and went home pleased with his reception and seventeen meetings (all very large). He gave him also a further report on the progress of the new party:

We have just agreed on a constitution for the SWRP and we can now move ahead systematically. We are having monster meetings and as you'll see we are steadily creeping over the city.

A fortnight later he was able to report that

Each week we are starting new branches here, and by the time classes (Scottish Labour College classes; *NM*) are re-opened I fancy we'll have the classes, who ever may control the machinery. Then a very severe struggle will start for control.

In this letter he also informed Clunie that he was again

standing for the town council in a by-election at Townhead ward.

Once again his address for this election, which took place in August, was of more than parochial interest, ending again with the demand for a Scottish Workers' Republic:

> One course is open to us in Scotland. Let us declare for a Workers' Republic in Scotland. A Republic would absolve us from responsibility towards England, should she declare war on France. That would protect us from air and other attacks, but would not secure the workers a livelihood. Hence the need for a *Workers' Republic.*
>
> The workers ought at once to select representatives from all over Scotland to form a Workers' Parliament in Glasgow, with powers and support to take control of all industries, set all the fit to work, control all the products, distribute these products as required for production or human consumption, and export all surplus goods for those of other lands needed by us in Scotland.
>
> That would be a political and economic revolution.

As a result of this venture, another branch of the SWRP was set up in Townhead, consisting of about forty members, mostly young people. The first secretary was a young Veterinary College student, John Mitchell, who had been his election agent. After Maclean's death young John joined the Communist Party and remained a loyal member until his death two years ago. Shortly before he died, he wrote out his recollections of this short experience with Maclean, whom he admired and reverenced all his life. What impressed him most was Maclean's warmth and simplicity and lack of condescension towards these raw, young recruits. They called him 'John' and he was a friend to them all, encouraging them and pushing them on to get up on their feet and start expressing themelves, and he had them outside on the soap box as soon as they gained sufficient confidence. In the winter all felt it their cardinal duty to attend the economics and industrial history classes. After young John Mitchell left the party, another youngster, Jenny McNeill, took over as secretary for a few years until the branch petered out. She preserved the Minute Book, however, and this is the only record of the business affairs of the party that remains, as far as I know.

66/The last two months

In August events occurred which might have proved a turning-point in his life, had death not intervened. He wrote to us on 24 July, insisting that when we came on holiday to Glasgow on 4 August, we should stay at home with him. He also had some interesting information to give us about a recent visitor:

> The Glasgow Fair Holidays are now past and gone for another year, and your father spent his at home for the first time in his history, I think. I had staying with me a Negro called Neil Johnston all the week; but we spent it very quietly, going no farther away than Eaglesham. . . .
>
> Neil Johnston comes from the Barbados Is, away in the West Indies, and he was telling me all about life there and in other islands in that warm region—Haiti, San Domingo, St Thomas, Jamaica, Cuba, etc. He learnt English, Spanish, Portuguese, French and German out there, and he can speak Dutch, Danish and Flemish too. Now, you chicks, learn from this black man. Study your geography, history, arithmetic and languages, so that you may be able to move around. . . .

During that holiday, of which I have few recollections except that he was by this time so shabby that I was ashamed to walk down the street with him, his personal life took a turn for the better. He met mother for the first time for years at Aunt Lizzie's home, and was shocked by her appearance. She had been having a bad time. Living in Rulewater was like going back about 150 years in time to a pre-capitalist world, where the village 'dominie' was regarded as a dangerous rebel because he supported the Liberal cause! Here, although Jean and I were enjoying life more than ever before, she was like a fish out of water. Aunt Rose would make it clear, whenever she was irritated, that she thought mother had ruined not only her own life but also the lives of the whole Wood family by marrying that man Maclean, whose ideas were quite beyond her ken.

The previous winter Mother had been very ill with pleurisy, which must have left her, although nobody was aware of this at the time, with a tubercular lung, which eventually healed up naturally. In later life it flared up again and killed her. In the meantime she was down in both health and spirits, and when Maclean wrote to

her on 28 August, after we had all gone back home, he expressed
his feelings:

> When at Lizzie's I tried to study your face and I felt that it was
> that of a broken person. Had your separation from home at Bon-
> chester improved your apearance and spirits I would have been
> content to leave things alone, but your appearance has left me
> far from comfortable, to put it mildly.
>
> When you were here, I was afraid to ask you to stay as I had
> no sure source of income to guarantee a passable existence. On the
> other hand I am annoyed at Jean's awkwardness and timidity due
> to a rural life and the need for city experience.
>
> I have revolved the matter several times over, and have come
> to the conclusion now to leave it to you to definitely decide on
> your course of action, whether you'll stay at B or return home.
>
> So far as my activities are concerned, they must go on even
> more intensely than before, as my livelihood is now completely
> dependent on my public efforts. As you know perfectly well the
> authorities will preclude me from any position at all.
>
> Again I'm going to make an effort for re-instatement, but the
> prospects aren't at all rosy as the Authority is hiding behind the
> surplus of teachers. . . .
>
> Above everything else I feel sure you are longing to be here, and
> that satisfies me that I am doing the right thing in penning this
> letter as I am doing. No one more than me would wish to see you
> shake off the depressing load and become the genial soul you were
> long years ago.

Mother replied immediately with heartfelt relief:

> This is a real red letter day, and a turning point surely in our
> lives! I have been waiting for such a letter to come for some time
> now, so I must have had the presentiment that *you* had a longing
> for me to be back home. Am I right? I take it that you would not
> have asked me unless your trust in me is firm once more. I have
> been through hell these last four years because you lost faith in
> me. It has been very hard.
>
> I never realized how sweet Home was until I lost it, or how
> comforting (I can't get another word) Hubby was until I lost him.
> Need I say more! . . . As you say, the finance will be a difficulty.
> I am afraid for that part of it, but have faith that you will fall in
> for a position suited to your ability.

Other matters delayed his immediate reply, and mother
hurriedly sent a reproachful letter, to which he replied with complete re-assurance:

> You know perfectly well that were you not my sole concern I
> would have paired up with another woman ere this. That I have

not, surely shows where my love lies. Need I write more? *Come* a thousand times *come* by the first bus and train, and I trust I'll give you a welcome warmer than words.

But it wasn't as easy as all that, as mother explained.

Aunt Rose had spent about £200 on getting a comfortable home together for us, as she had previously lived in lodgings during the week, going home to Hawick at the weekends. Mother felt she would have to stay at least until her sister found a suitable housekeeper. Moreover, Aunt Rose had grown very fond of Jean and myself, and was going to find parting with us a big wrench.

Various letters on this subject passed between them, and in one Maclean apologized for not being able to send any money:

> Owing to a hitch on Sunday night my drawings were down very heavily and consequently I'm unable at the moment to forward anything.

He was already making plans to have the house cleaned up preparatory to our return, and explained also that the cost of distemper, etc for 'doing up' the house had been extra heavy. He informed her also that a deputation from the Party was going to see the Education Authority regarding his re-instatement—'I'll keep pegging away at them on the matter'.

Towards the end of September mother had to go to Glasgow to look after her two small nieces, whose mother was ill, so she was able to spend some time with her husband, and when she went back to the borders, she wrote back saying how very sorry she had been to leave Glasgow. He replied:

> Yes, last week-end was the best I've had for four years at least and naturally I'd wish it every week-end till the end of time. So haste ye back again.

Going on to tell her about his political activities he mentioned that he had burst his throat speaking at Rutherglen, and would have to take it easy during the winter, except for the November elections, which the SWRP planned to contest in at least a dozen wards. His success in previous by-elections in defeating Labour Party candidates had so aroused Labour Party hostility that he had been faced with an entirely new development:

> I hear that Bailie Geo Smith is slandering me at his election meetings. I am in the pay of the Moderates, so he says! I think you might write him and tell him how much I get!

He mentioned this also in a letter to Clunie on 4 September:

Wm Shaw claims he has a letter sent by a Maryhill member of our party to a Maryhill Moderate councillor. If he has it, or even a copy, it shows collusion on his part.

In the next letter he pursued this question:

Bailie Geo Smith in the Bijou Picture House openly said I was paid by the Moderates. In his ward (N Woodside) I have told the electors not to give him a hearing until he proves his statement or withdraws the lie . . . My West Regent St meeting ever grows. Now at least 3,000 pack up the street. It is a great sight and is most encouraging, tho' money is absolutely scarce.

In his next letter on 5 October, he wrote about the position of the Scottish Labour College:

So far as the SLC work in Glasgow is concerned I'm at logger-heads with the Committee over their 'constitution', one that is tying them up instead of fostering education. I've had to attack them twice at W Regent St and I think that will do good. Publicity I find my only safeguard against the opposition parties.

I gave four nights a week, and not one class has been started yet. There's business ability for you! The adverts in *Forward* are largely show, in both Glasgow and Lanarkshire. Had I left my Sunday class to the Committee it, too, would have had a belated start. Happily I got the Ardgowan Picture House and have pushed the advertisement of the class. In the past I used to issue 10,000 leaflets announcing the class. This time the Committee has issued nothing meantime. Fortunately the manager of the Ardgowan has advertised it in the leaflet I enclose and on the screen this week. He caters for Kinning Park and Kingston, so that a wide area is thus tapped. Latterly I've been getting about 3,000 at W Regent Street, the **biggest crowds ever held Sunday after Sunday in Glasgow**, (my emphasis) and at these I've pushed the class as well as at the Monument every Sunday afternoon.

The Committee wish the course to be 12 lectures for 2/6, but I'm insisting on at least 20. . . .

The SWRP, I expect, will have at least a dozen candidates up in November, and we are using all our speakers as candidates, so as to put on the utmost pressure. . . . The capitalist reactionaries for the moment are swinging politically into power, but the next swing will be more decided to the 'left' (red), and then may rapidly evolve a situation calling us into power . . .

The size of my Sunday night audience is largely due to the fair interpretation of evolving events in general and in detail. As things are going, a growing number of Glasgow people are quite alive; and should a crisis arise I feel sure the people will come to me for guidance. That is one tremendous advantage of the continuity of meetings and concentration of efforts on Glasgow. . . .'

Meantime Labour College work was going on as usual. On 14 October he wrote mother telling her about it:

> During last week I started a class on Wed afternoons at Partick, and one on Thursday evenings in the Rev R Lee's church hall in the East End. A very good start was made, about forty at each. On Sunday afternoon last about 100 turned up to enrol in the Central Class. I expect about 200 soon. A large part of the week I've spent in the Mitchell Library reading up about ancient Crete and Egypt, a most pleasant change for me recently.

In this letter he showed the only sign of depression of spirits that he ever manifested, as far as my researches indicate, because it began:

> Excuse my delay in replying to your last one, but the wretched weather, a worse throat, and an almost empty pocket just about make one sink into one's self and cut entirely with the rest of the world. . . .
>
> I've just had a letter from Guy Aldred, who appears to be in a much worse plight than myself, but if the winter proceeds as it appears to do then it is going to be a very hopeless one with no sure promise that you'll be back here at Xmas, much as I'd wish so.

This letter was so entirely unlike him, and so distressed mother that she immediately replied:

> Your letter arrived this morning, but what a gloomy one and so hopeless. I want to sit down and have a right good cry, but have no time for that. I want so much to be beside you, and yet how can I take the girls from here meantime? Surely you are getting less money than ever this last month or so! . . . Your health appears to me to be going down or you would not be feeling like that (I was in that condition last November, and could not get my spirits up at all. A strong tonic from the doctor made me feel quite different). Do look after yourself, Johnnie. For if anything happened to you now, after that little glimmer of hope you have given me, I would go down through myself, and what about Jean and Nan? We must live and help to give them a good start in life. We must make up our minds to let the two rooms—bedroom and parlour. Two business girls, I could surely get—that would always pay the rent. If your throat is so bad, you will have to give up speaking and take a holiday. . . . Could none of your friends give you a clerking job to tide us over until your throat gets a thorough rest? . . . To finish off. I am not on with you standing as a candidate in your present condition. Again it is wasting

your health when it should be given to your wife and bairns. No one would be better pleased than me to help for the common good, but you *can't help* effectively when the home is not right . . . Do get someone who has no bad throat to stand in your place. Your time will come again.

Maclean replied immediately, again trying to reassure her:

I fear that you have become over-alarmed at the tone of my last letter. There is no fear of depression, except that of depression of income. The situation here is so dependent on that in Germany and the continent generally, where things are rapidly moving from bad to worse, that I am apprehensive of a winter severer than any that has gone by yet.

He was actually suffering from semi-starvation. Most of his supporters were either unemployed or working with pitifully low wages and there was nothing to spare for collections or literature. It was round about this time also that he had no money to pay his rates, and our furniture would have been sold off if Tom Johnston (of *Forward*) had not come to his aid with money from some fund for this purpose. In her obituary, Sylvia Pankhurst, who came up from London to speak for him during his election campaign, described what she found:

HE WAS A FIGHTER: that is the first thought that comes to mind as one hears of John Maclean's death. One is surprised to learn that he was only 44 years of age, for he had been long in the forefront of the struggle, his hair was white and his rugged face deeply lined. . . .
    He had gathered round him latterly a big movement in Glasgow. When we saw him a month ago he was holding great meetings and seemed stronger and more confident than ever. Yet he lived the bare, lonely life of an ascetic. Parted from his wife and children, by the financial difficulties which followed his dismissal from his school post, on account of his political activities, he lived quite alone, doing his own cooking and housework. . . . He was talking enthusiastically of the nourishing properties of pease brose, which in English is plain pease flour porridge, when last we saw him, declaring that 'pease brose' was one of his daily meals. His tones bespoke his cheerful frugality, which was only too near to want.

Confirmation of his diet came to me recently from Mrs Janet Loan, who wrote telling me about her late husband's friendship with Maclean. Born in 1902, Sandy Loan came under the influence of Maclean while still quite young (probably one of 'John Maclean's bright young things' as the young members of the SWRP came to be known):

Maclean schooled him in Marxism and they lived together for a while. . . . they lived off *porridge and dates* . . .*

My husband idolized the memory of John Maclean so much that he very rarely spoke about him, would refuse to enter into any controversial conversation about him, and guarded his image as if he were a saint . . . He put Maclean on the same level as Lenin and, although he was a 'hard' type would freely weep about Maclean (when he had a pint or two) without any embarrassment . . . He never really got over the death of Maclean, which haunted him throughout his life.

Sandy Loan was only one of the many helped by Maclean in that dreadful winter. In his obituary George Lansbury recalled:

Only a few days before his death, even when he himself was bodily sick, he went to a slum home to see a sick child whom he found without warmth or food or a doctor. He sent for all these, paying for them out of what he had in his pocket, afterwards going to the Labour rooms to borrow the money for the tram fare home.

The *Glasgow Herald* gave the SWRP a good write-up, prior to the municipal election at the beginning of November, under the title of 'Red Menace':

Never before has the challenge of the extremist been so bold. Doubtless he counts on the dire distress of this unemployment period giving him an electoral ear ready to listen to his red remedy for all the ills of the time.

The writer listed the names of the candidates—John Ball, Norman MacNeill, Colin Maclean, John Maclean, Peter Marshall, Allan Hannah, Frank Shevlin, Tom Smith, Edward Rennie, Tom Macgregor, and Tom Hitman.

As a last round-up prior to the election, the Trades Council organized a big demonstration in the City Hall on Unemployment, the principal speakers to be George Lansbury and Robert Smillie, two old friends of Maclean's. But that did not prevent Maclean from deprecating their recent performances in the working-class movement, and from issuing a leaflet poking fun at the Labour Party efforts on unemployment. The leaflet was entitled 'George Lansbury and Robert Smillie to the Rescue', and exposed the action of the Poplar Guardians, of whom Lansbury was the most famous, in refusing legitimate requests of the Unemployed Workers' Organization, who locked the guardians in the building. Police were summoned and batoned the unemployed deputation, fifty-two

---

*   Dates were then very cheap

of whom were wounded. The Guardians were all Labour men, except two, and they also included two Communists, Edgar Lansbury and Maclean's old BSP colleague A A Watts. Maclean went on to ask:

> Has George been brought to remind us of what 'LORD PROVOST SIR PATRICK DOLLAN' will do to the unemployed of Glasgow?

He also pointed out that Bob Smillie had been the most powerful personality in the Scottish labour movement:

> Now he is an English MP when Scotland is on the road to Independence. What can he do for the Unemployed? He retired from the position of President of the Miners' Federation in the spring of 1921 when he knew Sir Adam Nimmo (of Redding slaughter fame) and his coal barons were about to attack the miners. The miners are down and out. The Lanarkshire miners refuse to join up again, not even for 'Bob'.
>
> If these Lanarkshire miners have lost faith in their old leader, should the Unemployed trust him? We say, 'No, a Thousand Times No!'
>
> Trust the Scottish Workers' Republican Party, and VOTE RED LABOUR.

In his last letter to Clunie of 28 October, he described what happened at the City Hall:

> On Wednesday last the Trades Council had a demonstration in the City Hall on Unemployment with Lansbury and Smillie as principal speakers. *The Workers' Dreadnought* by good luck gave a full description of the Poplar battle, so the SWRP decided to issue a leaflet . . . These we gave out at the TC demonstration. The police, present outside in large numbers, prevented our announced counter-demonstration, so I asked our folks to go inside. Smillie got a hearing. Trouble began when John Robertson MP* rose to speak: but when Hannington (CP and Secy of Unemployed Comm) rose to take Lansbury's place (absent) and to explain away the Poplar incident the row got so hot that the meeting had to be abandoned. . . . We are having ours on Friday and yesterday I had a wire from Sylvia Pankhurst that she's coming on Friday.

On that same day he also wrote to mother, giving her more or less the same account, and explaining that James Hamilton was paying Sylvia's expenses and was giving her hospitality at his own home. Later he gave her the result:

---

*   Previously a pro-Hyndman member of the BSP

Sylvia came on Friday, and after tea at the Ca'Dora she arrived in the City Hall all right, but naturally tired. The City Hall was filled and if it had been free for the unemployed we could have filled it three times over. The ILP are using every filth against me in the campaign and are persistently spreading the lie that I'm in the pay of the Moderates!

On the eve of the election, Maclean issued another hard-hitting leaflet, with some noteworthy points. He pointed out that:

The worker who votes for the upholders of the system of society that allows him to be robbed of the larger part of the wealth produced by him and his fellows, is clearly a simpleton.

Rule by Force

In country after country in Europe the robbing capitalists are setting up political dictatorships, the better to rule and rob the workers. The latest country to do so is Germany. The German Parliament is to be broken up, and Dr Stresemann, with a handful of political puppets, will boss Germany for Stinnes and other big capitalists.

Beware the Fascisti

The start of the Fascisti in Britain shows that, when the moment arrives, Baldwin, the Duke of Northumberland, and all the other propertied class politicians will do likewise by sending Parliament about its business.

Baldwin's Balderdash

To stave off the evil day, Baldwin, in his Manchester speech on 2 November, offers Tariff Reform, Ill-Health Insurance Reforms, Unemployment Insurance Reforms; in fact a general reform of British Imperial Capitalism, to retain the loyal support of the insane type of workers.

The Real Motive

Baldwin's game is to tighten up the British Empire in the coming terrific trade war against the United States, embitter the wage-earners against the Yankees. . . .

The Pinks Entrapped

The Pink Labourists have played on mothers' milk, housing, rents, and other reform superficialities to gain popular support so as to make Ramsay MacDonald or Clynes Prime Minister of Britain. The Town Council Labourists, in a minor key, have done the same to make Pat Dollan the 'Lord' Provost. Baldwin is covering up his real game by urging that he is out for more reforms than the 'Pinks'.

Our Revolutionary Contention

We 'Reds' have always contended that, to save capitalism from death, the Moderates (Tories and Liberals), would patch and reform capitalism lavishly, if need be.

That is why we insist on the Social Revolution ie, the ownership of all wealth-making agencies by mankind in common.

The more who vote 'Red', the more crumbs of reform will fall from the masters' table. **Even supposing you only wish piece-meal reforms, the best way to get them is not to vote for the 'Pinks', who sacrifice Socialist principles to emphasize vote-catching reforms, but to vote for the 'Reds', who place principle before patch-work proposals. Every working-class vote cast for a 'Pink' is a vote lost.** (My emphasis.)

The Root of Our Wrongs

If all our social ills are due to the continuous robbery of the workers, it is obvious that reforms can in no way solve our difficulties. Only Social Ownership can do so. If you are too cowardly to vote 'Red', you will be too cowardly to face the secretly organizing British Fascisti. . . .

This is now, a different policy from the tolerant one towards Labour Party candidates expressed a year ago.

Recent experiences of Pink Labour's total inadequacy in coping with capitalism now made it necessary, according to Maclean, to draw a distinct line between revolutionary and reformist socialism.

No sooner was this municipal campaign over than he began his parliamentary one. He told mother in a letter on 4 November:

I'll contest the Gorbals, let the General Election come when it may.

Her dismayed reaction came immediately:

You fill me with dismay at the thought of you contesting the Gorbals. It is just throwing yourself away, and money that is needed to keep your family. I am up against it here—the loneliness and depressing atmosphere is more than I can stand. Last winter I said I would never come through another such horror. I keep sticking it for the sake of the children, but I am at the end of my tether. I have constant headaches. My mind is made up. It must end or it will finish me. I have decided to come home at Xmas, and if you can't manage to get a job, then I intend to strike out for myself and go in for nursing or something that will give me some independence and that will be a bit cheerier. We will need to arrange about the children in some way.

But the return letter gave mother news that made her angry, rather than depressed:

Yesterday I received a letter from the secretary of the SLC saying I was on the short list of six for a Glasgow appointment. However, they are jamming me by inserting a clause to the effect that the tutor must take no active part in politics. That condition I'm refusing to accept, so the fight in that quarter will now really begin.

My only hope of economic security (of a kind) at present is from the masses, and so I must ever keep in the fight. I am therefore standing again in the Gorbals. The press suggests that the date of the election will be on Wed or Thurs, 5 or 6 Dec.

Now, any chance I have of holding my own against the deluge of ILP lies against me at the Nov election, eg, that I was in the pay of the Moderates, your severance from me, etc, is thro' your immediate return home and appearing in public with me.

If you cannot come I'll be blackened worse than ever, and will be economically damned. If that is so, I have made up my mind for the worst—that we'll never come together again.

If I go down, I must go down with my flag at the mast-top. Nothing on earth will shift me from that. Now, there's the tragedy for you, as clearly and bluntly as I can put it.

If it's your duty to be here, as I maintain it now is, I contend it is your duty to stand shoulder to shoulder with me in the hardest and dirtiest battle of my life. If we have to go under we had better go under fighting together than fighting one another.

Realizing that this is the greatest crisis in our lives I cannot find words to say more.

If you come I'd prefer you to come at once and walk right in.

Whatever course we follow, remember that you are the only woman I love and can now love.

Mother's response was immediate, and predictable. She was extremely distressed that Maclean was refusing to give up political activity in order to obtain the SLC position:

It will just be the limit if you refuse the chance of a tutorship. *It will be very wrong of you and that's that.* You have been burning the candle at both ends for too long and it would just be a godsend if you had no time to take an active part in politics for a year or so at least. Think what it would mean for us—for any sake *don't* refuse it . . .

However, in spite of her anger, she intended to stand by him, and wrote:

I will come back to you this week-end, Johnnie, but Jean and Nan will follow on later, if we can get the wherewithal to feed them. Fancy, *coming home* at long last.

But, in spite of that, she pleaded on him to give up his election campaign:

It is your duty to stand by me and leave the election alone for this time. Let your friends know that your wife's health will not stand the excitement of an election. That will not damn you, but the very opposite.

She arrived back to find him in an alarming condition, with his health now completely ruined by malnutrition and constant political activity. Although suffering from severe sinus trouble and a chronic sore throat, he was outside every night speaking, often in a dense November fog. Accustomed as he had been all his life to health and strength, he seemed quite unable to realize his own weakness. Indeed, he continued to the end to be much more concerned about the well-being of others. Neil Johnston from Barbados told mother later in an emotional letter of sympathy:

I have had an overcoat for the last six months which was lent to me by your husband. Can you be so kind as to let me retain it as a remembrance of him whom I shall always remember as the truest and best friend I had in Europe.

That, of course, was Maclean's only overcoat, and here he was outside speaking without one in the depths of a very severe winter! He thought, typically, that Neil Johnston had needed it more than he did. One of his last actions was just as typical. Just before he took ill, he called on Aunt Lizzie on his way to an outdoor meeting. It was intensely cold and foggy, and his brother-in-law, a railway worker, was just going out to work. Maclean was anxious about him, insisting that he must wrap himself up properly, as he was not a strong man. When asked why *he* hadn't done so, he brushed the question aside as being irrelevant. Two or three days later he had to be lifted from his open-air platform, mortally ill with double pneumonia, and carried home. Mother had arrived, only to nurse him through his first and last illness.

His last election address, dated 30 November, the day he died, had been written ten days previously, and bore witness to his passionate belief in communism and that it could come to Scotland only through separation from England. If any reader is still under the impression that his Marxist world outlook had changed in any way because of his support for Scottish independence, surely extracts from this last election address should dispel that illusion:

For the wage-earning class there is but one alternative to a capitalist war for markets. The root of all the trouble in society at present is the inevitable robbery of the workers by the propertied class, simply because it is the propertied class. To end that robbery would be to end the social troubles of modern society. The way to end that robbery is the transfer of the land and the means of production and transport from the present possessors to the community. Community ownership is communism. The transfer is a Social Revolution, not the bloodshed that may or may not accompany the transfer.

Russia could not produce the World Revolution. Neither can we in Gorbals, in Scotland, in Great Britain. Before England is ready I am sure the next war will be on us. I therefore consider that Scotland's wisest policy is to declare for a republic in Scotland, so that the youths of Scotland will not be forced out to die for England's markets.

I accordingly stand out as a Scottish Republican candidate, feeling sure that if Scotland had to elect a Parliament to sit in Glasgow it would vote for a working-class Parliament.

Such a Parliament would have to use the might of the workers to force the land and the means of production in Scotland out of the grasp of the brutal few who control them, and place them at the full disposal of the community. The Social Revolution is possible sooner in Scotland than in England. . . . Scottish separation is part of the process of England's imperial disintegration and is a help towards the ultimate triumph of the workers of the world.

Conclusion

The spontaneous tribute paid to John Maclean at his funeral by thousands of Scottish workers did not turn out to be an empty gesture. As soon as possible there was set up a Memorial Committee representing the General Council of the Scottish TUC, the Glasgow Trades and Labour Council, the Scottish co-operative movement, the Scottish Labour College, and socialist organizations. Two of his dearest friends, Tom Anderson, and James Figgins (later to become General Secretary of the NUR), were elected president and secretary respectively, while William Shaw, secretary of the Glasgow Trades and Labour Council was appointed treasurer. Bob Smillie became honorary president, Robert Stewart of the SCWC hon vice-president, and James Maxton hon secretary.

No time was lost in sending round the following circular:

We direct this appeal to your members in an endeavour to fittingly commemorate the life's work of one of Labour's most heroic advocates.

Comrade John Maclean, MA, died on 30 November 1923. His period of work embraced his youthful as well as his more mature years, and his earnestness and virility in the Workers' Cause never diminished. Throughout his life he was intimately connected with the Co-operative and Socialist wings of Labour's endeavours, and many prominent members of Trade Union, Co-operative and Socialist organizations bear witness to the value and inspiration of his tutorship.

His convictions were based on profound knowledge of social questions, for which, on five occasions, he suffered imprisonment. For the great Cause of the Workers he gave up the things most men count precious. He died having given his all for the sake of others.

The chief object of this Memorial Fund is to make adequate provision for his dependants, who shared his sacrifice; and the Committee, which is of a most representative character, working in conjunction with many prominent members of Labour's Army and under the direct supervision of all Working-class organizations, appeals to all to give most generously.

John Maclean gave help to those in need without question as to their particular beliefs, and we trust the same spirit will prompt your members to do likewise in recognition of his life's work.

There was a magnificent response to this appeal, and for a number of years mother received £3 a week, which at that time was a comfortable income and probably more than that received by the majority of the donors. She gradually recovered a modicum of health and happiness as the nightmare years receded into the past and lived until 1953.

A new Memorial Committee was formed at the beginning of this year, 1973, to commemorate the fiftieth anniversary of John Maclean's death. With the help of the John Maclean Society and the General Council of the Scottish TUC, it has raised enough money by public subscription to build a large Cairn, erected near the Old Town's House of Pollokshaws, where he held so many outdoor propaganda meetings more than sixty years ago. The site was donated by Glasgow Corporation, and the Cairn unveiled by Glasgow's Lord Provost on the first Sunday of December, the traditional Commemoration Day. The Cairn bears the following simple inscription:

In Memory of John Maclean
Who was born in Pollokshaws on 24th August 1879,
And died there on 30th November 1923.
FAMOUS PIONEER OF WORKING-CLASS EDUCATION,
HE FORGED THE SCOTTISH LINK IN THE
GOLDEN CHAIN OF WORLD SOCIALISM.

The cause of world socialism for which he lived has not yet been won, but I am quite confident that the Scottish working-class will play an honourable and noteworthy part in its achievement.

Bibliography

John Maclean's private papers are held by the National Library of Scotland, Edinburgh.

The place of publication is London, unless otherwise given.

G Aldred, *John Maclean, Martyr of the Class Struggle*, Glasgow, Bakunin Press 1932

T Anderson, *John Maclean*, Glasgow Proletarian Press 1930

R P Arnot, *A History of the Scottish Miners from the Earliest Times*, Allen & Unwin 1955

Max Beer, *A History of British Socialism*, G Bell & Son 1919–20, 2 vols.

T Bell, *John Maclean, a Fighter for Freedom*, Glasgow, Communist Party Scottish Committee 1944

E H Carr, *A History of Soviet Russia*, Part I: *The Bolshevik Revolution 1917-23*, Penguin 1966

James Clunie, *The Voice of Labour, the Autobiography of a House Painter*, Dunfermline, the author 1958

J Connolly, *Socialism made Easy*, Dublin, Socialist Labour Press 1917

P B Ellis, *A History of the Irish Working Class*, Gollancz 1972

R C K Ensor (ed), *Modern Socialism*, 3rd ed Harper 1910

W Gallacher, *Revolt on the Clyde, an Autobiography*, Lawrence & Wishart 1936

——— *The Last Memoirs*, ed Nan Green, Lawrence & Wishart 1966

H J Hanham, *Scottish Nationalism*, Faber 1969

T Johnston, *The History of the Working Classes in Scotland*, Glasgow, Forward Publishing Co 1922

——— *Scots Noble Families*, Glasgow, Forward Publishing Co 1909

W Kendall, *The Revolutionary Movement in Britain 1900-21*, Weidenfeld & Nicolson 1969

G Lansbury, *My Life*, Constable 1928

E Larkin, *James Larkin, Irish Labour Leader*, Routledge & Kegan Paul 1969

V I Lenin, *On the Road to Insurrection*, CPGB 1927

——— *Imperialism, the Highest Stage of Capitalism*, Moscow, Foreign Languages Publishing House 1947

——— *'Left Wing' Communism, an Infantile Disorder*, CPGB 1920

——— *One Step Forward, Two Steps Back*, Lawrence & Wishart 1941

R Luxemburg, *Reform or Revolution*, Bombay, Modern India Publications 1951

John Maclean, *Avenge Bloody Friday*, Glasgow, BSP Scottish District Council 1919

────── *The Coming War with America*, Glasgow, BSP Scottish District Council 1919

────── *Condemned from the Dock*, Glasgow, BSP Scottish District Council 1918

────── *Co-operation and the Rise in Prices*, Glasgow, SDF Scottish District Council 1911

────── *The Irish Tragedy*, Glasgow, the author 1920

────── *A Plea for a Labour College for Scotland*, Glasgow, Scottish Labour College Provisional Committee 1916

────── *The War after the War*, Glasgow, Scottish Labour College 1918

John McNair, *James Maxton, the Beloved Rebel*, Allen & Unwin 1955

H McShane, *Remembering John Maclean*, Glasgow, John Maclean Society 1972

W H Marwick, *Labour in Scotland, a Short History of the Scottish Working Class Movement*, Glasgow, Scottish Secretariat 1949

R K Middlemas, *The Clydesiders*, Hutchinson 1965

E R Pease, *The History of the Fabian Society*, A C Fifield 1916

P & I Petroff, *The Secret of Hitler's Victory*, L & V Woolf 1934

P Snowden, *Socialism and Syndicalism*, Collins 1913

────── *Labour and the New World*, Cassell 1921

J Strachey, *What are We to Do?* Gollancz 1938

H Tracey (ed), *The Book of the Labour Party*, Caxton 1925 3 vols.

L Trotsky, *History of the Russian Revolution*, transl Max Eastman, Gollancz 1934

────── *Where is Britain Going?* Allen & Unwin 1926

W Wolfe, *Scotland Lives*, Edinburgh, Reprographia 1973

Newspapers and Periodicals

The Call, The Communist, Communist International, Daily Record (Scottish), Daily Worker, Forward, Glasgow Herald, Justice, The Labour Leader, Nineteenth Century, Plebs, Pollokshaws News, Pollokshaws Review, Scottish Co-operator, Scottish Review, The Socialist, Vanguard, The Worker, The Workers' Dreadnought, United Scotsman.

Index